Edwardian Occasions

Also by Samuel Hynes

The Pattern of Hardy's Poetry
The Edwardian Turn of Mind

Edited by Samuel Hynes

Further Speculations by T. E. Hulme
Critical Writings of Arnold Bennett
Romance and Realism by Christopher Caudwell

Edwardian Occasions

Essays on English Writing in the
Early Twentieth Century

Samuel Hynes

New York
Oxford University Press
1972

To Liz

Contents

Contents

The essays in this book were written over the past ten years, and on a diversity of occasions; if they nevertheless have a unity, it is the unity of one mind thinking about one period of literary history. I have found the Edwardian period distinct and interesting, for reasons that I have tried to set down in my introduction, and the essays that follow might be considered as examples of what has interested me among the writers and literary problems of the time. The reader who reads the book through should get an impression of the English literary situation in the early years of this century, though it will be only an *impression*, with all the subjective bias that that term implies, and not a representation.

Half of these essays were first published in *The Times Literary Supplement*, and I am grateful to the editor, Mr Arthur Crook, both for the opportunity to write for him and for permission to republish these contributions. I also want to thank the editors of the Columbia University Press, *Commonweal*, *Modern Fiction Studies*, *Novel*, the *Sewanee Review*, and the *Yale Review* for their permission to reprint work first published by them. A few essays have been expanded or cut in minor ways, but I have not revised my opinions, not even the incomprehensibly obtuse remark that *Howards End* is Forster's most impressive novel. The Introduction and the last three essays are here published for the first time.

Acknowledgments

I am grateful to the following for permission to include the material indicated: Miss D. E. Collins, Methuen & Co. Ltd, and Dodd, Mead & Co., Inc., for 'The Ballad of the White Horse', from *The Collected Poems of G. K. Chesterton*; The Cresset Press, for 'Youth', from *The Collected Poems* of Frances Cornford; Miss Jennifer Gosse, for a letter by Sir Edmund Gosse; The Librarian of the British Library of Political and Economic Science, for quotations from the Passfield Papers; The Master and Fellows of Magdalene College, Cambridge, for letters by A. C. Benson; Mr Peter Newbolt, for a letter by Sir Henry Newbolt, from the Ashley collection of the British Museum; New Directions Publishing Corporation, and Faber and Faber Ltd, for quotations from *Personae* and *The Cantos* by Ezra Pound (copyright 1926 and 1934 by Ezra Pound); Mrs Jessie Orage, for two letters from A. R. Orage to H. G. Wells; Mrs Eva Reichmann, for caricatures by Max Beerbohm, and for Max Beerbohm's letter to Sir Edmund Gosse; The Royal Society of Literature, and its Secretary, Mrs J. M. Patterson, for quotations from the Society's archives; Mr Michael Yeats, for a letter by W. B. Yeats; 'The Old Man at King's', first published in *Commonweal* (21 February 1964), reprinted by permission of the editors of *Commonweal*; 'Pound and the Prose Tradition', first published in the *Yale Review*, (summer 1962), copyright Yale University Press, published, in a different version, as 'Whitman, Pound, and the Prose Tradition,' in *The Presence of Walt Whitman*, ed. R. W. B. Lewis, Columbia University Press (New York: 1962), pp. 110 to 136; 'Ford and the Spirit of Romance', first published in *Modern Fiction Studies*, copyright 1963 by Purdue Research Foundation, Lafayette, Indiana; 'The Whole Contention . . .', first published in *Novel* (fall 1967), reprinted by permission of the editors; 'The Epistemology of *The Good Soldier*', first published in the *Sewanee Review* (spring 1961), and 'Conrad and Ford: Two Rye Revolutionists' (January–March 1965).

Both reprinted by permission of the editors and of The University of the South; Eleven essays from *The Times Literary Supplement* are reprinted by permission of the Editor: Nos 1, 2, 4, 6b, 7a, 7b, 8, 9, 10b, 10c, 11.

Edwardian scarcely exists as a literary term. Most of us are fairly sure of what we mean by *Victorian*, and *Modern* and even *Post-modern* have been given a good deal of defining attention lately, but Edwardian still identifies at most the cut of a suit, or perhaps a kind of opulent interior décor. This may be because the Edwardian period was too short to attract scholarly specialists: every English department has its Victorianists and its Modernists, but who has ever heard of an academic Edwardianist? Or it may be that Victorian and Modern can be made to spread out, and cover the intervening years so completely that no transitional term seems necessary. After all, Meredith and Swinburne both lived until 1909, and by then Pound was in London, and Joyce had finished writing *Dubliners*: where, then, is the hiatus that will contain Edwardianism?

Yet the time between the turn of the century and the First World War does seem to have the qualities that make a literary period: a shape – a beginning, a middle, and an end, a consciousness of its own separateness from what went before and what followed, and a body of literature that expresses that consciousness. One must accept the historians' view that such divisions of time are always arbitrary; nevertheless men do seek in history for the temporal patterns that shape their own lives, and find commencements and terminations in great events, and perhaps one might argue that historical periods exist when men think they do, and that a sense of a terminus *is* a terminus. Men have always felt a bit apocalyptic at the end of a century, and at the death of a monarch, and wars and other disasters have brought feelings of finality, and it is not surprising that Englishmen saw signs of an ending around 1900, in the date and in the death of the old queen, and in 1910, when Edward died, and again in 1914, at the beginning of the First World War.

In 1900 a long reign was drawing to a close, during which two vast changes had occurred in English life and thought: discoveries in geology and biology had changed the way men thought about their place in the universe, and a transformation of the economic bases of society had changed the nature of human communities. Obviously the changes were not completed by the turn of the century – they are still going on – but by 1900 they had disordered customary and familiar assumptions about life enough to affect intellectual and literary consciousness, and to turn the minds of thoughtful men towards problems of consequences: how to live in a scientific universe, and how to live with industrialism. One finds everywhere in Edwardian writing the sense of disturbing change, and the essential Edwardian mood is sombre – a feeling of nostalgia for what has gone, and of apprehension for what is to come – and this is true even of writers whom one might expect, for intellectual reasons, to be more optimistic. An example is J. W. Mackail, a classical scholar who was also a socialist and an admirer of William Morris. Mackail wrote, in a lecture on Morris delivered in 1900:[1]

> The times are strange and evil, round us and within us we may see without much searching all the signs that hitherto have preceded great revolutions in human history . . . The end of the century, now close upon us, might well seem to any highly kindled imagination, the visible index of some approaching end of the world. To those who hope for and work towards human progress, whether or not they call themselves by the name of Socialists, the outward aspect of the time is full of profound discouragement. Nor is the discouragement confined to them. It was said to me lately, by one whose memory goes back with clearness over fifty years, that one great difference between that time and this is the general loss of high spirits, of laughter, and the enjoyment of life. If that be so, it is not without reasons. We may see all round us how vainly people try to drown in increasing luxury and excitement the sense that joy and beauty are dwindling out of life; with what pitiful eagerness they dress themselves up in pretended enthusiasms, which seem to bring little joy to the maker or the user. The uneasy feeling is abroad that the Nineteenth Century, which has done such wonderful things, and from which things so much more wonderful were hoped, has been on the whole a failure. Fifty years ago men's minds were full of ideals. Some of them have come to nothing.

Others have received a strangely disenchanting fulfilment. Cinder heaps smoulder where there once were beacon fires. Everywhere is re-action triumphant.

The death of Victoria in the following year added to this sense of the melancholy ending of an era. Arthur Balfour, speaking on that occasion before the House of Commons, was being rhetorical when he described the nation's grief, but reached beyond convention when he went on to name its causes:[2]

> I suppose that, in all the history of the British Monarchy, there
> never has been a case in which the feeling of national grief was
> so deep-seated as it is at present, so universal, so spontaneous.
> And that grief affects us not merely because we have lost a great
> personality, but because we feel that the end of a great epoch
> has come upon us – an epoch the beginning of which stretches
> beyond the memory, I suppose, of any individual whom I am
> now addressing . . .

That is the point, surely; few could remember when Victoria had not been queen, when England had not been rich and the Empire powerful. But that historical continuity had ended, and Englishmen knew that it had; 'The Victorian Era', C. F. G. Masterman wrote in 1901, 'has definitely closed.'

For literary people, as for politicians, the end of the century seemed to coincide with a radical change, at least in retrospect. 'Then in 1900', Yeats recalled, 'everybody got down off his stilts; henceforth nobody drank absinthe with his black coffee; nobody went mad; nobody committed suicide; nobody joined the Catholic church; or if they did I have forgotten. Victorianism had been defeated.'[3] H. G. Wells, surveying the contemporary novel in 1911, made the Boer War the dividing line between Victorian fiction (a fiction of assurance and moral confirmation) and a modern kind of novel concerned with doubts and problems. And even Virginia Woolf, though she was hard on Edwardian novelists, assumed that they had been preceded by a different kind of fiction, which was Victorian, and which had come to an end.

This sense of a radical social and literary change is common in the Edwardian period, but not all Edwardians placed it at the beginning of the decade. For example A. R. Orage, a shrewd journalistic observer of his time, argued that in fact Edward's reign had been merely a continuation of Victoria's, and that the important change came at his death:[4]

The last genuine link with the Victorian age has been broken with the death of King Edward VII. Nobody who will reflect for a moment on the circumstances of the Queen's death and on the historic as well as family relationship in which the late King stood to the late Queen, will fail to realise at once that King Edward was spiritually the mere executor of Queen Victoria. The impulse of her epoch flowed over, as it were, and merged in his reign, begun actually before her death, colouring it with the peculiar tones of the Victorian era. King Edward VII was adored almost as much as the son and successor of his mother as for his own qualities and merits.

This fact, indeed, puts the seal of difference on the two accessions to the throne which the last ten years have witnessed. The accession of Edward VII was neither felt to be, nor in fact was it, a leap in the dark or a plunge into a new period. Everything that the late King did on the throne had been anticipated and expected, both from the evidence of his own public life and from the impetus given to his times by the long reign that drew to a close in him. But the situation is strangely different at this moment, and all the surrounding circumstances mark it off as unique in English history for many a generation. For if it is felt, as it clearly is felt, that the era of Victoria is indeed and at last over, who is so bold as to dare forecast the nature of the epoch that is now opening?

Reading this editorial of May 1910 one cannot help recalling Virginia Woolf's later assertion that 'on or about December, 1910, human character changed'. The argument in both cases is that it was *here*, at the time of Edward's death, that the crucial break between generations came, that *this* was the radical change of consciousness.

It is generally assumed that Mrs Woolf chose December 1910 because of the first Post-Impressionist show, then open in London, but one might note any number of other events of the same general time: Blériot's first flight across the Channel in July 1909; the beginning of suffragist militancy in the fall of that year; Lloyd George's 'People's Budget' in November 1909; the strikes in the mines in September 1910 and on the London docks the following summer; the Parliament Bill in August 1911. The point is simply that one could make a case for a significant change in English life and thought at either the beginning or the end of Edward's reign, and that in either case one could find literary persons who were conscious of the change, and of its social roots and consequences.

There would be one fundamental difference between the cases, however: that is, in the expressed sense of a change in the formal properties of literature itself. Among the remarks by literary persons that one might gather concerning the end of the nineteenth century, none, I think, would speak of technique. Not only Wells – one would scarcely expect him to worry about such matters – but Yeats as well looked to changes in society, in human relations, in an imaginative 'world', and the consequences for the artist of those changes. And this, I take it, is a fundamental fact about the Edwardian decade, understood as a literary period: it was concerned with the state of society, and acknowledged the urgency and force of social change, but it was *not* concerned to effect a *literary* revolution.

Virginia Woolf quite correctly perceived this essential Edwardian quality, though she gave it an incorrect interpretation. Of the books of Wells, Bennett, and Galsworthy, she wrote:[5]

> Yet what odd books they are! Sometimes I wonder if we are right to call them books at all. For they leave one with so strange a feeling of incompleteness and dissatisfaction. In order to complete them it seems necessary to do something – to join a society, or, more desperately, to write a cheque.

Her point is that these writers were concerned with social reality, with – as I put it before – how to live in a scientific universe and how to live with industrialism. And one cannot deny that this is true, if one considers *Ann Veronica* and *Tono-Bungay*, *Anna of the Five Towns* and *The Old Wives' Tale*, *The Man of Property* and *The Island Pharisees*. All are about social problems, and since social problems are not resolvable within any novel, none is as closed, as finished, as an aesthetic sense like Mrs Woolf's might wish.

Wells's own definition of the fiction of his time makes much the same point from the other side:[6]

> to-day [he wrote in 1911], while we live in a period of tightening and extending social organisation, we live also in a period of adventurous and insurgent thought, in an intellectual spring unprecedented in the world's history. There is an enormous criticism going on of the faiths upon which men's lives and associations are based, and of every standard and rule of conduct.

And it is inevitable that the novel, just in the measure of its sincerity and ability, should reflect and co-operate in the atmosphere and uncertainties and changing variety of this seething and creative time.

This notion of literature 'co-operating' in the social thought and mood of its time seems to me particularly Edwardian. The idea has its roots, of course, in traditional theories of the social function of literature, but Wells's formulation of it strikes me as different in important ways. For what Wells seems to be saying is that literature and historical events share a common temporality, that they co-exist in the flux of time. Literature is not an agent of change (as Shelley would have put it) nor is it a manifestation of eternal truths; rather it is a reflector of the process of which it is itself a part. This is a theory that places literature altogether in history, and subject to the same forces of change and decay, and in that sense it reflects the spirit, and the time-consciousness, of the period.

Take, as examples, two characteristically Edwardian works: Shaw's *Man and Superman* and Wells's *The New Machiavelli*. Shaw's play begins with an elaborate stage direction, which locates Roebuck Ransden in time. 'How old is Roebuck?', Shaw asks.[7]

The question is important on the threshold of a drama of ideas; for under such circumstances everything depends on whether his adolescence belonged to the sixties or to the eighties. He was born, as a matter of fact, in 1839, and was a Unitarian and Free Trader from his boyhood, and Evolutionist from the publication of the Origin of Species. Consequently he has always classed himself as an advanced thinker and fearlessly outspoken reformer.

Ramsden is classified, not only by the furniture of his mind but by the furnishings of his study: Shaw mentions busts of John Bright and Herbert Spencer, a portrait of Richard Cobden, and photographs of Martineau, Huxley, and George Eliot. Obviously this elaborate stage direction has no relevance to production (how many theatre-goers could recognize a photograph of James Martineau from the fourth row?); it is simply a device for introducing into the published text the theory that a man's mind is the product of his place in history. Ramsden was an advanced thinker in his time, who has been succeeded by John Tanner and his *Revolutionist's Handbook*; but neither represents fixed or final values. Hence there can be no hero in the temporal world of the play, only a heroine representing the creative principle of evolution; Don Juan, the true Shavian hero, can exist and talk only in eternity.

The New Machiavelli is even more explicitly historical; it contains a history of English public education in the nineteenth century, a sketch of the economic history of Staffordshire, and a version of the actual political history of the Edwardian years. Historical figures appear, sometimes slightly disguised (the Webbs become the Baileys, Balfour becomes Evesham), and historical events are inserted directly into the fabric of the novel. Wells's history is different from Shaw's, because he is *inside* it (his principal character, Remington, lives through a good deal of Wells's personal experience, and articulates his political ideas), but he shares many of Shaw's assumptions: that thought is historically conditioned, that men and societies evolve, that the artist is legitimately concerned with the shape of the future (which is to say that Wells and Shaw were prophets as well as historians).

This preoccupation with history seems to me a striking characteristic of much important Edwardian literature. It derives, I think, from the most important scientific and philosophic thought of the nineteenth century, and implies a post-Darwinian, post-Hegelian way of looking at the linear shape of time. Two aspects may be distinguished: nostalgia, the sense of the pastness of the past (as in the passage from Mackail quoted above, and in Hardy, Edward Thomas, Belloc, Chesterton, Forster); and temporality, the sense of the passage of time, the unique historical existence of the present moment in its relation to past and future (I note the careful dating of actions in Shaw, Wells, and Bennett, and – an extreme case – in Ford's *The Good Soldier*). Much of the best writing of the period is social history, the recording of the historical moment; Forster is brilliant at fixing the historical fact of suburbanism, Frank Harris is at his best as a social historian, Bennett is only excellent when preserving the historical reality of the Five Towns. Joyce's *Dubliners* is in this sense very Edwardian, and so are the late novels of Henry James.

Perhaps such meticulous care for the historical moment is only possible in a time that is conscious of its uncertain continuation; if self-consciousness is a product of anxiety, there is ample evidence that a good many Edwardians brooded gloomily over England's (or civilization's) future. One of the best Edwardian books on contemporary society, Masterman's *The Condition of England*, ends with these comfortless words:[8]

Humanity – at best – appears but as a shipwrecked crew which has taken refuge on a narrow ledge of rock, beaten by wind and wave; which cannot tell how many, if any at all, will survive when the long night gives place to morning. The wise man will still go softly all his days; working always for greater economic equality on the one hand, for understanding between estranged peoples on the other; apprehending always how slight an effort of stupidity or violence could strike a death-blow to twentieth-century civilisation, and elevate the forces of destruction triumphant over the ruins of a world.

One finds the same spirit in many other writers, and increasingly as the Edwardian years passed – most strikingly in Belloc and Chesterton, but also frequently in Wells, in Galsworthy, in Forster, and in Conrad. It is difficult to think of an important Edwardian optimist. So that if 'Edwardian' is to be used as an adjective identifying a literary *tone*, that tone must be one of social awareness and anxious concern. The best single expression of this Edwardian mood is in a book published in 1905, in the middle of Edward's decade – Masterman's *In Peril of Change*.9

Expectancy and surprise [Masterman wrote] are the notes of the age. Expectancy belongs by nature to a time balanced uneasily between two great periods of change. On the one hand is a past still showing faint survivals of vitality; on the other is the future but hardly coming to birth. The years as they pass still appear as years of preparation, a time of waiting rather than a time of action. Surprise, again, is probably the first impression of all who look on, detached from the eager traffic of man. The spectator sees him performing the same antics in the same grave fashion as in all the past: heaping up wealth which another shall inherit, following pleasure which turns to dust in the mouth, and the end weariness: thinking, as always, that he will endure for ever, and calling after his own name the place which shall know him no more. But surprise passes into astonishment in confronting the particular and special features of the age. Here is a civilisation becoming ever more divorced from Nature and the ancient sanities, protesting through its literature a kind of cosmic weari-ness. Society which had started on its mechanical advance and the aggrandisement of material goods with the buoyancy of an impetuous life confronts a poverty which it can neither ameliorate or destroy, and an organised discontent which may yet prove the end of the Western civilisation. Faith in the invisible seems dying, and faith in the visible is proving inadequate to the hunger of the Soul.

Masterman here describes an important feature of the Edwardian years – the consciousness of men at the time that they were living in a transitional period. And this perhaps accounts for what seems to me an unusual feature of the literary history of the period: that the sense of an ending and the sense of a new beginning do not coincide, but are separated by about ten years, the length of Edward's reign. Here again Mrs Woolf's essay, 'Mr. Bennett and Mrs. Brown', is instructive. In that essay she has high praise for the art of the great Victorians, but she seems to regard Edwardian novelists as artless, as writers *between* styles. 'Men and women who began writing in 1910 or thereabouts', she writes, 'had this great difficulty to face – that there was no English novelist from whom they could learn their business.'[10] And Mrs Woolf's friend, T. S. Eliot, says much the same in a late, retrospective essay: 'In the first decade of the century the situation was unusual. I cannot think of a single living poet, either in England or America, then at the height of his powers, whose work was capable of pointing the way to a young poet conscious of the desire for a new idiom.'[11]

Modernism did not rise out of Victorianism, then, as Romanticism did out of the eighteenth century; there was an interim, and that interim we may properly call The Edwardian Period. If we return once more to Mrs Woolf we will find in her useful essay the proposition that the change of character that occurred 'on or about December 1910' was a consequence of a change in human relations, between master and servant, between husband and wife; that is to say, the roots of formal change were in social change, and not, as one might have expected her to argue, in Cézanne and Dostoevsky. And the consciousness of that social change is surely the contribution of Edwardian literature to the modern movement.

By 1910 the moving spirits of the modern movement in England were at work: Pound and Joyce, Hulme and Epstein and Lewis had begun their revolution, though it was not yet very visible. The years between 1910 and the war were a time when many artists believed that a new era of English art was possible. Harold Monro thought so, as much as Pound and Wyndham Lewis did, and Ford had thought so when he founded (and quickly lost control of) the *English Review*.

Bloomsbury thought so, too, and supported Roger Fry's efforts to publicize Post-Impressionism, and the attempts of various Bloomsbury painters to paint like Frenchmen. What they all meant by the new art varied, but they had one common article of faith – that it would not be social. There is not, in any of the pre-war expressions of the modern movement, any concern for society, or for the phenomena of social change that were so important to writers of the previous generation; art as an instrument of social record or of social change is replaced by new conceptions of an aristocracy of artists, and an autonomous art of aesthetic values.

When Mrs Woolf condemned the Edwardian novelists, she did so in terms of two values that have become associated with her own world of Bloomsbury: the Edwardians, she said, did not offer aesthetic experience, and they did not deal with human relationships. Implicit in this criticism are crucial negative assumptions about literature: that it should not concern itself with the larger historical world, that it should not treat what Wells called 'Problems', that it should not pretend that art can alter life. The art that she proposed instead would be self-contained, like consciousness; it would abandon man's historical existence as a possible subject. Behind this assumption about art lies a loss of belief in the movement of history that is a central fact of modern consciousness, and in terms of which the Edwardian period can be seen as transitional. For if we say that the period was marked by a sense of history as the medium of change, we must also note that during those crucial years belief in the positive movement of history faded. And it would be more than simply a neat conclusion to propose that when that belief had ceased to be an important mover of men's actions, the Edwardian period was over.

In that case we can find a fit symbolic end to the period in July 1914, one month before the war began, with the appearance of the first issue of *Blast*. For *Blast* both records and celebrates the end of tradition and of the historical sense. 'Life is the Past and the Future', Wyndham Lewis wrote in that first issue: 'The Present is Art', and the whole effort of the journal, and the Vorticist movement that it publicized, was to reject all time but the present. Among the aspects of English life 'blasted' are 'years 1837 to 1900' – the modern treatment of the Victorian period as an object of derision seems to begin here – but there is no period of English history that is 'blessed'; 'Our vortex is not afraid of the Past', Lewis wrote: 'it has forgotten its existence.'[12]

The new world of art – the world in which we feel uncertain but at home – was already in existence when the First World War began. That war, as everyone agrees, accelerated the transition from older attitudes to new, but it did not initiate the new. If the war had not come, things would have happened differently: Vorticism might have become a major movement, Hulme might have become what he wanted to be, 'a heavy philosopher', Bennett might have had an influence on the next generation of novelists – one can extend the possibilities infinitely. What *did* happen was that the modern movement was cut off for four years, and when it did flower, after the war, it was different – more cynical, less assertive about points of morality and value, and most of all, determined to reject everything that could be identified with pre-war England ('Mr. Bennett and Mrs. Brown' is a characteristically post-war utterance). Many fine writers were caught in that rejection; but perhaps even more important, an idea of art was dismissed that might have lent vitality to the post-war literary world.

It does no good to regret history; all we can do is to try to understand it. A proper understanding of 'Edwardian' as a literary term, identifying the literary qualities of an historical period, ought to lead to a revaluation of some works that are now neglected, at least by fashionable critics. But beyond this it may suggest a connection between the present and the past, a relevance of that troubled period to our own time; and the drawing of such connections is surely one of the principal tasks, one of the great responsibilities, of the scholar and the critic.

Notes

1 J. W. Mackail, *William Morris* (Hammersmith: The Doves Press, 1901), pp. 18–19.
2 *Hansard* (Commons), vol. 89 (25 January 1901), cols. 19–20 Compare Arnold Bennett's journal entry for 2 February: 'This morning I saw what I could, over the heads of a vast crowd, of the funeral procession of the Queen. The people were not, on the whole, deeply moved, whatever journalists may say, but rather serene and cheerful.' *The Journals of Arnold Bennett* (London: Cassell, 1932), vol. 1, p. 110.
3 'Introduction', *Oxford Book of Modern Verse* (New York: Oxford University Press, 1936), pp. xi–xii.
4 'Notes of the Week', *New Age*, vol. 7 (12 May 1910), p. 26.
5 'Mr. Bennett and Mrs. Brown', in *The Captain's Death Bed* (New York: Harcourt, Brace, 1950), p. 105.
6 'The Contemporary Novel', reprinted in *Henry James and H. G. Wells*, ed. Leon Edel and Gordon N. Ray (London: Hart-Davis, 1958), p. 147.

7 From the opening stage direction of Act One.
8 *The Condition of England* (London: Methuen, 1909), p. 303.
9 *In Peril of Change* (London: T. Fisher Unwin, 1905), pp. xii–xiii.
10 *The Captain's Death Bed*, p. 104.
11 'American Literature and Language', in *To Criticize the Critic* (New York: Farrar, 1965), p. 58. The essay was written in 1953.
12 'Our Vortex', *Blast*, no. 1 (1914), p. 147.

Frank Harris:
The Complete Literary
Rascal

Frank Harris belongs to a fascinating, if not very important, class of writers – the Literary Rascals. His peers are Doctor Johnson's friend Savage, and poor Chatterton, and Baron Corvo, all writers of small talent and large ambitions, all vain and resentful of the world's indifference, and all more appealing for what they were than for what they wrote. As a class the Literary Rascals are not likely to accumulate doctoral dissertations, or even examination questions; but for the curious reader they offer curious rewards, and none more than Harris.

His origins are typically obscure: he was born, under a different name, in one of two countries, on one of several dates (1856 seems the most likely one). When he was fourteen he emigrated to America, where he lived a life of romantic adventure (in both senses of *romantic*, by his account) before enrolling as a law student at the University of Kansas. The years of his early manhood are somewhat cloudy, but in the late 1870s he was back in Europe, studying in Germany and Greece, with time off to serve as a war correspondent. He appeared in London in the early 1880s, became editor of the *Evening News* in 1883 (some said by seducing an influential man's wife), married a rich widow and moved up to the more respectable *Fortnightly Review* (and to Park Lane). In 1894 he took over the *Saturday Review*, and for a few years made it the most distinguished journal in England. But like most rascals Harris's staying powers were not great, and in a few years he was once more out of a job.

When Harris left the *Saturday* he left the pinnacle of his success, and, though he was scarcely forty, he never regained such eminence; for the next twenty years he moved from one editorship to another, each less respectable than the last, wrote a great many books, engaged in an increasing number of controversies, quarrels, and lawsuits, and at last, having, as Shaw remarked, quarrelled with everyone but Shakespeare, fled to France. He spent the 1914–18 War in the United States, where he wrote pro-German propaganda, and later returned to Nice to spend the last decade of his life. He died in 1931.

In this picaresque, and on the whole unsuccessful, career Harris was sustained by the rascal's chief solace – a complete and unwavering vanity; he never ceased to believe in, and to proclaim, his own genius. He thought his stories were better than Maupassant's, his plays better than Shaw's; as a critic he placed himself with Ben Jonson, Goethe, and Coleridge – the four critics, he asserted, who had understood Shakespeare. And when an admirer dared to compare *My Life and Loves* to Casanova, Harris replied: 'Casanova! My dear man, Casanova is not worthy to untie my boot-strings!'

As his fortunes declined, his sense of his own greatness increased. In the books from *The Man Shakespeare* on, Harris-the-Prophet, or, as he was fond of describing himself, 'God's spy', becomes increasingly prominent. The Shakespeare book announced the approach of the 'Kingdom of Man on Earth', in which, it was clear, Harris would play the role of messiah, and the later writings show an increasing fondness for references to Christ, often as an implied analogy to Harris (in the *Life and Loves*, for example, he remarks 'I, too, had to be about my father's business', and refers to his 'disciples' and his 'Beatific Vision'). Augustus John, after reading the first draft of Harris's *Oscar Wilde*, asked the author 'what the devil he meant by dragging in Jesus Christ on every other page?' The answer is obvious: for Harris, Christ was a Harris-figure.

One's natural reaction to such egomania is to dismiss the author of it all as simply a crank; but Harris will not quite submit to such dismissal. Though his own estimates of his importance were wildly inflated, he was nevertheless a significant figure in the literary history of his time. It is not surprising that his real excellences were in those activities in which personal vanity is least freely expressible – in his editing, and in his journalistic reporting. His editing of the *Fortnightly* was able, but not distinguished, but the *Saturday Review* for the few years that he ran it was the best paper of its kind, and a glance at the list of contributors – Shaw, Wells, Stephen Crane, Arthur Symons, Cunninghame Graham, and, of course, Max Beerbohm – shows that Harris had, for a time at least, an acute sense of literary promise.

Of Harris's nearly thirty books, only the biographical writings are readable today. Both the Wilde and the Shaw biographies are well done (though there is some evidence that the excellence of the Shaw owes more to Harris's ghost-writer, Frank Scully, and to Shaw himself than to Harris); and a clever editor could select one volume of very interesting sketches from the five volumes of *Contemporary Portraits*. Harris's biographies have been called impressionistic sketches, and this is a fairly accurate description, but one should add that in each frame there are always *two* faces at once, like a double-exposed negative: one is the ostensible subject, the other Harris's small-town-seducer's face, saying 'Look at me, I'm more interesting, more important, a better writer and a better lover than my subject ever was'. Such portraiture can scarcely be called objective, but it is often extremely entertaining, in the way that indiscreet gossip is.

It is not surprising that Harris's best writing should have this gossipy quality, for many of his acquaintances – including Max Beerbohm in a caricature – have testified that he was 'the Best Talker in London'. He was evidently a born teller of tales, and to this gift his years in America seem to have added skill in that characteristically American art form, the dirty joke (according to Harris he endeared himself to King Edward VII with such stories, though the examples he offers in *My Life and Loves* are not likely to make even a commoner laugh). But he did not write his stories as well as he told them, and when he turned from fiction to criticism and ideas he wrote very badly indeed. Harris did not have a mind equipped for fine discriminations, and his prose reflects his mind; his style is crude and aggressive, forceful at times, but full of hasty compromises with banality of phrase and triteness of idea. (Like most vain men Harris found even his own platitudes fascinating because they were his.) But his style reveals something more than vanity; it reveals his complete lack of sensitivity. He had, one feels, neither a sensitive ear, nor a sensitive eye, nor a sensitive heart ('On Harris', Shaw observed, 'delicacy was thrown away'). When he was aware of suffering, as in Wilde's case, he was capable of great loyalty and generosity; but he does not seem often to have been aware of other people, except as they reflected himself. There is a revealing confession of this fact in his 'portrait' of Olive Schreiner. Harris had met her, and had found her attractive; he then introduced her to George Moore and to his astonishment saw that she was very much impressed, 'Curiously enough', he wrote, 'her admiration for Moore brought my interest in her to an untimely end. No one could be really important to me who admired Moore so intensely.' The interesting thing is that he found such an obvious response to wounded vanity curious.

Harris's egotism is the defining characteristic of his mind. When circumstance or subject kept his ego at bay he was capable of good work: but when he made himself his subject his writing became preposterously inflated, uncontrolled, inaccurate, and at last simply dull. *My Life and Loves*, the work of his declining years, is a very revealing book, but not, one feels, in quite the way that Harris meant it to be. The best of it – the narrative of his early life and some of the portraits and anecdotes of the London years – is vigorously and vividly done. This is Harris the talker, and reading these pages one can believe Harris's boast that he had been invited to every great house in London. But reading the worst of the book – the crude, vulgar, vain worst – one can also believe Wilde's rejoinder to that boast: 'Yes, Frank – *once*.' Unfortunately there is more of the worst than of the best in the book, and long before the end the Best Talker in London has become the Biggest Bore.

An account of Life and Loves would, one might expect, involve other people, but Harris had the egotist's instinct for treating people as aspects of himself, and his 'portraits' became progressively more self-regarding and less distinct as he grew older. This instinct is also, of course, the instinct of the pornographer (who is merely the egotist at the keyhole) and it is not surprising that Harris, when he turned from his triumphs in society to his triumphs in bed, wrote about sex in the manner and style of the cheapest Soho trash. This is not to say that *My Life and Loves* is a pornographic book in any sense that the Director of Public Prosecutions would accept, but simply that its attitudes toward human sexual experience associate it with *What the Chambermaid Saw* rather than with *Lady Chatterley's Lover*. The faceless anonymity of the women involved, the emphasis on super-human sexual powers, the invariable success of the seducer – these are all characteristic of the pornographic attitude. Pornography dehumanizes sex by treating whole human beings as merely organs, and Harris's book is pornographic in this sense. The 'truths' that he claims to reveal are not general truths about sex, but rather inadvertent exposures of his own emotional limitations. Psychologists may find the book a useful example of the Don Giovanni Complex (or perhaps rather the Leporello Complex, for, like most sexual braggarts, Harris would rather count than conquer); but seekers after the truth about sexual love will search in vain through these vain pages.

My Life and Loves is a poor thing, and an unworthy record of its author's life and character. During his best years Harris must have been an impressive man – certainly men of judgment freely testified to their admiration for him. Arnold Bennett called Harris 'one of the most extraordinary men I ever met'; Wilde dedicated *An Ideal Husband* (a most ironic choice) 'To Frank Harris, a slight tribute to his power and distinctions as an artist, his chivalry and nobility as a friend'; and Shaw wrote his friend's epitaph: 'Here lies a man of letters who hated cruelty and injustice and bad art, and never spared them in his own interest.'

Though these are the praises of friendship, yet they point to real virtues. But it was Harris's flaw that he could not rest content with the praises of others; his vanity, as he once confessed, was as abnormally developed as his ambition, and no praises, not even his own, could satisfy it. *My Life and Loves* is a ponderous, gross book, a monument to that abnormal vanity, and not to the whole man; it would be a pity if such a complex and often entertaining literary rascal were to be remembered, not by his best writing, but by this, nearly his worst.

The original version was first published in *The Times Literary Supplement*, 12 November 1964.

2

H.G. and G.B.S.

In Beatrice Webb House, at Leith Hill, Surrey, a stained-glass window commemorates the Edwardian makers of the Fabian Society. Shaw is prominent there; with Sidney Webb he is hammering out a new world on the Fabian anvil, while in a row below, the lesser Fabians kneel before an altar made of the works of Shaw and the Webbs. Only one figure offends the mood of energetic piety that the window playfully expresses; in the lower left-hand corner H. G. Wells cocks a snook at the whole tableau (and one notices then that one of the reverent kneelers is irreverently reading Wells's *New Worlds for Old*).

The Fabian window was commissioned by Shaw in 1910, and it is a properly Shavian version of the Society's situation at that time; Shaw-the-Maker, cheerful and dominating; and Wells-the-Mocker, impudently opposing, but nearly out of the picture. One can imagine another window, commissioned by Wells, in which the roles of hero and imp would have been reversed, and the altar made of *Anticipations*, *A Modern Utopia*, and *The Faults of the Fabian*; and if events had taken a different turn this window would have had its validity, too. But the point to be made is that in any representation of the most significant political group of the Edwardian period, the two best-known writers of the time would necessarily have figured. One cannot avoid seeing them as public faces in public places.

It is surely this quality of public and various activity, of enormous energies scattered in many causes, that has left both Shaw and Wells with such unstable reputations. Shaw expected a 'period of staleness and out-of-dateness' after his death, but this is not in fact what has happened; critics have gone on writing about him, his plays are revived, and professors lecture on his works, but his place in English letters is still uncertain, and no settled canon of his writings has emerged (is *Saint Joan* a good play? should *Back to Methuselah* have been revived? is there any life left in *Mrs. Warren's Profession*? has anyone here read

Everybody's Political What's What?). And the same is true of Wells –
so many books, so few established judgments. That Wells's novels are
readable and Shaw's plays playable is apparently not enough; Wells
has not found a secure place in the histories of modern fiction, and
Shaw figures among modern dramatists as an example of nineteenth-
century technique. Nor has either had any formal influence on his
chosen form (though both thought of themselves as innovators).

Certainly the critical commonplaces of the Age of Eliot do not
work very well in these hard cases: the autonomy of the work of art,
the impersonality of the artist, the importance of significant form – in
these terms, Shaw and Wells simply don't pass. For one thing, they
took the wrong matters seriously: Wells worried about the specializa-
tion of function, but not about the form of the novel ('I was disposed to
regard a novel as about as much an art form as a market place or a
boulevard'); and Shaw, though he worked hard at the structure of
governments, let his plays come as they would ('I have never claimed a
greater respect for playmaking than for the commoner crafts'). At a
time when the idea of the Conscious Artist was becoming current,
neither writer was content to play that role with a seemly single-
mindedness: Wells wrote more than a hundred books, but only half
of them could be called fiction, and some of those are scarcely novels;
and Shaw wrote far more non-dramatic prose than plays.

Most of all, Shaw and Wells are as far from the ideal of the impersonal artist as could be. Wells drew so shamelessly on his own life and
the lives of his acquaintances for material that his works can be read
virtually as a hundred-volume autobiography; and Shaw not only
thrust Shavian characters into his plays to speak his piece, but surrounded them with even more Shavian stage directions, and then
attached most Shavian prefaces that were often longer than the play.

Paradoxically, though their fictions were like life, their lives had the
quality of fiction. Shaw created a public role for himself of such precise
definition that he could give it a name, and having created 'G.B.S.'
could refer to him thereafter as a tedious, but useful fiction. And
'H.G.' was a similar sort of invention – a scientific prophet with lower-
class manners and a gift for publicity. One might take it as a measure of
the distance of the actual men from their inventions that both could
write mocking third-person biographies of their public selves. Shaw's
begins, characteristically: 'I declare at once that Shaw was the just
man made perfect.' Wells is equally characteristic in his ironic self-
denigration: 'First we have to realize that this Mr H. G. Wells, in

spite of the inexplicable prestige he has contrived for himself, is an individual of the lowest extraction and the most haphazard education.'

These are self-caricatures as bold and simplified as the figures in Low's cartoons, and one's first response to them is that though they might have written the lesser works, they could not have created *Man and Superman* or *Kipps*. But perhaps this is the point, that neither Shaw nor Wells played the artist's role in public. We must take them, if we take them at all, on other terms – beard and knickerbockers, limp moustache and baggy eyes, and all. Those other terms are complex, because the men are complex, and the twentieth century seems to have no critical machinery adequate to deal with a playwright-philosopher-politician-novelist-phonetician, or a novelist-romancer-scientist-philosopher-historian.

One might propose as a beginning that Shaw and Wells are best regarded, not as a playwright and a novelist, but as two Edwardian polymaths. *Edwardian* because, though Shaw was forty-five when Edward ascended the throne, and Wells wrote more than half of his books after Edward died, both men represent that point of intersection between Victorian and Modern, and both express in their lives and works the preoccupation of that time; like the Webbs and Galsworthy and Forster, they carried the advanced ideas of the late-Victorian reformers into the twentieth century, and watched them grow out-of-date and useless there. *Polymaths* because they believed that man could seize knowledge in a wide embrace, and that through much knowing he could affect the future of his species, and earn a place in the story. Both were humanists in the most generous and impressive sense, engaging themselves in human affairs as agents rather than as critics. They suffered, to use Shaw's term, from *Weltverbesserungswahn* – a rage to better the world.

Since their medium was the written word, they were both polemicists in everything they wrote. There is no useful distinction to be made between Shaw's prefaces and his plays, or between the Wells of *Tono-Bungay* and the Wells of *The Open Conspiracy* – all are polemical, for if one aspires to turn words into actions, then all words are equally instrumental. (This is what Virginia Woolf found so unsatisfactory in Wells's novels: 'in order to complete them it seems necessary to do something – to join a society, or, more desperately, to write a cheque'. Mrs Woolf did not include Shaw among her bad Edwardian examples, but she might have – he was as guilty of what she condemned as Wells was.)

The effect of polemical intentions on judgment is nicely illustrated in the relations between Shaw and Wells and Henry James. Both men quarrelled with James, and neither understood what he was getting at. Shaw, writing to explain why the Incorporated Stage Society was rejecting a James play, said:

> I, as a socialist, have had to preach, as much as anyone, the enormous power of the environment as a dead destiny. We can change it: we must change it: there is absolutely no other sense in life than the work of changing it. . . .

and he urged James to forsake art and join with the forces of change. And Wells, though admired by James, cruelly attacked him in *Boon*, and later, mulling over his relations with the Master, concluded that James 'had no idea of the possible use of the novel as a help to conduct'. To which James would no doubt have replied that Wells had no idea that the novel might nobly exist *without* uses.

It might be argued – and indeed it has been argued – that in both men the polemicist eventually dominated the artist. One could find considerable evidence for this view in their later writings, and especially in those vast works of the 1920s, *Back To Methuselah* and *The World of William Clissold* – two distended, ill-constructed, undramatic monsters over which Creative Evolution and The Open Conspiracy have spread like some dreadful Wellsian plague, and have left imagination quite dead.

But even in such cases, the canons of aesthetics seem inadequate bases for condemnation. 'You cannot be an artist', Shaw wrote in an early letter, 'until you have contracted yourself with the limits of your art.' Neither he nor Wells found that contraction easy, and it is a necessary condition of just judgment of either writer that the critic realize that the limits of the art cannot be held. One must see Wells, not as a spoiled Dickens, but *sui generis*, as a complete Wells; and similarly with Shaw. The coordinates of art are too strict to contain them, and to say simply that *Back to Methuselah* is a bad play, or *William Clissold* a bad novel, is to have missed the point. Perhaps an aesthetics of polemics is what is called for.

On the other hand, one must not let a preoccupation with polemical concerns blind one to essential excellences in both writers. There must be many readers of Shaw who first discovered that discursive prose could be pleasurable by reading his prefaces, and who learnt there the meaning of style. And though no one is likely to miss the fact that

Shaw was a gifted comic dramatist, it is worth noting that he was at least as good in comic narrative: 'The Life and Death of Uncle William', for example, in Shaw's Preface to *Immaturity*, is as good as Sterne. And in Wells, behind and below the myths of science and the satirical grotesques of society, lies a gift for particularizing ordinariness and imagining new actualities that makes the comparison with Dickens legitimate.

The polemical road may lead to fame – artists don't visit Stalin, but polemicists do, and both Shaw and Wells did – but it also leads to disappointment. These two men had set out to change the world, and how far had they succeeded? Shaw had played his part in the Fabian Society, and had lived to see the Labour Party governing England; but how many of the words he wrote had touched that change? And did he admire what socialism had come to? Wells had imposed his views of history on more people than any other historian ever reached, and by writing frankly about sex, and frankly living his convictions, he had contributed to the sexual revolution in this century; but these were not the achievements he had imagined.

No, in spite of their endeavours, mankind remained unreformed. 'Man is so far a failure as a political animal', Shaw observed, and Wells, in a novella of the 1930s, has a psychiatrist darkly conclude:

Man is still what he was. Invincibly bestial, envious, malicious, greedy. Man, Sir, unmasked and disillusioned, is the same fearing, snarling, fighting beast he was a hundred thousand years ago. These are no metaphors, Sir. What I tell you is the monstrous reality.

It was as though *The Island of Doctor Moreau* had come true.

One must conclude that both men lived too long. They belonged to the Edwardian era, when optimism was still possible, and they lived to see the failure of their hopes. 'I have produced no permanent impression', Shaw once said, 'because nobody has ever believed me'; and almost nobody ever did. And Wells said sadly, near the end of his life, that he was tired of talking in parables to a world engaged in destroying itself.

But if both had a sense of ultimate failure, they expressed it very differently, and the difference points to a fundamental difference of temperament. Compare, for example, the epitaphs that they imagined for themselves. Shaw's was to be

Hic Jacet
BERNARD SHAW
Who the devil was he ?

while Wells proposed for his own,

'God damn you all. I told you so'.

There was a cosmic indifference in Shaw that made it possible for him to contemplate being forgotten, and even to provide for that eventuality in his will. It was not coldness (though careless men mistook it for that), for Shaw had, if not a warm heart, then a warm intellect; it was, rather, an abnormal tolerance for reality. Wells didn't have it – the actual made him furious (perhaps one does not invent futures unless the present is intolerable), and he spent his life – both his public life and his private one – in trying to exchange new worlds for old. And it was Wells who came in the end to despair; his last book, *Mind at the End of its Tether*, is a cry of anguish and pain, like that last Martian howling alone on Primrose Hill in *The War of the Worlds*. Whereas Shaw, like one of his Ancients, waited for death with at most a slight irritation that it was so long in coming.

If Shaw and Wells, viewed as artists, rank below the very greatest, this is partly because they refused to be *merely* artists, and partly because they nevertheless invite comparison with the best: Shaw is one of the Great Irishmen, and shares the ambience of Joyce and Yeats, and Wells's novels are in the greatest English tradition; if neither is at the top, yet both are in honoured company, Shaw himself said: 'Either I shall be remembered as a playwright as long as Aristophanes and rank with Shakespeare and Molière, or I shall be a forgotten clown before the end of the century.' But there is a third possibility: to be remembered as a man who was great in the multitudinousness of his imagination, and who realized his greatness in the amplitude of his work. Writing of Charles Doughty, Shaw remarked that 'there must have been something majestic or gigantic about the man that made him classic in himself'. Perhaps that is the best way to treat Shaw and Wells, as giants who were classics in themselves. Few men of letters have lived such fully engaged lives in the world, and put that fulness into their work, so that here one can rightly say that the work is the man. The truest and most useful judgment of either will be that which encompasses the life and the work together, as one record of a great imagination.

The original version was first published in *The Times Literary Supplement*, November 1969.

3

The Whole Contention Between Mr Bennett and Mrs Woolf

For most readers, Arnold Bennett's literary criticism probably exists – if it exists at all – only as a reflection in his enemy's eye. Virginia Woolf's 'Mr. Bennett and Mrs. Brown' has become the standard example of her kind of impressionism; it is included in anthologies of modern criticism, and is mentioned in histories of modern literature. But who attends to Bennett's criticism? Not one of his eight critical books is in print either in the United States or in England, and his hundreds of articles have simply disappeared. The colorful, opinionated, influential artist that was Arnold Bennett has faded into the author of one Edwardian novel, and the defeated antagonist of a fierce bluestocking.

A consequence of this state of affairs is that Mrs Woolf's essay has come loose from its context, and is read as though it were a complete, objective statement of the differences between two writing generations. But in fact it is neither complete nor objective: it is simply one blow struck in a quarrel that ran for more than ten years, and was far more personal than generational. Reading 'Mr. Bennett and Mrs. Brown' as a separate critical document is like watching the third round of a fifteen-round fight. We will understand both the essay and the combatants better if we understand the whole of their quarrel.

In 1917, when the quarrel began, Bennett was 50, successful, and astonishingly prolific. He had been writing novels at the rate of one a year for nearly twenty years; he had had five plays produced; and in his spare time he had turned out a vast amount of lively popular journalism. He wrote rapidly and easily, budgeted his time, and counted his words – that is to say, he was a professional. He was probably the best-known English novelist of the time; as he noted with satisfaction, his name on a poster sold newspapers, and strangers recognized him on the street. His evident pleasure in this sort of fame helped to establish what is still the dominant image of Bennett, as the self-satisfied provincial philistine who would write on any subject for two shillings a word, and who kept a yacht and a mistress on the proceeds.

But if there is truth in this version of Bennett, it is not the whole truth. There was another and more important side to him as a writer. One can see the other Bennett most clearly in the early critical writings, and especially in the columns that he contributed to the *New Age* under the pseudonym of Jacob Tonson (he collected some of the best in *Books and Persons*). These casual weekly pieces, most of which Bennett wrote for nothing, did much to make Edwardian England conscious of the twentieth century. Bennett was one of the few Englishmen in that insular time modern enough to be aware of what was happening in Europe, and he used his column to spread the news. He was the first English critic to testify to the greatness of *The Brothers Karamazov* (he had read it in French before Constance Garnett's translation appeared); he praised *The Cherry Orchard* when it was first performed in London, and scolded the audience for walking out; and he recognized the significance of the first Post-Impressionist show in London, not only for painters, but for all artists, including himself. He was a shrewd judge of his fellow novelists, and most of his judgments of writers like James, Conrad and Galsworthy will stand without revision. In all these matters he had what one might call *modern* intuitions.

When Bennett wrote about the novel, he was likely to make two main points: one, that the novelist should consider his audience; and two, that the novel is a serious art form. In the popular image of Bennett the first point has been stressed and the second ignored; consequently he appears as at best a skillful hack (this is the point of Ezra Pound's portrait of Bennett as 'Mr. Nixon' in *Hugh Selwyn Mauberley*). But the essence of Bennett's theory of the novel was that both these points should be made:[1]

there is a theory [he wrote in 1901] that the great public can appreciate a great novel, that the highest modern expression of literary art need not appeal in vain to the average reader. And I believe this to be true – provided that such a novel is written with intent, and with a full knowledge of the peculiar conditions to be satisfied; I believe that a novel could be written which would unite in a mild ecstasy of praise the two extremes – the most inclusive majority and the most exclusive minority.

Here Bennett is testifying to his belief in what he called 'the demo-
cratization of art'; but it is important to note that the critical standards
that the passage imposes remain those of *literary* art. A few years later,
reviewing a book by Sturge Moore, Bennett wrote:[2]

> His value is that he would make the English artist a conscious
> artist. He does, without once stating it, bring out in the most
> startling way the contrast between, for example, the English
> artist and the Continental artist. Read the correspondence of
> Dickens and Thackeray, and then read the correspondence of
> Flaubert, and you will see. The latter was continually preoccupied
> with his craft, the two former scarcely ever – and never in an
> intelligent fashion. I have been preaching on this theme for years,
> but I am not aware that anybody has been listening. I was going
> to say that I was sick of preaching about it, but I am not. I shall
> continue. . . .

The striking thing about this passage is the number of ways in which it
echoes the views, and even the phrases, of Edwardian writers with
whom Bennett is not usually connected – James, for example, and
Conrad and Ford. One can find the idea of the 'conscious artist', the
comparison of English and Continental attitudes, the admiration for
Flaubert's dedication and the contempt for Thackeray, all in Ford's
The English Novel, and similar remarks are scattered through the essays
and introductions of James and Conrad. The best of Bennett's novels
– *Clayhanger, The Old Wives' Tale, Riceyman Steps* – are built on these
critical principles, and the best of his criticism unambiguously pro-
claims his serious commitment to art. If one considers Bennett in these
terms – in terms, that is, of his *best* work and his most thoughtful
critical statements, then one must conclude that his place among
Edwardian novelists is with the Conscious Artists, and not with
Galsworthy and Wells. If this is true, then ironically he belongs among
the literary ancestors of Virginia Woolf.

In 1917 Mrs Woolf was younger, less known, and less productive
than Bennett. She had written one novel, which had not sold well. She
also wrote reviews and articles, as Bennett did, but she shunned the
publicity that might have attended literary journalism; much of her
reviewing was anonymous in *The Times Literary Supplement*, and other
pieces were signed with initials. To all her writing, whether a novel or
a short review, she gave the same meticulous attention; a single paragraph of an unimportant review might go through a dozen drafts

before it pleased her. She worked slowly and painfully and at great emotional expense, and she was excessively sensitive to criticism of what she had written. And what was true of her art was also true of her life: she was a reserved, fastidious, aristocratic woman who found human relationships difficult, and who stayed within the familiar and protective limits of her Bloomsbury circle.

Clearly Bennett and Mrs Woolf were antithetical in all the important particulars of their personalities. It is equally obvious, I think, that they were *not* antithetical in their views of their common art. Their quarrel, when it came, rose out of their personal differences, and not out of their aesthetic convictions; but it soon lost definition, and became an untidy and bitter wrangle that marred both their lives for more than a decade.

The first document in the case is an unsigned review of Bennett's *Books and Persons*, which Mrs Woolf wrote for the *TLS* in July 1917. It is on the whole a favorable notice. What it *says* is that Bennett is a creative artist and a knowing professional writer, and that his reviews have the vitality of speech. But it implies a rather different set of propositions: that Bennett in 1917 was out-of-date, that he was allied with second-rate Edwardian writers, and that he lacked the sensitivity of a well-bred person (for which one should read 'Bloomsbury'). None of these things are quite explicit, but then Mrs Woolf's critical writing never was; if Impressionism at its best expresses a delicate sensibility responding to the presence of art, at its worst it offers endless opportunities for innuendo and ill will. In this short review Mrs Woolf suggests that Bennett made the reputations of Galsworthy and Wells by over-praising them, and thus she at once creates the 'Edwardian' group that she would later attack, and marks them as inferior. She praises Bennett's criticism, but adds that it is 'not at all what we are accustomed to hear spoken at dinner-tables and in drawing-rooms. It is the talk of a writer in his work-room, in his shirt-sleeves.' So the praise of his professionalism becomes a denigration, of a kind most likely to chafe Bennett's Five Towns pride.

Two years later Mrs Woolf repeated and elaborated her case against Bennett in an unsigned essay, 'Modern Novels', also in the *TLS*. The essay is a sketch of the criticism of Bennett, Wells, and Galsworthy that was later elaborated in 'Mr. Bennett and Mrs. Brown': it attacks the three writers for their 'materialism', calls Bennett the worst culprit of the three, and – in a figure that recurs in later essays – compares Bennett's novels to well-built houses in which nobody lives.

It is worth noting that at this stage Mrs Woolf was willing to concede (though with qualifications) Bennett's skill at characterization:[3]

> His characters live abundantly [she wrote], even unexpectedly, but it still remains to ask how do they live, and what do they live for? More and more they seem to us, deserting even the well-built villa in the Five Towns, to spend their time in some softly padded first-class railway carriage, fitted with bells and buttons innumerable; and the destiny to which they travel so luxuriously becomes more and more unquestionably an eternity of bliss spent in the very best hotel in Brighton.[3]

As so often in Mrs Woolf's criticism, the point is blurred by fancy, but there is surely a note of class-conscious disapproval in the well-built villa and the Brighton hotel.

While there is no evidence that Bennett read either the essay or the review, or guessed the identity of their author, it seems unlikely that a man so conscious of his status would have missed a notice in the *TLS*; and London literary life being what it is, it is equally unlikely that he would not have known who his critic was. But if Bennett did know, he cannot have been much upset, for he took four years to retaliate. It was not until March 1923, that he referred to Mrs Woolf in print. Then, in an article called 'Is the Novel Decaying?', he cited *Jacob's Room* as an example of the sort of thing the new novelists were doing. 'I have seldom read a cleverer book,' he wrote. 'It is packed and bursting with originality, and it is exquisitely written.' But, he added, the novel had one flaw: 'the characters do not vitally survive in the mind, because the author has been obsessed by details of originality and cleverness.'[4] The point is not one that most readers of Mrs Woolf would dispute – even her friend E. M. Forster agreed that she was not much good at characterization – but Mrs Woolf disputed it. By choosing characterization as a critical issue, Bennett had inadvertently chosen the battlefield for the quarrel that followed.

Two months after Bennett's article appeared, Mrs Woolf was still brooding over his offense. In her diary for June 19 she wrote:[5]

> People, like Arnold Bennett, say I can't create, or didn't in *Jacob's Room*, characters that survive. My answer is – but I leave that to the *Nation*: it's only the old argument that character is dissipated into shreds now; the old post-Dostoevsky argument. I daresay it's true, however, that I haven't that 'reality' gift. I

insubstantize, willfully to some extent, distrusting reality – its cheapness.

The *Nation and Athenaeum* was the instrument through which Mrs Woolf had decided to strike back – quite naturally, since her husband was its Literary Editor. On 1 December 1923, an article by Mrs Woolf appeared in its pages, titled 'Mr. Bennett and Mrs. Brown'. This is not the much-anthologized essay of the same title, however; it is a shorter and very different first draft. The differences are worth pausing over.

In this first rebuttal, Mrs Woolf moved directly, if a little clumsily, to the attack. 'The other day', the essay begins,[6]

> Mr. Arnold Bennett, himself one of the most famous of the Edwardians, surveyed the younger generation and said: 'I admit that for myself I cannot yet descry any coming big novelist.'

This quotation from 'Is the Novel Decaying?' is followed by two paragraphs of further summary and quotation (or rather, of *mis*-quotation, for Mrs Woolf was not over-scrupulous in controversy, and revised and rearranged Bennett's words to suit her needs), which prepare the ground for a vigorous counterattack. As the basis for her defense, Mrs Woolf chose the point on which Bennett had criticized *Jacob's Room* – the point of characterization. Yes, she agreed, the novel *is* a remarkable machine for the creation of human character, and yes, vivid characterization *has* disappeared from English fiction. But the culprits were not of her generation. During the Edwardian years, two things had happened: first, sensitive men had become aware of the iniquities of the Victorian social system; and second, Mrs Garnett's translations of Dostoevsky had appeared. Social awareness turned novelists into reformers; Dostoevsky destroyed their conventional notions of what a 'character' was. Together these two influences altered writers' minds and, Mrs Woolf suggests, the effect was to make them better men, but worse artists.[7]

> The Edwardian novelists therefore give us a vast sense of things in general; but a very vague one of things in particular. Mr. Galsworthy gives us a sense of compassion; Mr. Wells fills us with generous enthusiasm; Mr. Bennett (in his early work) gave us a sense of time. But their books are already a little chill, and must steadily grow more distant, for 'the foundation of good fiction is character-creating, and nothing else', as Mr. Bennett says:

and in none of them are we given a man or woman whom we know.

One must admire the skill of the in-fighting here – the use of Bennett to abuse Bennett, and the parenthetical dismissal of all his later work – but it scarcely amounts to a theory of fiction.

Mrs Brown, the illustrative figure in the second version of the essay, appears in the first only at the end, and confusedly there, as though she were an afterthought. She has no identity, no distinct appearance, no mysterious story; she is simply a name. What does the young novelist do, Mrs Woolf asks, when he finds himself disagreeing with Wells, Galsworthy, and Bennett concerning the character of Mrs Brown?

. . . it is useless to defer to their superior genius. It is useless to mumble the polite agreements of the drawing-room. He must set about to remake the woman after his own idea. And that, in the circumstances, is a very perilous pursuit.

For what, after all, is character – the way that Mrs. Brown, for instance, reacts to her surroundings – when we cease to believe what we are told about her, and begin to search out her real meaning for ourselves? In the first place, her solidity disappears; her features crumble; the house in which she has lived so long (and a very substantial house it was) topples to the ground. She becomes a will-o'-the-wisp, a dancing light, an illumination gliding up the wall and out of the window, lighting now in freakish malice upon the nose of an archbishop, now in sudden splendor upon the mahogany of the wardrobe. The most solemn sights she turns to ridicule; the most ordinary she invests with beauty. She changes the shape, shifts the accent, of every scene in which she plays her part. And it is from the ruins and splinters of this tumbled mansion that the Georgian writer must somehow reconstruct a habitable dwelling-place; it is from the gleams and flashes of this flying spirit that he must create solid, living, flesh-and-blood Mrs. Brown. Sadly he must allow that the lady still escapes him. Dismally he must admit bruises received in the pursuit. But it is because the Georgians, poets and novelists, biographers and dramatists, are so hotly engaged each in the pursuit of his own Mrs. Brown that theirs is at once the least successful, and the most interesting, hundred years. Moreover, let us prophesy: Mrs. Brown will not always escape. One of these

days Mrs. Brown will be caught. The capture of Mrs. Brown is
the title of the next chapter in the history of literature; and, let
us prophesy again, that chapter will be one of the most important,
the most illustrious, the most epoch-making of them all.

That is the whole of Mrs Brown in her first appearance; she simply
flits through the conclusion of the essay, like a Georgian Ariel, wooing
novelists away from Caliban-Bennett. It is not a happy fancy.

But then, the first version of 'Mr. Bennett and Mrs. Brown' is not
very impressive in other respects, either. It has few virtues and many
faults, and those of kinds that are not often found in Mrs Woolf's
critical writing – faults of clumsiness, of ill-temper, of failure of
imagination. The essay seems hastily done; and yet her diary shows that
Mrs Woolf was at work on it six months before it appeared. And
apparently Mrs Woolf did not find the piece unsatisfactory; she
published it in three places in three months – once in England and
twice in the United States. Then she set about to re-write it, for
delivery as a lecture at Cambridge, where she read it to the girls of
Girton College in May 1924.

The argument of this, the familiar second version of the essay, is
essentially that of the first; like the first, it begins with a misquotation
of Bennett's 'Is the Novel Decaying?', though it is a different misquotation. But from there on, the strategy is very different. Most
noticeably, Mrs Brown's part in the show has been expanded from her
brief appearance as Ariel to a starring role in a dramatic vignette about
a clean old lady in a Waterloo train. The scene takes up a good deal of
space, and one may wonder why an imaginary character should so
dominate an essay concerned with the art of the novel. The ostensible
answer is that Mrs Woolf is demonstrating by example how human
character has changed, and the inadequacy of the old methods of
characterization to deal with the new task. But Mrs Brown quickly
expands beyond this function, and one may conclude that her real role
in the essay is simply to *be* an imagined character; Mrs Woolf, still
brooding over her lack of 'that "reality" gift', is demonstrating that
she has it, by creating a character right before our eyes. It is a demonstration designed not only to prove that she can create character, but
to show the superiority of her method to Bennett's (which is ridiculed
in a lengthy and somewhat misleading analysis of a passage from *Hilda
Lessways*).[8] But in fact, if we examine Mrs Brown carefully, we will
find that she is put together in pretty much the same way that Hilda is,

out of physical description and details of a characteristic environment; 'I thought of her in a seaside house, among queer ornaments' is not unlike Bennett's account of Hilda's house.

The tone of the second version is also remarkably changed. Perhaps Mrs Woolf had recovered her temper; or perhaps she realized that cheerfulness and charm were better weapons in a lady's hands than abuse. In any case, she managed in her revised version to ridicule, patronize, and actually distort Bennett's writing without raising her voice. Like the first version, this essay was published and republished: first in T. S. Eliot's *Criterion* (where it was called 'Character in Fiction'), then as the first pamphlet in the Hogarth Essays series, and again the following summer in the *New York Herald Tribune*. For one paragraph of mixed praise and criticism of *Jacob's Room*, Bennett had reaped six separate published attacks and one lecture.

In the summer of 1924, Bennett and Mrs Woolf appeared together in a symposium, 'What is a Good Novel?', published in *The Highway*, a socialist journal of adult education. Each took the occasion to reaffirm and harden previously stated critical views. Bennett repeated his opinion that good fiction depends on character-drawing, plotting, and 'an effect of beauty'; Mrs Woolf argued that 'a good novel need not have a plot; need not have a happy ending; need not be about nice or respectable people; need not be in the least like life as we know it', and renewed her attack on the use of exhausted conventions. Neither writer mentioned the other, but one can sense a critical drawing apart; for the first time, the critical attitudes they take are orthogonal. It is at this point, I think, that the two become self-consciously representatives of opposed schools; and it seems clear that it was Mrs Woolf who had forced the breach.

Bennett was aware of both of Mrs Woolf's replies, but he did nothing to extend the quarrel, even though Eliot proposed in September 1924 that Bennett reply to 'Character in Fiction' in the *Criterion*. In May 1925, Mrs Woolf provided a new target in *Mrs. Dalloway*, but Bennett did not comment on the book for more than a year. Then, in November 1927, Leonard Woolf reviewed Bennett's *Lord Raingo* unfavorably in the *Nation*. The Woolfs and Bennett met shortly after at a dinner at H. G. Wells's. According to Woolf, Bennett contributed nothing to the conversation except to stutter, at frequent intervals, 'W-w-woolf d-d-does not l-l-like my novels'. Bennett's own note on meeting the Woolfs was: 'Both gloomy, these two last. But I liked both of them in spite of their naughty treatment of me in the press.'[9]

And he regretted that he had not been seated where he could 'have a scrap with Virginia Woolf'.

He found his opportunity later the same month, when he began a new series of weekly 'Books and Persons' articles for the London *Evening Standard*. His second and third articles were addressed to young writers, and the latter of these focused particularly on Virginia Woolf, and on the Woolf-Bennett quarrel.[10]

> The real champion of the younger school [he wrote] is Mrs. Virginia Woolf. She is almost a senior; but she was the inventor, years ago, of a half-new technique, and she alone, so far as I know, came forward and attacked the old. She has written a small book about me, which through a culpable neglect I have not read. I do, however, remember an article of hers in which she asserted that I and my kind could not create character. This was in answer to an article of mine in which I said that the sound drawing of character was the foundation of good fiction, and in which incidentally I gave my opinion that Mrs. Woolf and her kind could not create character.

This is a fairly accurate account of the origins of the controversy, though one may doubt whether Bennett was in fact guilty of 'culpable neglect'; certainly he had read both versions of 'Mr. Bennett and Mrs. Brown' in the periodicals in which they first appeared.

Bennett then moved on to a more direct criticism of Mrs Woolf's books:[11]

> I have read two and a half of Mrs. Woolf's books. First, 'The Common Reader', which is an agreeable collection of elegant essays on literary subjects. Second, 'Jacob's Room,' which I achieved with great difficulty. Third, 'Mrs. Dalloway', which beat me, I could not finish it, because I could not discover what it was really about, what was its direction and what Mrs. Woolf intended to demonstrate by it.
>
> To express myself differently, I failed to discern what was its moral basis. As regards character-drawing, Mrs. Woolf (in my opinion) told us ten thousand things about Mrs. Dalloway, but did not show us Mrs. Dalloway.

The reader familiar with 'Mr. Bennett and Mrs. Brown' will recognize that final charge: it is simply a paraphrase of Mrs Woolf's judgment of *Hilda Lessways*.

From this point on, the public side of the argument was all Bennett's. The weekly column in the *Standard* provided him with a platform, and an appropriate stance. For as Bennett proceeded in his anti-Woolf campaign, he saw it more and more as a quarrel between popular art and coterie art, and for the champion of the popular a popular evening paper was an ideal medium. He was addressing the People – the tube-riders and commuters – and he addressed them as one of themselves, an ordinary bloke who wrote novels, and who knew what he liked.

Between 1927 and 1930 Bennett reviewed three books by Mrs Woolf, and disliked them all. He liked *To the Lighthouse* the best – thought it her best book – but having said that, he withdrew his praise in a series of slurring qualifications: Mrs Ramsay *almost* amounts to a complete person, the story is wilful and seemingly designed to exhibit virtuosity, the middle part doesn't work, the style is tryingly monotonous.[12] The following year he was more aggressively hostile to *Orlando*: the book was 'fanciful embroidery, wordy, and naught else', it lacked imaginative power, and it was even ungrammatical.[13]

That same year (1928) Bennett had another opportunity to advance his cause; he was asked to write on 'The Progress of the Novel' for the *Realist*, a journal on which he was a member of the editorial board.[14] The essay that he wrote is a recapitulation of his later views of the novel, but the form that his views took seems keyed to Mrs Woolf's criticisms of his own work. What he was writing was one more – and as it turned out, the last – refutation of 'Mr. Bennett and Mrs. Brown'. He therefore began his essay with a defense of social criticism: 'The chief mark of the serious novelist, after fundamental creative power, is that he has a definite critical attitude towards life.' (Mrs. Woolf had complained that the Edwardian novelists' books were incomplete: 'in order to complete them it seems necessary to do something – to join a society, or, more desperately, to write a cheque.') Bennett countered by praising novelists who were critics of life: Balzac, Wells, and Galsworthy (Mrs Woolf's two other Edwardian victims, linked to an unquestioned master). But Bennett continued, 'Simply to ask whether they are image-breakers or image-makers would be too simple and too crude'. (Mrs Woolf had described Joyce as 'a desperate man who feels that in order to breathe he must break the windows'.) He looked for examples of 'the constructive spirit' in modern fiction, and found it in the novels of Galsworthy and Wells.

Bennett had always admired Wells, but his praise of Galsworthy seems pretty clearly a reaction to Mrs Woolf, for in earlier essays his judgments had been on the whole unfavorable (and more in line with his own high standards). He wrote of *The Man of Property* and *The Country House*, for example, 'personally I do not consider that either of Mr Galsworthy's novels comes within the four-mile radius of the first-rate', and he objected to Galsworthy's treating oppressors with less sympathy than the oppressed – i.e., he disliked his social criticism; but those opinions were uttered in the days before Mrs Woolf, when Bennett was in his own eyes an artist, and not a *popular* artist.

At the end of 'The Progress of the Novel', having defended Edwardianism, Bennett turned to the young. And there, between R. H. Mottram and Henry Williamson, he found room for a few words on Mrs Woolf.

> Virginia Woolf has passionate praisers, who maintain that she is a discoverer in psychology and in form. Disagreeing, I regard her alleged form as the absence of form, and her psychology as an unco-ordinated mass of interesting details, none of which is truly original. All that I can urge in her favor is that she is authentically feminine, and that her style is admirable. Both these qualities are beside my point.

This would seem to be the definitive and final dismissal of his antagonist, but one further opportunity presented itself, and Bennett took it. In October 1929 Mrs Woolf published *A Room of One's Own*, and Bennett commented on it, and on her, in the *Standard*. 'If her mind were not what it is', he wrote, 'I should accuse her of wholesale padding. This would be unjust. She is not consciously guilty of padding. She is merely the victim of her extraordinary gift of fancy (not imagination).'[15] This distinction is a new one in Bennett's criticism; what it seems to distinguish is the kind of mind that could create Mrs Brown (fancy) from the kind of mind that had created Hilda Lessways. A more significant, and unfortunate, distinction is the one Bennett makes between himself and Mrs Woolf:

> She is the queen of the high-brows; and I am a low-brow. But it takes all sorts of brows to make a world, and without a large admixture of low-brows even Bloomsbury would be uninhabitable.

Here the class bias that had been implicit in the quarrel from the beginning nearly reached the surface. This is sad, because Bennett was not a low-brow, either socially or artistically. But he had been despised in public by a lady, and voluntary vulgarity was one defense against her; and so he abdicated his place among serious artists, and widened the gap between two excellent kinds of fiction.

Even after such severe words, the two combatants met socially, and apparently amiably. In December 1930, they were together at dinner; Bennett's journal-note was 'Virginia is all right; other guests held their breath to listen to us.' In her diary, Mrs Woolf was less generous: 'This meeting I am convinced was engineered by B. to "get on good terms with Mrs. Woolf" – when Heaven knows I don't care a rap if I'm on terms with B. or not.' She ridiculed his stutter, his vanity, his art. 'I like the old creature', she noted. 'I do my best, as a writer, to detect signs of genius in his smoky brown eye. . . .' But she concluded that she did not feel him to be a creative artist. The whole entry makes unpleasant reading – most unpleasant because it is gratuitous cruelty and aggressiveness recorded for the private eye alone.

Three months later Bennett was dead. Mrs Woolf recorded the event in her diary:[16]

Arnold Bennett died last night; which leaves me sadder than I should have supposed. A lovable genuine man; impeded, somehow a little awkward in life; well meaning; ponderous; kindly; coarse; knowing he was coarse; dimly floundering and feeling for something else; glutted with success; wounded in his feelings; avid; thicklipped; prosaic intolerably; rather dignified; set upon writing; yet always taken in; deluded by splendor and success; but naive; an old bore; an egotist; much at the mercy of life for all his competence; a shopkeeper's view of literature; yet with the rudiments, covered over with fat and prosperity and the desire for hideous Empire furniture; of sensibility. Some real understanding power, as well as a gigantic absorbing power. These are the sort of things that I think by fits and starts this morning, as I sit journalising; I remember his determination to write 1,000 words daily; and how he trotted off to do it that night, and feel some sorrow that now he will never sit down and begin methodically covering his regulation number of pages in his workmanlike beautiful but dull hand. Queer how one regrets the dispersal of anybody who seemed – as I say – genuine: who had direct contact with life – for he abused me; and I yet rather wished him to go on abusing me; and me abusing him. An element in life – even in mine that was so remote – taken away. This is what one minds.

A curious, exposed comment. Mrs Woolf twice says that Bennett was *genuine* – a quality which she associated with grossness, coarseness, and appetite. He had 'direct contact with life', and that gave him, perhaps, the 'reality gift' that Mrs Woolf doubted in herself, the gift that she despised and envied. But Bennett was also the critic who had abused her, and even at his death she had to go on abusing him back, sneering in private at his 'shopkeeper's view of literature' and his vulgar taste in furniture.

There is one further comment in the diary, and it is a revealing one. In May 1933 – two years after Bennett's death – Mrs Woolf was preparing to write *The Pargiters*, the book that eventually became *The Years*.[17]

> I think I have now got to the point where I can write for four months straight ahead at *The Pargiters*. Oh the relief – the physical relief! I feel as if I could hardly any longer keep back – that my brain is being tortured by always butting against a blank wall – I mean *Flush*, Goldsmith, motoring through Italy. Now, tomorrow, I mean to run it off. And suppose only nonsense comes? The thing is to be venturous, bold, to take every possible fence. One might introduce plays, poems, letters, dialogues: must get the round, not only the flat. Not the theory only. And conversation: argument. How to do that will be one of the problems. I mean intellectual argument in the form of art: I mean how give ordinary waking Arnold Bennett life the form of art?

The whole of the contention is in that final phrase: for Mrs Woolf, Arnold Bennett represented Life – ordinary, waking life. For Bennett, Mrs Woolf represented Art – highbrow, bloodless, supercilious art. These are the poles of a quarrel that has little to do with generations, of Edwardians vs. Georgians, though it has a lot to do with the history of the novel in the twentieth century. The quarrel between Bennett and Mrs Woolf publicized the divorce of art from ordinariness in the novel, and thus helped to create a coterie audience for Mrs Woolf (which was certainly bad for her reputation). It also speeded the decline of Bennett's reputation as a novelist, and this is even worse for Bennett, who deserves the place that Mrs Woolf denied him, among the conscious artists.

Notes

1 *Fame and Fiction* (New York, 1901), p. 16.

2 'Books and Persons', *New Age*, vi (24 March 1910), 494.

3 'Modern Novels', *TLS* (10 April 1919), p. 189. A revised version entitled 'Modern Fiction' was included in *The Common Reader* in 1925.

4 *Cassell's Weekly*, II (28 March 1923), 47. The essay is reprinted in *Things That Have Interested Me*, third series (New York, 1926), pp. 160–3.

5 *Writer's Diary* (New York, 1954), p. 56.

6 *Nation and Athenaeum*, xxxiv (1 December 1923), 342.

7 *Ibid.*, p. 343.

8 For an excellent analysis of Mrs Woolf's methods, see Irving Kreutz, 'Mr. Bennett and Mrs. Woolf', *Modern Fiction Studies*, viii (summer 1962), 103–15.

9 Woolf, *Beginning Again* (London, 1964), p. 124; Bennett, *Journal* (New York, 1933), p. 910.

10 *Evening Standard* (2 December 1926), p. 5.

11 *Ibid.*

12 *Evening Standard* (23 June 1927), p. 5.

13 *Evening Standard* (8 November 1928), p. 5.

14 *Realist*, i (April 1929), pp. 3–11.

15 *Evening Standard* (28 November 1929), p. 5.

16 *Writer's Diary*, pp. 165–6.

The original version was first published in *Novel*, fall 1967.

4

Orage and the *New Age*

Alfred Orage was a man who, as Shaw observed, 'did not belong to the successful world'. He was an editor who never ran a profitable paper, a socialist who backed Guild Socialism against the Fabians, an economist who preached Social Credit against the Keynesians, a literary critic who found *Ulysses* repellent and disliked the poems of Yeats, a mystic who expected the Second Coming. In thirty years of public life he never supported a winning cause, or profited from a losing one; the movements that consumed his energies are dead, and so are the journals that he edited, and the books that he wrote.

Yet when Orage died in 1934 he was remembered, and mourned, by many men more celebrated than he. The memorial number of the *New English Weekly* (of which he was the founder and first editor) included elegiac notes from Eliot, Chesterton, Shaw, A. E., Pound, Wells, Augustus John, Richard Aldington, Herbert Read, Middleton Murry, G. D. H. Cole, Frank Swinnerton, Edwin Muir, and St John Irvine, all expressing a sense of loss, and all for different reasons. Eliot praised the literary critic, A.E. the *guru*, Pound the economist; others admired Orage's brilliance as an editor, his flair for discovering talent, his prose style, his disinterestedness, his obstinacy. There is no doubt that to his contemporaries Orage was important; the question is, what importance, if any, remains?

One might say, first of all, that Orage is important as a representative of a type – the lower-middle-class provincial intellectual who turned up in considerable numbers around the beginning of this century and gave a new thrust and tone to English literary life. He belongs, that is, with Wells and Bennett and Lawrence. And he had all the characteristics of the type; he was learned but half-educated, arrogant and quick to take offence, charming but humourless, grimly serious about art and ideas ('a judge of literature cannot afford to indulge in witticisms', he said, and he never did). He was extremely susceptible to conversion, and it could be said of him, as Wells remarked of Nietzsche, that he was so constituted that to get an idea was to receive a revelation. He had many revelations, and like Wells and Lawrence he had a messianic itch to turn his revelations into dogmas. Part radical reformer and part heterodox evangelist, he helped to give Edwardian intellectual life its characteristic tone of strenuous but sombre zeal.

Orage is most representative of his type in the variety of his enthusiasms. Like many another man of his time he had gone to the two sources of Victorian values – science and liberalism – and had found them bankrupt.

> Spencer and Darwin had mechanized the world [he wrote] and carried the industrial revolution into thought. Tennyson on his lawn had prettified it and hung it with paper garlands. But nothing could conceal the fact that the new world was repellent and that *nothing* was better than the only certainty promised by it.

For a born believer like Orage, such nihilism was not in fact possible, and he turned instead to newer, less orthodox systems in search of values. In his earlier years he was a Theosophist, a Nietzschean, and a Fabian Socialist; later he tried psychoanalysis, Social Credit, and Gurdjieff's 'institute' at Fontainebleau. Some of his spiritual restlessness one must attribute to the temper of the time, but the eccentric forms in which it was expressed is a function of the type; a man like Orage, rooted neither in a traditional education nor in a fixed social role, will regard society and its ideas as infinitely revisable because he has no stake in either. And he will set few limits on the intellectual instruments that he employs to re-build society and its ideas so that they will include him.

Orage's own roots were in Yorkshire, and in poverty. His father was an improvident schoolmaster who died when his son was a year old, and his mother supported her family by taking in washing. Alfred, the clever child of the family, was encouraged by the local squire, who sent him to a teachers' training college. He became, like Lawrence, a schoolmaster, and settled in Leeds. There he joined the Theosophical Society, the Fabian Society, and a 'Plato Group', and helped to found the Leeds branch of the Independent Labour Party and the Leeds Arts Club. This is a remarkable range of intellectual activities for a provincial city in the 1890s, but for Orage it was insufficient. In 1906 he left Leeds, his teaching career, and his wife, and went up to London to become a full-time intellectual.

In London Orage entered into political activities, and became at once two kinds of socialist: he joined the Gilds Restoration League, and he re-joined the Fabian Society. His intentions as a socialist are made clear in a letter that he wrote to Wells in July 1906:

I beg to enclose for your consideration a draft of the objects of a *Gilds Restoration League*. You have, I know, advocated at the Fabian Society and elsewhere a propaganda of Socialism among the middle classes. The main objection to Socialism which I have found amongst those classes is to its materialism. This, of course, is due to the accident that Socialism has been largely bound up with trades unionism. Which in its turn has been necessarily an economic protestant movement. Thus the real obstacle to middle class conversion to Socialism is the fear that it may involve government by trades union officials.

The defect of the Trades Union movement is felt however quite as much by many Socialists as by non-Socialists. Most of the artists and craftsmen I have met are in favour of the Labour Programme on grounds of Justice but *not* on grounds of art. As explained in the enclosed draft the Arts and Crafts Movement while really as much a social reform movement as trades unionism, has nevertheless kept itself since Morris' day aloof from actual politics. And this absence of the artists and craftsmen *as* artists from the Socialist movement really accounts for the objections raised by the middle classes. The object of the proposed *Gilds Restoration League* is to bring about a union between the economic aims of the Trades Unionists and the aesthetic aims of the craftsmen. Hitherto, the collectivist proposals have been designed solely to make economic poverty impossible; it is necessary to design them not only to make economic but also aesthetic poverty impossible. This, of course, would involve a considerable modification of the usual Collectivist formulas, on the lines, I think, sketched in your *Modern Utopia*. However, I am proposing to issue the enclosed in printed form and over a wide area during the coming autumn: and to call together all those who are interested for the purpose of discussing the best methods of procedure.

As a member of the Fabian Society, I should have been glad to see that Society take up the present propaganda; but I am afraid the major part of the Fabians is too rigidly bound to the collectivist formulas to make such a hope practicable.

This William-Morrisy mixture of romantic medievalism and aestheticism may strike one as improbable, and as altogether incompatible with the statistical rationalism of the Fabian Society, but socialism in 1906 was a slumgullion of fads and dissensions that could accommodate any view, so long as it was unconventional. It was, Orage later recalled,

> a cult, with affiliations in directions now quite disowned – with theosophy, art and crafts, vegetarianism, the 'simple life', and almost, one might say, with the musical glasses. Morris had shed a medieval glamour over it with his stained-glass *News from Nowhere*, Edward Carpenter had put it into sandals, Cunninghame Graham had mounted it upon an Arab steed to which he was always saying a romantic farewell. Keir Hardie had clothed it in a cloth cap and a red tie. And Bernard Shaw, on behalf of the Fabian Society, had hung it with innumerable jingling epigrammatic bells – and cap. My brand of socialism was, therefore, a blend or, let us say, an anthology of all these, to which from my personal predilections and experience I added a good practical knowledge of working classes, a professional interest in economics which led me to master Marx's *Das Kapital* and an idealism fed at the source – namely Plato.

If this socialist anthology seems an odd account of a Fabian, one need only remind oneself that the society began as The Fellowship of the New Life, a front-parlour discussion group that included communists, spiritualists, psychic researchers and single taxers, and that for a long time it remained receptive to members from the queer fringes of radicalism.

Orage's conception of his role in the Fabian Society became clear very quickly; he was to be a leader of the philosophical and aesthetic wing. With his friend Holbrook Jackson he created the Fabian Arts Group, with the ostensible aim of making an appeal to 'minds that remained unmoved by the ordinary Fabian attitude', and of providing 'a platform for the discussion of the more subtle relationships of man to society which had been brought to the front in the works of such modern philosopher-artists as Nietzsche, Ibsen, Tolstoy, and Bernard Shaw'. One might think that the Fabian leaders, faced with this frank contempt for their methods and opinions, would have discouraged Orage, but instead they encouraged him to buy a paper. In the spring of 1907 Orage and Jackson raised enough money to buy the *New Age*, a failing weekly of uncertain convictions and no circulation, and the *Fabian News* announced the birth of a new socialist journal, to be run strictly 'on Fabian Lines'. If the Fabians had paused to consider the sources of Orage's funds, they might have viewed the birth of his paper with less confidence; he had got £500 from Shaw, but the other £500 had come from a theosophical banker in the City. This curiously mixed parentage one may take as symbolical; for from birth the *New Age* was at best a bastard socialist.

The *New Age* gives Orage another kind of importance. He edited it, almost without help, for fifteen years. During those years he published a more impressive list of contributors than any other British journal: among more than 700 were Belloc, Bennett, Bierce, Brooke, Burns, Carpenter, Chesterton, Cunninghame Graham, Havelock Ellis, Ervine, Galsworthy, Gogarty, Harris, Hulme, John, Mansfield, Murry, Pound, Herbert Read, Sassoon, Shaw, Sickert, Swinnerton, Webb, Wells, West, and Zangwill; art work reproduced included drawings by Epstein, Gaudier-Brzeska, Wyndham Lewis, Sickert, and Picasso. 'Great editorship', Orage said, 'is a form of creation, and the great editor is measured by the number and quality of the writers he brings to birth – or to ripeness.' By this standard, Orage was the greatest English editor of this century; nowadays, when that title is often awarded to Ford Madox Ford for his *English Review*, it is worth noting that Ford ran his review for little more than a year, lost £5,000, and was fired, while Orage kept the *New Age* going for fifteen years with an initial investment one-fifth the size of Ford's, and resigned. Ford was brilliant, but Orage lasted.

Orage's notion of a great editor says nothing about ideas, principles, or editorial policy, and the paper that he edited had little intellectual coherence; it was, like its editor's socialism, an anthology of views. It first appeared as 'an Independent Socialist Weekly' with impeccable socialist credentials – the first issue carried letters of congratulation from Sidney Webb, Edward Pease (the Secretary of the Fabian Society), and Prince Kropotkin. But it also contained an editorial that those congratulators must have read with sinking hearts. 'Socialism as a progressive will', the editors observed,

> is neither exclusively democratic nor aristocratic, neither anarchist nor individualist. Each of the great permanent moods of human nature, as imperfectly reflected in the hierarchy of society, has its inalienable right to a place in the social pyramid.
> Believing that the darling object and purpose of the universal will of life is the creation of a race of supremely and progressively intelligent beings, *The New Age* will devote itself to the serious endeavour to cooperate with the purposes of life, and to enlist in that noble service the help of serious students of the new contemplative and imaginative order.

This untidy mixture of socialism, Nietzscheanism, and mysticism is a fair expression of Orage's untidy thought, and the journal that he edited was similarly eclectic. It published, for example, the reactionary philosophical essays of T. E. Hulme as well as the heretical socialism of Wells, and found space both for Ford's support of women's suffrage and Orage's fierce opposition to it. If it had an editorial policy at all, it was simply an open-door policy. 'One used to write to *The New Age*', Belloc later recalled, 'simply because one knew it to be the only paper in which the truth with regard to our corrupt policies, or indeed with regard to any powerful evil, could be told.' And when Hulme was asked why he wrote for such a radical journal, he replied simply, 'Because they'll print me'. The *New Age* may have set out to be an 'independent socialist weekly', but the emphasis was on 'independent', and one can see why the Webbs soon gave up hope of seeing it run on Fabian lines, and founded the *New Statesman* to serve that purpose.

The greatest appeal of such a farraginous chronicle was to people like Orage, provincial intellectuals in search of a faith, and it is not surprising that such people made up a substantial number of both its contributors and its readers. The regular writers – the now for-gotten journalists who attended Orage's salon in the basement of the Chancery Lane ABC – were mostly, like Orage, poor intellectual outsiders. And the subscribers included people like young D. H. Lawrence, who shared the paper with the Eastwood intelligentsia and liked it more for its literature than for its politics. One may guess that it was far better read in Eastwood than in Westminster, because it meant more there; it was the voice of rebellion and liberation, not clear, perhaps, but loud.

This point of authorship and audience may in part account for the fact that the *New Age*, for all its vigour and occasional distinction, seems to have had little impact on the direction of English thought in its time. But a more important factor is that it had little direction itself. Eclecticism may stimulate, but it does not move, and the *New Age* left behind vivid impressions of its editor's personality, but no impressions of its policies.

When Orage left the journal in 1922, he left a remarkable record of achievements. He had run a weekly for fifteen years virtually without capital. He had persuaded most of the important writers of the time to write for him, and to write for nothing (Arnold Bennett, that most cash-conscious of writers, wrote a weekly piece in the *New Age* for eighteen months without payment). He had not only published Ezra Pound, but had made him into a music critic. He had encouraged many young writers, and had published the first works of a number who later made names for themselves, including Katherine Mansfield, Richard Aldington, and Middleton Murry. He had taught and demonstrated the importance of good writing, the style, as he called it, of 'brilliant common sense'. But most important, he had brought new ideas to a new audience, and had helped to redefine the English intellectual class.

Having said so much, one should note also the *New Age*'s limitations. It never published an excellent poem, rarely a good story. It opened its pages to a good deal of rubbish, simply because it was *new* rubbish. In the post-war years Orage indulged his strong mystical streak, and published the incomprehensible writings of a Serbian prophet called Mitrinović; at the same time he was giving space to Major Douglas and Social Credit, and the result was a concentrated unreadability that diminished Orage's reputation, and nearly destroyed the paper.

Orage's own contributions were sometimes examples of the brilliant common sense that he preached, and these won him the admiration of distinguished contemporaries like Chesterton, who described Orage as 'a man who wrote fine literature in the course of writing fighting journalism', and Eliot, who admired him both as a leader-writer and a critic. For Orage these elements – the literary quality, the editorial vigour, and the critical judgment – were not distinct, and his ideal writing was a prose that would combine them all. Recalling his 'Readers and Writers' columns in the *New Age*, which he wrote weekly for seven or eight years, Orage wrote:

> My original design was to treat literary events from week to week
> with the continuity and policy ordinarily applied to comments on
> current events; that is to say, with equal seriousness and from a
> similarly more or less fixed point of view as regards both means
> and ends. This design involved of necessity a freedom of
> expression distinctly out of fashion . . .

When he achieved this goal, he was very good indeed, and his two
books of these essays – *Readers and Writers* and *The Art of Reading* –
do give a lively sense of the literary politics of those years. But the art
of the leader-writer is a transitory one, and it is not surprising that
Orage's essays are not read now; for by treating literature as current
events, he had guaranteed his own swift obsolescence. But even when
they were written many of his pieces must have seemed unworthy of
his talents, for his doctrine of free expression encouraged vigorous
writing at the expense of judgment and restraint, and he was capable of
crude brutality in his criticisms, and of windy vagueness in his philoso-
phizing. As his causes failed and his voice lost authority, he became
more and more negative in his own defence, and less readable.

Orage's last years, after his resignation from the *New Age*, are puzzling
and sad. He became a disciple of Gurdjieff and laboured for him for a
year at Fontainebleau. Then he went to New York as Gurdjieff's
representative and stayed six years, teaching and raising funds for the
'institute'. In 1931 he returned to England to found a new paper, the
New English Weekly, which he edited until his death.

The *New English Weekly* clearly set out to be another *New Age*,
and was greeted as such by the dozens of old admirers who wrote
their testimonies for the first issue – A.E., Epstein, Henry Nevinson,
Swinnerton, Herbert Read, Gogarty, Havelock Ellis, Eric Gill, T.
Sturge Moore. These were the readers, and in most cases the writers, of
Orage's first paper, and what they hoped for was more of the same.
To a considerable degree they got it: Pound returned with Cantos
and economic theories, Major Douglas contributed his own economic
essays, A. J. Penty, from the Gild Restoration days, was still around
offering alternatives to communism. But the times had changed, and
so had Orage; his mind was fixed on economic issues, and economics,
even in the 1930s, could not make a paper lively. He continued to
demonstrate his good eye for promising young writers – one finds
Walter Allen, Basil Bunting, Erskine Caldwell, Emily Hahn, Storm

Jameson, Stephen Potter, and Michael Roberts in early issues – and he had improved his taste in poetry (or his advisers) remarkably, with poems by David Gascoyne, Dylan Thomas, and William Carlos Williams, but he never found a formula, or an audience, that would make the paper succeed.

Looking back over Orage's life, one can see that his need to follow was as great as his need to lead, and that his submission to Gurdjieff's beliefs and discipline was inevitable. But to the unconverted the spectacle of a strong mind capitulating is depressing, and Orage's later life seems a waste of a lively intelligence. In his memoir of Orage, Eliot remarked his 'restless desire for the absolute'; the desire one may call a strength in Orage's character, but the restlessness dissipated that strength, drove him aimlessly from faith to faith, and made his life, in the end, incoherent. 'Gurdjieff once told me', Orage said, 'that he knew my ambition. He said I wanted to be one of the "elder brothers" of the human race, but that I had not the ability it required.' That observation will do for Orage's epitaph.

The original version was first published in *The Times Literary Supplement*, 25 April 1968.

5

Conrad and Ford:
Two Rye Revolutionists

As Edwardian England recedes farther and farther into the past, it becomes easier for us to see how revolutionary that *belle époque* really was. Among other changes, a revolutionary change took place in the way that Englishmen – at least *some* Englishmen – thought about the novel. The geographical center of the revolution was at Rye, where Henry James was living, with his co-revolutionists scattered about the neighborhood: Conrad at Pent Farm, Ford at Winchelsea, Crane at Brede Place (and the counter-revolutionary Wells sneering at Sandgate). Important English writers do not ordinarily fit very neatly into schools, but the Rye Revolutionists were, in a loose way, a kind of school, held together by common theories about fiction, by common likes and dislikes, as well as by the odd fact that none of them was altogether an Englishman (in the novel, as in poetry, the defences of nineteenth-century convention had to be breached by an invasion of foreigners).

The group around James – by which I mean in his vicinity, for certainly nobody sat at his feet – shared a sense of European roots (Flaubert and Turgenev were their patriarchs, Tolstoy their anti-Christ) and a common contempt for 'the national English novelist', the literary tradesman who produced what Ford contemptuously referred to as *nuvvles*. They agreed that a novel should be rendered action, from which the novelist rigorously excluded himself, and, most importantly, they believed that the writing of fiction could be a high and noble calling – a calling made noble not by the high-minded morality of its content, but by the perfection of its art. 'In this matter of life and art', Conrad wrote, 'it is not the Why that matters so much to our happiness as the How. As the Frenchman said: "*Il y a toujours la manière*".' That Frenchman's remark might stand as the slogan of the Rye Revolutionists: there is always the manner, the way of doing it. We can see how thoroughly their revolution has carried the day if we consider how self-evident and incontrovertible their principles now seem: a revolution has succeeded when its battle cries have become platitudes.

To learn those principles, the best place to go to is still the critical writings of James. James belongs – and he is the only novelist who does belong – among the great English artist-critics, with Dryden and Coleridge and Eliot. His is the first order of criticism, the kind that, like a lens, magnifies to reveal; the criticism of his fellows is of the second order, the kind that, like a mirror, reflects the observer. If one reads the criticism of Ford and Conrad, then, one does so to learn, not about The Novel, but about the novels of these two writers, and to discover, perhaps, something of their principles and intentions. This is a perfectly good reason for reading such criticism, and a sufficient justification for publishing it; still the fact remains that if neither Ford nor Conrad had written novels, their criticism would not be worth the reading.

The amount of Conrad's writing that could be called literary criticism is relatively small: there are the essays collected in *Notes on Life and Letters*, the prefaces to the first collected edition, some letters, and a scattering of notes to other men's works. Conrad was not by nature a theorist; he mistrusted rational processes and abstract discourse, and regarded his own work as the product of instinct and intuition: 'One does one's work first', he wrote, 'and theorizes about it afterwards.' But in fact he didn't theorize about it, because his mind was not equipped to do so; most of his critical writing is either simply appreciative (as in the essay on James) or reminiscent (as in the long, moving tribute to Stephen Crane) or – in the case of the prefaces to the collected edition – pale imitation of James. Here and there one finds a sharp aphoristic remark (as when he describes James as 'the historian of fine consciences'), but almost never a sustained argument.

One must conclude that though Conrad was an emotionally complex man, he was intellectually simple. His aesthetic principles, like his philosophical principles, were few and plain: a half-page of note paper would contain all the ideas that he had. One could begin with this remark from a letter to Cunninghame Graham:

> There is no morality, no knowledge and no hope: there is only the consciousness of ourselves which drives us about the world that, whether seen in a convex or a concave mirror, is always but a vain and floating appearance.

This near-solipsism is a philosophical stance that Conrad shared with many of his contemporaries, and certainly it defines a line of English fiction from James to Virginia Woolf. If there is only the consciousness of ourselves, then the only possible matter of fiction is consciousness, and the sensations that consciousness records. And that is precisely Conrad's understanding of his art – as he says in the much-quoted passage from his Preface to the *Nigger*:

> My task which I am trying to achieve is, by the power of the
> written word to make you hear, to make you feel – it is, before
> all, to make you *see*. That – and no more, and it is everything.

To hear, to feel, to see – if that is everything, it is so only in a world limited to the apprehension of sense data. The world that Conrad's novels propose is such a world – a world of isolated consciousnesses, each open to the rich, mysterious data of experience, but closed to one another. Conrad did not believe in the illuminated heart, and though he recorded the 'vain and floating appearance' of the world with scrupulous exactitude, he left the motives and awarenesses of his characters shrouded in obscurity and cloudy rhetoric – not because he could not invent clear motives, but because he could not imagine a human relationship in which motives would be mutually comprehensible (his Heyst is a paradigmatic figure – a man alone on an island below the horizon, visible to other men only as a cloud of smoke).

The *Nigger* Preface contains Conrad's whole aesthetic; he wrote it very early in his career, but he never evolved beyond its propositions. The artist, he said, draws from his own experience the sense data that will appeal to the feelings of his readers; the appeal is to 'that part of our being which is not dependent on wisdom', and must therefore be made by conveyed impressions, and not by persuasion: hence before all to make you see. In philosophical defence of this anti-rational aesthetic, Conrad proposed an analogy between art and life: both are inspiring, difficult, and 'obscured by mists'; art therefore offers men models of life's mysteries, rather than the superior ordering of experience that most aesthetic systems would propose. For Conrad, the artist has no superior wisdom: he lives in the commonplace world 'in which, like the rest of us, he has that share which his senses are able to give him'. (Note that the senses are the sole agent of knowledge here.) He is subject to no moral imperatives except one, which the aesthetic implies: he must be true to his own sensations.

It is through this truth-to-sensations that Conrad introduces the idea of *craft*. The true rendering of one's perceptions requires an austere and rigorous technique, and the elimination of elements that are not fundamentally sensational; the authorial voice, for example, must go, not because it is inartistic, but because it implies assumptions about the nature of truth that are invalid; similarly, a chronological ordering of events is wrong because it is untrue to the realities of perception, in which human histories do not come to us in straight lines.

The forms of Conrad's novels are therefore difficult and obscure by intention. Even James was a bit staggered by the difficulty of *Chance*, which, he observed, 'places the author absolutely alone as the votary of the way to do a thing that shall make it undergo the most doing' (*toujours la manière*), and he plainly could not understand why Conrad should so gratuitously violate 'the general laws of fiction'. The answer is that Conrad had set out to render experience as he perceived it, with all the limitations and difficulties of perception built into it: 'In doing this book', he wrote in the preface to *Chance*, 'my intention was to interest people in my vision of things, which is indissolubly allied to the style in which it is expressed.' This is the central point about Conrad as a thinker-about-fiction: that his forms emerged from his vision of things, and not from theories.

It is this sense of the art-life relationship that most separates Conrad from James, co-revolutionists though they were. For James, art was artifact, the unique creation of the considering mind: surely that is the point of his elaborately embryological prefaces – to demonstrate the complete disparity between the germ of initial idea and the intricately finished work. But for Conrad, art was subject to the same pressures and uncertainties as life, and was to be lived in the same way. Consequently his thoughts about fiction are thoughts about life – interesting for what they reveal about Conrad's mind at work, but not generally illuminating of the novel as a genre.

Ford used to claim that he had shared in the composition of some of Conrad's novels. Whether this claim is true or not, he certainly did have a major share in the composition of Conrad's reputation as a Conscious Artist. Much of the cloud of anecdote and theoretical terminology that has gathered about Conrad has come from Ford's *Joseph Conrad, A Personal Remembrance* – anecdotes that make Conrad a Polish Flaubert, and terms like *cadence* and *progression d'effet* and *time shift* that do not occur in Conrad's critical writings, and for which we have only Ford's word. But though Ford's impressions were trustworthy, his word often was not – a point which he freely acknowledged in the Conrad book by calling it a novel. Ford's Conrad is a fictional character who might very well have written Conrad's novels, but didn't, and who expresses theories that Conrad might very well have expressed, but didn't, at least not in those fancy terms.

The relation between Ford and Conrad during their years of collaboration, and their individual contributions to the Rye Revolution, have been obscured – probably forever – by Conrad's reticence and Ford's romancing. From the evidence, though, it must have been something like this: Conrad, the older, more experienced, more dedicated writer, provided the conception of the artist, and the 'European' concern with form; Ford provided an easy command of English idiom, an intelligent audience for Conrad, and eventually the critical formulations of the ideas that they discussed. In the many years that followed the collaboration, it was certainly Ford who carried the message of the Conscious Artist to the younger generation; his *English Review* made the new ideas public property, and the role he played, for the last thirty years of his life, of an 'old man mad about writing' was influential in the best ways. I doubt that any English writer of our time, excepting James, had more to do with the establishment of the novel as a serious art form in England than Ford did; but he accomplished what he did by example, and by direct personal influence, and it is not possible to argue that his critical writings had, or could have had, such an effect. And if one examines his novels against Conrad's, observing that Conrad was experimenting with disordered time and shifting point of view as early as *Lord Jim*, while Ford did nothing comparable until *The Good Soldier*, one must conclude that the ideas were probably Conrad's.

Not that Ford was merely a disciple; he had his own ideas, and a definably individual approach to the craft of writing. If, like Conrad's, Ford's ideas could be presented without distortion on half a page, this is not to suggest that these two were particularly impoverished minds – the same would be true of almost anyone. For Ford's half-page, I'd start with this sentence from *Thus to Revisit*: 'I am interested only in how to write, and . . . I care nothing – but nothing in the world! – what a man writes about.' And from *The Spirit of the People*: 'It is all one whether the artist be right or wrong as to his facts; his business is to render rightly the appearance of things.' And from his essay 'On Impressionism': 'I am a perfectly self-conscious writer: I know exactly how I get my effects.' The sum of these remarks is what Ford called

Impressionism – a theory of art that explains both Ford's writing strengths and his weaknesses. In so far as Impressionism means the right rendering of experience, it is like Conrad's practice; but Ford went a good deal further toward complete subjectivism than Conrad did. Ford's Impressionism denied external reality as an objective check on the artist's 'rendering'; for Ford (and he said it again and again) only the subjective state, the *impression* of appearance, mattered. But novelists, like the rest of us, must assume that the stone is there because we kick it. Ford's refusal to accept this check led to unnecessary inaccuracies in his writing, and even in his life; his enemies called him a liar because he did not let the facts of his own biography alone, and even his friends agreed that he could not remember even the greatest works of literature as they were written, but only as his transforming memory had re-created them.

It is easy to denigrate a man whose grasp on bread-and-butter reality is as fallible as that, and Ford had more than his share of denigration. Happily that time is past, and his reputation is solidly established; surely his five best novels will never again drop from the canon of important twentieth-century fiction. As for the rest of his long list of books, no amount of artificial respiration by admiring critics will bring most of them to life again, though a few deserve to survive – not the other novels and romances, perhaps, but the earlier memoirs, the book on the English novel, and the Conrad. None of these books is primarily valuable as criticism, and all are marked by Ford's characteristic disregard for facts; nevertheless, they are worth reading, first because they are all really about an attractive, semi-fictional character called Ford Madox Ford, and second because they are, as Ford would have said, 'written', intricately constructed examples of the fiction-making mind at work transforming reality. No one ever wrote memoirs as nearly like novels as Ford's, and as novels they should be read.

The original version was first published in *Sewanee Review*, January–March 1965.

6

Ford Madox Ford

a   The Epistemology of *The Good Soldier*

The problems involved in the interpretation of *The Good Soldier* all stem from one question: What are we to make of the novel's narrator? Or, to put it a bit more formally, what authority should we allow to the version of events which he narrates? The question is not, of course, particular to this novel; it raises a point of critical theory touching every novel which employs a limited mode of narration.

The point is really an epistemological one; for a novel is a version of the ways in which a man can know reality, as well as a version of reality itself. The techniques by which a novelist controls our contact with his fictional world, and particularly his choice of point of view and his treatment of time, combine to create a model of a theory of knowledge. Thus the narrative technique of Fielding, with the author omniscient and all consciousnesses equally open to him, implies eighteenth-century ideas of Reason, Order, and General Nature, while the modern inclination toward a restricted and subjective narrative mode implies a more limited and tentative conception of the way man knows.

When we speak of a limited-point-of-view novel, then, we are talking about a novel which implies a limited theory of knowledge. In this kind of novel, the reality that a man can know is two-fold; the external world exists as discrete, observed phenomena, and the individual consciousness exists. That is, a man is given what his senses tell him, and what he thinks. The 'central intelligence' is a narrow room, from which we the readers look out at the disorderly phenomena of experience. We do not *know* (as we know in Fielding) that what we see has meaning; if it has, it is an order which the narrator imposes upon phenomena, not one which is inherent there. And we can know only one consciousness – the one we are in. Other human beings are simply other events outside.

This seems to be equally true of first- and third-person narration in this mode; it is difficult to see an epistemological difference between, say, *The Ambassadors* and *The Aspern Papers*. James, however, favored the third-person method, and used it in all his major novels. He did so, I think, because it enabled him to take for granted, 'by the general law of nature', as he put it, 'a primary author'; it allowed him, that is to say, to retain a vestige of authority, even though that authority 'works upon us most in fact by making us forget him'. In fact, though the 'primary author' of James's novels is a rather retiring figure, we do not forget him, and from time to time he comes forward to realign us with the truth, to tell us what we know.

In the first-person novel, on the other hand, it is at least possible to eliminate authority altogether, and to devise a narrative which raises uncertainty about the nature of truth and reality to the level of a structural principle. A classic example is the one before us, and it is in these terms that I will examine Ford's narrative techniques.

The Good Soldier is 'A Tale of Passion', a story of seduction, adultery, and suicide told by a deceived husband. These are melodramatic materials; yet the novel is not a melodrama, because the action of which it is an imitation is not the sequence of passionate gestures which in another novel we would call the plot, but rather the action of the narrator's mind as it gropes for the meaning, the reality of what has occurred. It is an interior action, taking its order from the processes of a puzzled mind rather than from the external forms of chronology and causation. This point is clear enough if one considers the way in which Ford treats the violent events which would, in a true melodrama, be climactic – the deaths of Maisie Maidan, Florence, and Ashburnham. All these climaxes are, dramatically speaking, 'thrown away', anticipated in casual remarks so as to deprive them of melodramatic force, and treated, when they do occur, almost as afterthoughts. (Ashburnham's death is literally an afterthought: Dowell says on the last page but one, 'It suddenly occurs to me that I have forgotten to say how Edward met his death', and even then he does not give us an account of the actual suicide.)

The narrative technique of *The Good Soldier* is a formal model of this interior action. We are entirely restricted to what Dowell perceives, and the order in which we receive his perceptions is the order of his thought; we never know more than he knows about his 'saddest story', and we must accept his contradictions and uncertainties as stages in our own progress toward knowledge. At first glance, Dowell seems peculiarly ill-equipped to tell this story, because he is ill-equipped to *know* a tale of passion. He is a kind of eunuch, a married virgin, a cuckold. He has apparently never felt passion – certainly he has never acted passionately. He is a stranger to human affairs; he tells his wife's aunts that he does nothing because he has never seen any call to. And he is an American, a stranger to the society in which his story takes place.

But more than all this Dowell would seem to be disqualified as the narrator of *any* story by the doubt and uncertainty which are the defining characteristics of his mind. One phrase runs through his narrative, from the first pages to the last: 'I don't know'; and again and again he raises questions of knowledge, only to leave them unanswered: 'What does one know and why is one here?' 'Who in this world can know anything of any other heart – or of his own?'

The patent inadequacies of Dowell as a narrator have led critics of the novel to dismiss his version of the meaning of the events, and to look elsewhere for authority. Mark Schorer speaks of Dowell's 'distorted understanding', and James Hafley of his 'incoherent vision' and both look outside the narrator himself for objective truths to justify their judgments. But the point of technique here is simply that the factors which seem to disqualify Dowell – his ignorance, his inability to act, his profound doubt – are not seen in relation to any norm; there is neither a 'primary author' nor a 'knower' (of the kind of James's Fanny Assingham or Conrad's Marlowe) in terms of which we can get a true perspective of either Dowell or the events of the novel. There is only Dowell, sitting down 'to puzzle out what I know'. The world of the novel is his world, in which 'it is all a darkness'; there is no knowledge offered, or even implied, which is superior to his own.

In a novel which postulates such severe limits to human knowledge – a novel of doubt, that is, in which the narrator's fallibility *is* the norm – the problem of authority cannot be settled directly, because the question which authority answers: 'How can we know what is true?' is itself what the novel is about. There are, however, two indirect ways in which a sense of the truth can be introduced into such a novel without violating its formal (which is to say epistemological) limitations: either through ironic tone, which will act to discredit the narrator's version of events and to imply the correctness of some alternative version, or through the development of the narrator toward some partial knowledge, if only of his own fallibility (and indeed in an extreme case this may be the only kind of knowledge possible for him). Glenway Westcott's *The Pilgrim Hawk* and Eudora Welty's 'Why I live at the P.O.' are examples of the first device; each offers a sequence of events which are in themselves clear enough to the reader, and the irony lies in the disparity which we feel between the way the narrator understands these events and the way we understand them. The point made is thus a point of character, the revelation of a personal failure of perception.

The Great Gatsby is a fair example of the other sort. Fitzgerald's Nick Carraway learns as the action moves, and though he misunderstands and is surrounded by misunderstanding, in the end he knows something about himself, and about Gatsby, and about the world. The point made is a point of knowledge

It has generally been assumed by Ford's commentators that *The Good Soldier* belongs to the class of *The Pilgrim Hawk*; but in fact it is closer to *Gatsby*. Ford's novel is, to be sure, as ironic as Westcott's, but with this difference; that Ford's narrator is conscious of the irony, and consciously turns it upon himself. When he describes his own inactions, or ventures an analysis of his own character – when he says 'I appeared to be like a woman or a solicitor', and describes himself as 'just as much of a sentimentalist' as Ashburnham – he is consciously self-deprecating, and thus blocks, as any conscious ironist does, the possibility of being charged with self-delusion. Schorer errs on this crucial point when he says that 'the author, while speaking through his simple, infatuated character, lets us know how to take his simplicity and his infatuation'. For the author does not speak – the novel has no 'primary author'; it is Dowell himself who says, in effect, 'I am simple and infatuated' (though there is irony in this, too; he is not all *that* simple).

The case for reading the novel as Schorer does, as a comedy of humor, is based on the enormity of Dowell's inadequacies. There are two arguments to be raised against this reading. First, Dowell's failures – his failure to act, his failure to understand the people around him, his failure to 'connect' – are shared by all the other characters in the novel, and thus would seem to constitute a generalization about the human condition rather than a moral state peculiar to him. Alienation, silence, loneliness, repression – these describe Ashburnham and Leonora and Nancy, and even 'poor Florence' as well as they describe Dowell. Each character confronts his destiny alone.

Second, Dowell does have certain positive qualities which perhaps, in the light of recent criticism of the novel, require some rehabilitation.

For instance, if his moral doubt prevents positive action, it also restrains him from passing judgment, even on those who have most wronged him. 'But what were they?' he asks. 'The just? The unjust? God knows! I think that the pair of them were only poor wretches creeping over this earth in the shadow of an eternal wrath. It is very terrible.' And though he doubts judgment – doubts, that is, the existence of moral absolutes – he is filled with a desire to know, a compelling need for the truth to sustain him in the ruin of his life. In the action of the novel, the doubt and the need to know are equally real, though they deny each other.

Dowell has one other quality, and it is his finest and most saving attribute – his capacity for love; for ironically, it is he, the eunuch, who is the Lover. Florence and Ashburnham and Maisie Maidan suffer from 'hearts', but Dowell is sound, and able, after his fashion, to love – to love Ashburnham and Nancy, and even Leonora. It is he who performs the two acts of wholly unselfish love in the book – he crosses the Atlantic in answer to Ashburnham's plea for help, and he travels to Ceylon to bring back the mad Nancy, when Leonora will not. And he can forgive, as no other character can.

This is the character, then, through whom Ford chooses to tell this 'saddest story'. He is a limited, fallible man, but the novel is not a study of his particular limitations; it is rather a study of the difficulties which man's nature and the world's put in the way of his will to know. Absolute truth and objective judgment are not possible; experience is a darkness, and other hearts are closed to us. If man nevertheless desires to know, and he does, then he will have to do the best he can with the shabby equipment which life offers him, and to be content with small and tentative achievements.

Dowell's account of this affair is told, as all first-person narratives must be, in retrospect, but the technique is in some ways unusual. We know the physical, melodramatic world only at one remove, so that the real events of the novel are Dowell's thoughts about what has happened, and not the happenings themselves. We are never thrown back into the stream of events, as we are, for example, in the narratives of Conrad's Marlowe; dramatic scenes are rare, and tend to be told in scattered fragments, as Dowell reverts to them in his thoughts. We are always with Dowell, after the event.

Yet though we are constantly reminded that all the events are over and done, we are also reminded that time passes during the telling (two years in all). The point of this device is the clear distinction that the novel makes between events and meaning, between what we have witnessed and what we know. All the returns are in, but their meaning can only be discovered (if at all) in time, by re-examination of the data, by reflection, and ultimately by love. And so Dowell tells his story as a puzzled man thinks – not in chronological order, but compulsively, going over the ground in circles, returning to crucial points, like someone looking for a lost object in a dim light. What he is looking for is the meaning of his experience.

Since the action of the novel is Dowell's struggle to understand, the events are ordered in relation to his developing knowledge, and are given importance in relation to what he learns from them. Thus we know in the first chapter that Dowell's wife, Florence, is dead, hear in the second chapter of part II Dowell's account of that death (which he believes to be a heart attack), and only in part III learn, through Dowell's account of Leonora's version of the event, that it was in fact suicide. We move among the events of the affair, to stand with Dowell for a moment behind Ashburnham, then to Leonora, to Nancy, and back to Ashburnham, getting in each case an account, colored always by Dowell's compassionate doubt, of the individual's version of events. The effect of this ordering is not that we finally see one version as right and another as wrong, but that we recognize an irresolvable pluralism of truths, in a world that remains essentially dark.

There are, as I have said, certain crucial points in the narrative to which Dowell returns, or around which the narrative hovers. These are the points at which the two conflicting principles of the novel – Convention and Passion – intersect. The most important of these is the 'Protest' scene, in which Florence shows Ashburnham the Protestant document, signed by Luther, Bucer and Zwingli, which has made him what he is – 'honest, sober, industrious, provident, and clean-lived'. Leonora's reaction to this typical tourist scene strikes Dowell as a bit extravagant:

> 'Don't you see,' she said, with a really horrible bitterness, with a really horrible lamentation in her voice, 'Don't you see that that's the cause of the whole miserable affair; of the whole sorrow of the world? And of the eternal damnation of you and me and them. . . .'

He is relieved when she tells him that she is a Roman Catholic because it seems to provide an explanation of her outburst; and later his discovery that Florence was Ashburnham's mistress offers another, and more credible explanation. But neither explanation is really adequate. For Leonora is not simply reacting either to Protestantism or to adultery; she is reacting, in the name of a rigid conventionalism, to the destructive power of passion, which may equally well take the form of religious protest or of sexual license.

Ford once described himself as 'a sentimental Tory and a Roman Catholic', and it is in these two forms that convention functions in *The Good Soldier* (and in a number of his other novels as well). Society, as Dowell recognizes, depends on the arbitrary and unquestioning acceptance of 'the whole collection of rules'. Dowell is, at the beginning of his action, entirely conventional in this sense; conventions provide him with a way of existing in the world – they are the alternatives to the true reality which man cannot know, or which he cannot bear to know. From conventions he gets a spurious sense of permanence and stability and human intimacy, and the illusion of knowledge. When they collapse, he is left with nothing.

Leonora's conventions are her 'English Catholic conscience, her rigid principles, her coldness, even her very patience', conventions which are, Dowell thinks, 'all wrong in this special case' (it is characteristic of him that he refuses to generalize beyond the special case). Ashburnham's are those of a sentimental Tory – 'what was demanded by convention and the traditions of his house'. (A first draft of Ashburnham appears in *The Spirit of the People*, Ford's study of the English mind; there the scene between Ashburnham and Nancy at the railway station is offered as an example of the Englishman's characteristic reticence and fear of emotion.) It is by these conventions that the husband and wife act at crucial moments; but it is not conventions alone which bring about their tragedy. It is, rather, the interaction of Convention and Passion.

Passion is the necessary antagonist of Convention, the protest of the individual against the rules. It is anarchic and destructive; it reveals the secrets of the heart which convention exists to conceal and repress; it knows no rules except its own necessity. Passion is, of course, an ambiguous term. To the secular mind it is likely to suggest simply sexual desire. But it also means suffering, and specifically Christ's sacrificial suffering. I don't mean to suggest that Ashburnham is what it has become fashionable to call a 'Christ-figure' – I dislike the critical method which consists in re-writing novels as Passion Plays – but simply that the passionate sufferings of Ashburnham (and even of Leonora) are acts of love, and as such have their positive aspects.

Convention, as Dowell learns, provides no medium for the expression of such love. In conventional terms it is true, as Dowell says, that Edward and Nancy are the villains, and Leonora the heroine, but the expense of her conventional heroism is the defilement of what is best in her, and the destruction of what she loves, while the 'villains' are, in their suffering, blessed; the epigraph of the novel is their epitaph: *Beati Immaculati*, blessed are the pure.

Between the conflicting demands of Convention and Passion, the characters are, as Nancy says, shuttlecocks. 'Conventions and traditions I suppose', Dowell reflects near the end of the book, 'work blindly but surely for the preservation of the normal type; for the extinction of proud, resolute, and unusual individuals.' Passion works for the reverse.

In the action of Dowell's knowing, he learns the reality of Passion, but he also acknowledges that Convention will triumph, because it must. 'Society must go on, I suppose, and society can only exist if the normal, if the virtuous, the slightly deceitful flourish, and if the passionate, the headstrong, and the too-truthful are condemned to suicide and to madness.' Yet in the end he identifies himself unconditionally with Passion: 'I loved Edward Ashburnham', he says, 'because he was just myself.' This seems a bizarre assertion, that Dowell, the Philadelphia eunuch, should identify himself with Ashburnham, the English county squire and lover ('this is his weirdest absurdity', Schorer remarks of this passage, 'the final, total blindness of infatuation, and self-infatuation'). But in the action of the novel the identification is understandable enough. The problem that the novel sets is the problem of knowledge, and specifically knowledge of the human heart: 'Who in this world knows anything of any other heart – or of his own?' Dowell, in the end, *does* know another human heart – Ashburnham's, and knowing that heart, he knows his own. By entering selflessly into another man's suffering, he has identified himself with him, and identity is knowledge. He is, to be sure, ill-equipped for this knowledge; he lacks, as he says, Ashburnham's courage and virility and physique – everything, one would think, that goes to make an Ashburnham. But by an act of perfect sympathy he has known what Ashburnham was, and he can therefore place himself honestly in the category of 'the passionate, the headstrong, and the too-truthful'.

With this confession, the affair is over. The action in Dowell's mind is complete, or as complete as it can be in a novel built on doubt. The repeated questions, which Ford uses as Shakespeare uses questions in the tragedies, almost as symbols of the difficulty of knowing, disappear from the last chapter; but they are replaced, not by an emergent certainty, but by resigned admissions of the limits of human knowledge: 'I don't know. I know nothing. I am very tired' and 'I can't make out which of them was right. I leave it to you.' To know what you can't know is nevertheless a kind of knowledge, and a kind that Dowell did not have at the beginning of the affair. Of positive knowledge, he has this: he knows something of another human heart, and something also of the necessary and irreconcilable conflict which exists between Passion and Convention, and which he accepts as in the nature of things. Beyond that, it is all a darkness, as it was.

The original version was first published in the *Sewanee Review*, spring 1961.

b   The Conscious Artist

The division of literary careers into periods is more often than not simply an arbitrary convenience for critics – small bites, as we tell our children, are more easily chewed. But in the case of Ford Madox Ford we have support both from the man and from the work for dealing with him in two distinct periods, roughly before and after the First World War. During the first period Ford lived in and around London, moved in the literary circles of the time, wrote some forty books and a vast amount of literary journalism, and edited the *English Review*. After the war he lived in self-imposed exile in France and the United States, and found readers and admirers outside his native country.

The impression that one gets from Ford's writing – both his fiction and his reminiscences – is that the two periods were radically discontinuous; there are two quite distinct bodies of creative work, and there are two very dissimilar lives. Looking back on his pre-war years, Ford remarked late in life, 'Whatever I may have since written may be regarded as the work of a different man', and he symbolically affirmed this view by taking a new name after the war. His first life – the life of Ford Madox Hueffer – had ended, or so he thought, in ostracism by the English literary establishment, and both the publication history of his later work and the generally hostile tone of the obituary notices at his death suggest that this was not entirely a delusion. The second life – that of Ford Madox Ford – was the life of an alien and a wanderer.

Ostracism must have hurt Ford deeply, for his first desire (in so far as another man's desires can be inferred) was to be an English Man of Letters – something between Edmund Gosse and Maurice Hewlett. In the years before the war he pursued this goal by writing romances in the manner of Hewlett and weekly book-page essays in the manner of Gosse, by belonging to clubs and dining with editors and politicians, and by giving literary parties at his house on Campden Hill. By 1908 his goal must have seemed very near; he was thirty-five years old, he had written more than twenty books, and he was the editor of a review which, under his editorship, was to be the acknowledged best of modern English literary periodicals. David Garnett remembers him at this time:

> He was arrayed in a magnificent fur coat; – wore a glossy topper; drove about in hired carriages; and his fresh features, the colour of raw veal, his prominent blue eyes and rabbit teeth smiled benevolently and patronizingly upon all gatherings of literary lions.

A year later the review had a new editor, Ford was in court (and in the newspaper headlines) for non-support, and the London man-of-letters dream was over. From this time on Ford became more and more an outsider in his own land.

To understand the Ford of these early years it is important to recognize the particular nature of his dream. He was, as he put it, 'a man of no race and few ties'; what he wanted was to be supremely English. He was the son of a German, he was the grandson of a Pre-Raphaelite painter, and he was a Roman Catholic, and all these were liabilities in the eyes of the establishment. Much of his earlier work can be explained as moves in a campaign to demonstrate that he belonged where in fact he did not belong – in English society as a man of letters. Hence, for example, his trilogy on 'Englishness' – *The Soul of London*, *The Heart of the Country*, and *The Spirit of the People*; hence perhaps the volumes of English historical romance, and *The Cinque Ports*; and hence the hearty 'By Jove' clubman style of his popular romances. 'Ford used to say', Allen Tate has recalled,

> that he wrote his novels in the tone of one English gentleman whispering into the ear of another English gentleman: how much irony he intended I never knew; I hope a great deal.

One can resolve Mr Tate's uncertainty by referring to Ford's novels. In general, the answer is that no irony was intended in the novels written before the war; none could have been intended, for Ford's aim was clearly to write about English society from within it. Whether he indeed managed to write like an English gentleman must be a subjective judgment; certainly he did not write much of permanent value, excepting those historical novels in which the 'tone of an English gentleman' was not necessary.

To explain fully Ford's alienation from the English establishment one must add two other 'ungentlemanly' factors to those already mentioned. One was Ford's habitual romancing inaccuracy, which he elevated to the level of an aesthetic principle, and called Impressionism. Impressionism, for Ford, meant a subjective version of experience from which there could, or at least should, be no appeal to facts. He called his first book of recollections *Memories and Impressions*, and observed complacently in the dedication, 'This book is full of inaccuracies as to facts, but its accuracy as to impressions is absolute'; and in *The Spirit of the People* he wrote: 'It is all one whether the artist be right or wrong as to his facts; his business is to render rightly the appearance of things.' Ford seems to have regarded all facts, including the facts of his own life, as legitimately subject to reordering and improvement by the imagination. When he wrote about actual persons (as in his many volumes of memoirs) he wrote about his impressions of them, and lived happily enough with the resulting inaccuracies.

The curious consequence of this view is that Ford's fiction is often more accurate than his facts; the treatment of the Marwood brothers in *Parade's End* comes closer to biographical accuracy than anything Ford says about them in his autobiographical writings, while his personal remembrance of Conrad is flatly described in the Preface as a novel. The book on Conrad understandably annoyed readers like H. G. Wells, who held verifiable truth in somewhat higher esteem, and who felt that a remembrance should not be quite so frankly fiction. Other acquaintances of Ford complained that in his later years his view of his own life as a work of imagination which he could rewrite at will sometimes took the form of Etonian ties and casual references to 'the Guards' (he had gone to University College School and had served in the Welsh Regiment). This latter, peculiarly un-English behaviour confirmed to the establishment the rightness of the alienation which had by then thoroughly taken place.

Ford was as 'un-English' in his views of fiction as he was in his views of fact. He professed to despise the great tradition of Fielding, Thackeray and Dickens – writers of what he contemptuously called 'nuvvles' – and claimed as his literary ancestors Flaubert, Maupassant, and Turgenev. During the early years of the century, while he was living at Winchelsea, he associated with a circle of 'foreigners' in the neighbourhood – with Conrad and Henry James and Stephen Crane – who had designs on the novel quite alien to the English tradition. They regarded the novel as a work of art, and the craft of fiction as a high calling. H. G. Wells, for a time their neighbour, regarded them all with suspicion: 'Hueffer,' he remarked disparagingly, 'talked criticism and style and words'. It was no doubt in part the influence of these foreigners that led Ford to write 'the best French novel in English', *The Good Soldier.*

Ford's relation to Conrad had begun earlier, in 1898, when Conrad wrote to him, inviting him to collaborate. Ford's serious literary career began with this collaboration (and no doubt for some critics ended there). By 1898 he had, it is true, written six books, whereas Conrad had written only four; but Ford's books were three children's stories, a privately printed volume of juvenile verses, a very bad novel, and a biography of his grandfather, while Conrad's were *Almayer's Folly, An Outcast of the Islands, The Nigger of the Narcissus,* and *Tales of Unrest.* Nevertheless, Conrad came to Ford. His idea of collaboration seems, in retrospect, the desperate, impossible scheme of an impractical, penniless artist; it was to be a way of making a little money by inserting into his own kind of work something more marketable. In Ford, Conrad saw poetry and style, and no doubt from Ford's confident, man-of-letters manner he got the impression of literary facility and sensitivity to popular taste. During the years of collaboration Conrad worked his young partner cruelly hard, borrowed money from him, lived in his house, and on occasion ridiculed him behind his back; in later years he referred to Ford in the most denigrating terms. Conrad's letters suggest that he regarded the arrangement as a necessary exploitation of a useful, expendable young man; but to Ford it must have seemed a ruinous expenditure of money, emotion, and talent.

Ford emerged from the experience poorer than he had entered it, and in a state of nervous collapse, with nothing to show for the years of work, neither money nor serious work of his own. He had, however, acquired a good deal of knowledge, though not of a sort likely to advance his desire for a place in English society. He had learnt from Conrad what a Conscious Artist (to use a phrase Ford grew fond of) was, and what dedication to art might mean, and he had developed his own ideas of the craft of fiction, though he had not found a subject appropriate to them.

The break with Conrad coincided with Ford's greatest personal troubles, and with his loss of the *English Review*. The years that followed were productive ones – he published fourteen books between 1910 and the outbreak of the war – but they must have seemed to Ford the end of an unsuccessful career. In 1914 he took a 'formal farewell of Letters', and entered the Army with apparent relief. When he returned to writing, it was as a different man; Hueffer had become Ford, the clubman had become the alien. He had failed as a Man of Letters, and as an Englishman; but by failing, he made it possible to succeed as a writer.

Ford's own opinion of the work of his first 'life' is as severe as any critic's could be: 'I had never really tried to put into any novel of mine all that I knew about writing', he wrote later,

> I had written rather desultorily a number of books – a great number – but they had all been in the nature of *pastiches*, of pieces of rather precious writing, or of *tours de force*.

Then, 'on the day I was forty I sat down to show what I could do – and *The Good Soldier* resulted'. Ford regarded *The Good Soldier* as his best work, and most of his critics have approved this judgment. It is the first novel to which Ford applied all the techniques that had evolved during his long association with Conrad – the intricate organization of time, the manipulation of narration to express a limited narrative consciousness, the controlled notation of impressions, the authorial aloofness – and it demonstrates beyond question that his technical skills were of the first order. It is also the first work of Ford's alienation, the first to regard the subjects of class, love, manners and money from a position outside established English society. The hero remains the English Gentleman, but the narrator is an outsider (an American expatriate), and the 'tale of passion' that he tells is of a kind that gentlemen do not discuss in their clubs.

The Good Soldier brings together the three principal themes which preoccupied Ford, and which run through his best work: passion and its relation to love; class and society; and the morality of independent action. These themes are not ordinarily separable in his novels, for Ford was acutely aware of the ways in which they interrelate – how love bends under social pressure, how class determines attitudes and values, and compels renunciations, and how both love and class may influence an individual's attempts at free moral choice. One may find these themes in Ford's work as early as *The Benefactors* (1905); they are more fully developed in *A Call* (1910), and most elaborately worked out in the intricate structure of Ford's massive tetralogy, *Parade's End*.

Ford saw the passionate life as taking two possible forms, which he habitually represented in two contrasting women. One woman is warm and generous, self-abnegating, sacrificial. The other is passionate with a cold passion, and driven by an obsessive desire to possess; passion for this kind of woman is a torture because she craves, in Auden's phrase, 'Not universal love, But to be loved alone'. She is possessive, but she is also possessed, and there is something diabolic in the passion of her pursuit (in his historical romances Ford sometimes represented this woman as a witch). One might say of these two female types that they symbolize the two sides of a basic (perhaps the most basic) human conflict. One, because she asks nothing, symbolizes freedom and natural instinct; the other, asking everything, is order and restraint, society and conscience. All the sanctions are on the side of order; only the emotions favour freedom. It is worth noting that neither woman's appeal is essentially sexual, and that in fact Ford's novels have very little overt sexuality in them. Ford understood that as long as man is a thinking animal sex will always be sex-in-the-head.

Between these two kinds of passion Ford stretched his typical hero – the suffering English Gentleman, a man who is drawn naturally toward the consolations of the sacrificial woman, but is at the same time tied to his destroyer by his own conceptions of honour and rectitude. In this impossible situation, his only course is to suffer like a gentleman, neither complaining nor making scenes in front of the servants, for as long as his strength lasts. Ford offered no solution to this dilemma; the action ends when the strength of the sufferer ends. Ashburnham, in *The Good Soldier*, cuts his throat because he 'must have a bit of a rest'; Tietjens, in *Parade's End*, agrees to live with the woman he loves only after the war has reduced him to a penniless, half-mad outcast; and Grimshaw, in *A Call*, surrenders to his tormentor only because, as he says, 'I'm very tired; I'm very lonely, I've discovered that there are things one can't do – that I'm not the man I thought I was. . . .' This tortured, exhausted hero is perhaps what Ford had in mind when he called two of his novels 'tales of passion' – *passion* having in this case its radical sense of *passio*, suffering. In a perfect dilemma positive action is not possible. But suffering is.

In constructing his passionate triangles Ford put the power of society on the side of his predators. Sylvia Tietjens and Leonora Ashburnham act with the authority of the marriage contract behind them, and to the English Gentleman the rightness of this authority is not to be questioned. But Society has other powers as well; instinctive, passionate action is impossible because in the eyes of Society it would be scandalous, and because it would be ill-bred. And so Tietjens does not divorce his unfaithful wife, Ashburnham does not bolt with Nancy Rufford, Grimshaw submits to a woman towards whom he feels 'as cold as a stone'. (The same pattern of renunciation appears in other Ford novels as early as *The Benefactors* and as late as *The Rash Act* (1933).) The situation is tragic, but tragic in a way which Ford considered peculiar to modern society, which has taught its members not wisdom but only how to behave, and which has in fact made a morality of good manners. The tragedy must end, therefore, either in mute and well-mannered suffering, or in suicide, or, in *Parade's End*, in a complete break with society.

The theme of moral responsibility follows from Ford's idea of class and its commitments. 'What have we arrived at in our day and our class', asks a character in *A Call*, 'if we haven't learnt to do what we want, to do what seems proper and expedient – and to take what we get for it?' This morality of take-and-pay Ford imagined to be an essentially aristocratic morality; his Gentlemen practise it, and suffer because they do, but there is no suggestion in the novels that a less painful course might be better, and the characters who practise a more comfortable, permissive morality are treated as being wicked and vulgar – terms which for Ford, as for James, were virtually synonymous.

Ford's treatment of the problem of right action is thus not unlike Hemingway's – both writers start with the assumption that neither society nor nature offers standards of conduct which will at once preserve society and provide man with an opportunity to think well of himself – that is, to see his own actions as at once free and moral. The

Ford hero, like the Hemingway hero, chooses arbitrarily to surrender freedom of action in order to preserve a sense of personal honour, and does so by committing himself to a severe code of conduct which is not rationally justifiable. The Code of the Gentleman is unreasonable, and does not lead Ford's heroes to either happiness or virtue; it may save them from vulgarity and dishonour, but it does so at the expense of suffering and renunciation. But the world, as the narrator of *The Good Soldier* says, is a darkness, and the idea of honour is a small, possible light, by which a man may live a life of grace under pressure.

Ford's most ambitious statement of these themes is in the tetralogy to which he gave the collective title, *Parade's End*. In these four books, as much as in *The Good Soldier*, he put all he knew about writing, and all he knew about the passionate man of honour in a crumbling, dishonourable world. Whether *Parade's End* is as good as *The Good Soldier* depends on whether one prefers the limited, perfect performance or the large, imperfect one; certainly it is one of the great English novels of this century. Through the vast intricacies of its structure, the rich multiplicity of its characters, the large movements of its actions, Ford 'renders' the meaning of the First World War to England and the English – the moral and social changes that it effected, and the human sacrifice and suffering that it required. It is not, strictly speaking, a 'war novel' (unless *War and Peace* is also a war novel); rather it is a novel of social and personal disintegration, for which the war provided an historical analogue. Christopher Tietjens, the gentleman-hero, is the last Tory gentleman, driven out of the new society, which has no place for his old-fashioned ideas of honour and rectitude and duty.

One might consider *Parade's End* among Ford's historical fiction, beside his other many-volumed masterpiece, *The Fifth Queen*. Both works are long and intricate, and both depend for their architectonic strength upon the framework of actual history, a fact which suggests certain limitations in Ford's creative powers. Impressionism, as Ford understood it, was a method of organizing consciousness – it could give precise definition to states of mind, but it could not, and did not, order exterior space and time. The order of *The Good Soldier* is memory, imaginatively created, and in that novel memory is sufficient; but memory is always in danger of falling into self-regard, or into irrelevance and garrulity, unless the objective world imposes its own limits. History provided Ford with such limits, and made it possible for him to write two long novels which are spacious without being formless. It also provided him with defined personalities outside his own, characters with real existences independent of his memory, and thus preserved the aloofness which he regarded as a literary virtue.

Parade's End is the last of Ford's important fiction. The 'fourth book of the tetralogy was published in 1928; Ford spent the ten years that remained to him re-using his techniques and his anecdotes, repeating himself in an ever more garrulous and formless way. Of the last fourteen books only two rise above triviality: *The Great Trade Route* (1937) and *Provence* (1938) are interesting because they are unashamedly garrulous – the free associations of an old man with many memories. But at the end Ford had lost his ability to turn experience into imagination. The shape of memory and the shape of fiction had lost their distinctions.

An evaluation of Ford's achievement must begin with a few flat statements: he wrote five novels – *The Good Soldier* and the *Parade's End* tetralogy – which deserve a permanent place among the best of English fiction; he wrote the best historical romance of this century – *The Fifth Queen*; he wrote 'impressions' of his friends and his times which are charming and perceptive, if not always scrupulous about facts. But his importance does not stop with his writing. He was, by proclamation and performance, the Concious Artist, the 'old man mad about writing' who could say 'I am interested only in how to write', and mean it. If more often than not his work fell short of his principles, yet the principles and the aspiration toward them were noble. He had a vision of what the craft of writing might be, and by his generous example he influenced generations of younger writers, from Ezra Pound to Robert Lowell (his principal influence, one should note, was not on English writers). He was a brilliant editor, a friend and encouragement to other writers, an experimenter and a supporter of experiment. English letters would be the poorer if he had not lived.

The original version was first published in *The Times Literary Supplement*, 15 June 1962.

c   Ford and the Spirit of Romance

I'm struck! I scarce can credit what I see.
When future Chronicles shall speak of this,
They will be thought Romance, not History.
                    Colley Cibber, *Richard III*

'Maxwell Drewitt' is not a novel of incident, but a picture of life and
character. Its interest is not meant to lie in the skilful combination of the
abstractions of passion and situation, irrespective of concrete probabilities,
irrespective of real human motives in the common transactions of life;
in other words, it is not a romance.
            George Henry Lewes, 'Criticism in Relation to Novels'

I suggest not that the strange and the far are at all necessarily romantic:
they happen to be simply the unknown, which is quite a different
matter. The real represents to my perception the things we cannot
possibly *not* know, sooner or later, in one way or another . . . The
romantic stands, on the other hand, for the things that, with all the
facilities in the world, all the wealth and all the courage and all the wit
and all the adventure, we never *can* directly know; the things that can
reach us only through the beautiful circuit and subterfuge of our thought
and our desire. . . .
                    Henry James, Preface to *The American*

And looking back, we see Romance – that subtle thing that is mirage
– that is life. It is the goodness of the years we have lived through, of the
old time when we did this or that, when we dwelt here or there. Looking
back, it seems a wonderful enough thing that I who am this, and she
who is that, commencing so far away a life that, after such sufferings
borne together and apart, ended so tranquilly there in a world so stable –
that she and I should have passed through so much, good chance and evil
chance, sad hours and joyful, all lived down and swept away into the
little heap of dust that is life. That, too, is Romance!
                        Conrad and Hueffer, *Romance*

The word *romance*, as my bundle of epigraphs is meant to suggest,
and every scholar knows, is one of the trickiest of literary terms.
Perhaps this is why it has virtually disappeared from the vocabulary
of modern fiction-criticism – it has accumulated too many meanings
and associations to be critically precise. I do not think the term need
be thrown out, however; critics of the eighteenth and nineteenth

centuries found it useful and precise enough, and certainly we need some term to describe that mode of prose fiction as badly as they did. Graham Greene offered a substitute when he took to calling his own romances *entertainments*, but his term hasn't caught on, and modern critics have on the whole been content simply to call all works of prose fiction of an appropriate length *novels*, and to judge them by a single system of critical standards. As a result, we have lost a distinction which is useful both for descriptive literary history and for aesthetic judgment. In this essay I will be arguing that the romance-novel distinction is helpful in dealing with Ford's writings, but I don't mean to suggest that Ford is a special case; the same distinction can be used in discussing the works of Bennett or Wells, or Fitzgerald or Steinbeck. Behind the propositions that I will make about Ford, there is an implied argument for the revival of *romance* as the proper name for a recognizable literary kind.

If we set out to extract a definition of the genre from the examples of usage I have provided above, we must take as our first condition the peculiar relation of romance to reality. We acknowledge that this kind of fiction is nourished by falsehood when we call a person who improves on the truth a 'romancer'. Fictional romance alters the world as we know it, and creates in its place a 'world-of-the-work' which is simpler, and less abrasive than our own, and which consequently appeals to the human will to escape (as the novel, presumably, appeals to our will to know). The romantic escape is most readily achieved through physical removal, and the commonest type of romance is the kind Dr Johnson was talking about when he said of 'the fictions of the last age' that they 'will vanish, if you deprive them of a hermit and a wood, a battle and a shipwreck'. But one may also remove in time, and write historical romance, or simplify the present, and write contemporary romance; as James shrewdly observed, it is not the situation, but the assumptions made about reality, that make a book a romance or a novel. Of the two most popular modern forms of romance, one – the Western – is removed in time and space to an American 'Green World', while the other – the detective story – remains in a 'world-of-the-work' which is apparently a model of the real world, but is in fact morally rigged. Both are properly romances, for both offer us simplified worlds with simple problems, in which we can unerringly ally ourselves with right and innocence, and in which pure-and-simple justice is invariably done.

It seems obvious that this kind of fiction will always have a powerful popular appeal, but its existence does not get much attention from the literary historians, because it is an inferior kind, with no serious claims to greatness. Still, students of turn-of-the-century fiction will do well to remind themselves that romancers like Stevenson, Henty, Hall Caine, Rider Haggard and Hewlett were all better known, and more widely read in their day than James or Hardy or Conrad were. Conrad acknowledged this fact when he invited a clever young man called Hueffer to collaborate with him, and called their most ambitious joint work *Romance*; and Hueffer acknowledged it by writing, in the years before the First World War, a number of books which he subtitled 'romances', all in more or less direct imitation of current popular successes. The books which he specifically labelled romances are *An English Girl* (an imitation of James's *American*), *The Fifth Queen Crowned* (a mis-labelling, in my opinion, perhaps to make the book more attractive to the large romance-reading public), *The 'Half Moon'* (imitation Stevenson), *Ladies Whose Bright Eyes* (imitation Mark Twain), and *The Young Lovell* (imitation Maurice Hewlett). He should also have included *Mr. Apollo* (imitation Wells), and *Mr. Fleight* (imitation de Morgan, perhaps). Some of these are specifically derivative – *Mr. Apollo*, for example, is very like Wells's *The Wonderful Visit*, and *Ladies Whose Bright Eyes* takes its central gimmick directly from Twain's *Connecticut Yankee* – while others are more generally 'in the style of'. All (with the exception of *The Fifth Queen Crowned*, which I'll get to presently) are clearly romances, and tend to be wildly mis-valued if read as serious novels (several of Ford's recent critics have made this fundamental error).

The defining characteristic of *romance*, I have said, is the rigged world of the work. Ford rigged his romances in the two traditional ways – either by removing in time into historical romance, or by simplifying the world of the present. His contemporary romances are (as is generally the case with such works) tales of wealthy and fashionable society; thus one reality, the need for money, is removed at the start. Nothing is less romantic than money worries, nothing more romantic than vast wealth. Any problem, including the common romance-problem of love, is complicated by a lack of money, and simplification is the prime condition of romance; furthermore, it is difficult to sentimentalize real financial distress, and sentimentality is the normative romance emotion. 'The sentimental habit and the spirit of romance stood out to sea as far as possible, through the Victorian age', wrote Henry James, 'the moment the shore appeared to offer the least difficulty to hugging'; the rockiest of rock-bound coasts is economic reality, and so sentiment and romance properly avoid it. Thus one of the justifications for calling *The American* a romance, as James does, is that Christopher Newman has an inexhaustible supply of cash with which to buy his way into European society. Ford, in his imitation of James, did the Master one better; the hero of *An English Girl* is not simply a rich American: he is the richest man in the world.

Another unromantic reality is the unfortunate fact that sexual desires and social conventions frequently conflict. Sex can, of course, be treated in romance, but only if the obstacles to union are circumstantial, and without social or moral sanction (make Rosalind a married woman, and *As You Like It* becomes a problem play). In his romances, Ford sometimes got round the sex problem by treating it as the work of supernatural forces (he uses witchcraft in both *The Young Lovell* and *The 'Half Moon'* to explain erotic attraction); sometimes he simply ignored it. And indeed, the man-woman problem as romance defines it is not really so much sexual as it is matrimonial – when Jack gets Jill, the problem is solved. In *The English Novel* Ford ridiculed this idea of a complete romantic action, and contemptuously labelled it the 'nuvvle'; but he might better have called it *romance*, and admitted that he had done the same thing himself.

Anyone familiar with Ford's best novels will recognize that the 'unromantic realities' I have been discussing are the very themes which inform those novels – the need for love and the need for money provide those real and continuous and tormenting pressures under which Ford's exhausted heroes try to live with honor and grace. Thus in writing romances Ford was depriving himself of the very themes which he could treat most profoundly. Or alternatively, one might say that until he was forty, Ford had no themes, and that he consequently imitated not life, but other men's romances.

Ford's romances of contemporary life must be seen as romances, and not as would-be novels; but even as romances they are not very good, and none is anywhere near as good as the book it imitates. One clamorous weakness of the lot is the tone in which he chose to tell these stories. Allen Tate has recalled that 'Ford used to say that he wrote his novels in the tone of one English gentleman whispering into the ear of another English gentleman'. This scarcely describes the tone of *Parade's End* or *The Good Soldier*, but it does very precisely describe the tone (and the weakness) of *Mr. Apollo* and *An English*

Girl. In the romances Ford did not use the techniques of limited narration which he claims to have worked out with Conrad during their collaboration; the speaking voice of the romances is omniscient and anonymous, and, perhaps in consequence of this, it is also arch, stilted, and supercilious. (Perhaps those adjectives do describe the tone of a whispering English gentleman; but they do not describe a persona that Ford could handle well.)

The English Gentleman was a figure with which Ford was obviously fascinated: both Edward Ashburnham and Christopher Tietjens belong to the class. But if one turns from those two brilliant characters to Mr Blood, a principal figure in Ford's *Mr. Fleight*, and a man who, Ford tells us, 'a hundred years ago . . . would have represented the Englishman and the gentleman', one sees at once the difference between character and stock figure: Mr Blood is papier mâché – there is no blood in him. This inclination to settle for conventional types – including, in *Mr. Fleight*, an unpleasantly coarse treatment of the stock Edwardian Jew – is evident in all Ford's contemporary romances, and supports the thesis that, until he was 40, Ford had no direct experience to write about, or at least that if he had it, he chose not to write about it. The conventions of the romance genre committed him to a fictional world of fashionable London society which he could not have known well, and to a narrative tone which ran counter to his real gift for the subjective, impressionistic treatment of experience. The texture of these romances seems thin through lack of information (how many Mayfair interiors, one wonders, had he really seen), and the tone stiff and literary out of uneasiness.

Ford's historical romances are more uneven in quality than are his contemporary ones; that is, some are as bad as *An English Girl* – *The Young Lovell*, for instance, is a thin and tedious pastiche of Hewlett – but *Ladies Whose Bright Eyes* is only not first-rate because it is second-hand, and the *Fifth Queen* trilogy is some of Ford's best work (Conrad admiringly described it as 'a noble conception – the swan song of Historical Romance'). One explanation of the excellence of the trilogy is that it was based on genuine historical research – Ford's story was that he had prepared himself to write a life of Henry VIII, but was beaten into print by another historian, and so converted his material into fiction. If this is true – and the historical accuracy and detail of the series supports Ford's account – then one might conclude that the *Fifth Queen* is good because it is an imitation of real history, whereas *The Young Lovell* is bad because it is an imitation of historical romance.

But it does not seem precise to call the *Fifth Queen* books romances at all; they are, I think, properly novels. For one thing, the world of these novels is not rigged; passions are complicated, motives complex and obscure, evil a powerful human reality. Ford's major themes – the need for love, the need for money, and the need to behave well under pressure – are all there, and all treated without the simplification of romance. The books have the texture of actuality, a realized and vividly particular Tudor England of mud and cold, as well as of crowns and royal splendor. Ford was always at his best in dealing with conditions of human deprivation, and the story of Katharine Howard, as he tells it, was ideal for his talents. Another important factor is that this piece of history provided him with the religious conformation – the Catholic alienated by religion in a secular and hostile world – which he used to such effect in *A Call*, *The Good Soldier*, and (somewhat obliquely) in *Parade's End*. Religious loyalties provided Ford with a form for that honorable, though self-tormenting, ideal of behavior which is a central concern in his best work; it is worth noting that history did not provide him with a queen who was piously Catholic, but that he made her into one, and in so doing made romance into novel.

If *The Fifth Queen* is not, then, a romance in the sense that *The Young Lovell* is, there is nevertheless something fundamentally romantic in the standards of behavior which it proposes as right and honorable, and in this sense all Ford's principal heroes and heroines are romantics – romantics who find themselves in radically unromantic, and therefore destructive, circumstances. Ford's conception of the relation of man to his circumstances was a romancer's conception: circumstances may torment, but because they change they do not ultimately matter, and man can, by an effort of will, transcend them. Reality is ultimately subjective, life is mirage and Romance and subject to change as the mind changes. Time inevitably simplifies and orders experience, turning Reality into Romance; and once an event has occurred, it exists only in memory, and is subject therefore to a romanticizing process which Ford seems to regard as an inevitable, and not undesirable condition of existence. This is, I take it, the substance of the last paragraph of *Romance* which I quoted above; the dedicatory poem to the volume makes a similar point:

> If we could have remembrance now
> And see, as in the days to come

We shall, what's venturous in these hours:
The swift, intangible romance of fields at home,
The gleams of sun, the showers,
Our workaday contentments, or our powers
To fare still forward through the unchartered haze
Of present days . . .
For, looking back when years shall flow
Upon this olden day that's now,
We'll see, romantic in dimn'd hours,
These memories of ours.

Not a very good poem; but consider what it proposes – not that time remembered is the real order (as in Proust), but rather that romanticized memory is *better* than reality. It is as though, to adapt James's figure, experience were an infinite series of balloons, which are constantly being cut loose, and floating off, and which gain lustre and romantic color as they recede in time.

This romancing habit of mind Ford preserved to the end of his days; one can find it demonstrated liberally enough not only in his novels, but in his life. But as he matured (and he admitted that this came late) he learned to probe deeper into the *expense* of romance, and into the dramatic effects of the juxtaposition of romance and reality. He came to see his own world as one in process of transition from a past system dominated at the top by moral values – honor, fidelity, humaneness – which were assumed without question, to a new system dominated by unreined ego and materialistic values. The past is looked back to, from a debased present, in a way which we may call *romance*; in the mind of the romantic hero that past is sentimentalized, distorted, and colored by nostalgia, and it is his version of the past, his private romance, which Ford, through his limited-point-of-view techniques, gives us. Only by thus subordinating objective reality to subjective romance could Ford celebrate the quixotic behavior of his greatest figures, Ashburnham and Tietjens, for by any realistic, objective evaluation both are fools. But they nevertheless do embody, in their romantic versions of old honor, models of behavior which make honor possible in a dishonored world, and as such they are admirable and valuable.

We may object that Ford's Golden Age, an England governed by self-abnegating, honorable country gentlemen, is unrealistic and unhistorical, but such objections do not negate the value of the conception; such a Golden Age never existed, but it does exist, in Ford's novels, as an ideal. Ford used romance to lament the absence of noble values from his world, and his lament is both proper and moving. When Christopher Tietjens thinks of Herrick and Purcell, or when Mark Tietjens thinks of Groby Great Tree, the 'old time' comments powerfully on the new.

It was not until Ford found this structural use for his romancing habit of mind that he began to do excellent work. By the time he came to write *The Good Soldier* he had formulated that habit of mind, and had even given it a convenient, if somewhat imprecise name – he called it 'impressionism'. Ford's Impressionism is his theory of subjective reality applied to literary form; it is the method by which experience, transformed by romancing memory, may be rendered – the method, in short, of his major novels. But it is also the method of his autobiographical writings, his discursive books, and even his literary criticism, and it is not fanciful to describe books like *Thus to Revisit*, *England and the English*, and *Joseph Conrad*, as Romances (Ford himself called *Joseph Conrad* a 'novel', but the treatment of reality there makes romance seem a more precise term). The title of his first book of recollections – *Memories and Impressions* – would do for almost any of his 'non-fictional' books, and would accurately indicate the nature of the reality offered in them. Impressions are the appearances of things, subjectively recorded; memories are past impressions, colored by romance; neither has any necessary relation to verifiable fact, but together they compose what is valuable for an artist. Ford's deep indifference to objective truth has this view of reality and value at its foundation; it led him inevitably to romanticize his own life, and to reconstruct it as his subjective sense of it dictated. The resulting contradictions and inaccuracies quite naturally alienated his acquaintances: Wells called Ford's memoirs 'autobiographical unreality', and James ponderously denied Ford's existence. But if we read the books properly as non-fictional romances, experience transformed by memory, then events appear in a different light – as metaphors for subjective attitudes rather than as facts – and the truth is no more than Ford's true *impression* of his experience. His recollections of Conrad are inaccurate, but they are not quite lies: they are rather an idealized version of a relationship between 'conscious artists', a romance against which the present may judge itself. If we go to the book for that romantic image, we will not be disappointed.

Ford was a 'romancer', both in the literary and in the popular pejorative sense. As a writer of conventional fictional romances he was on the whole a poor performer. Nevertheless, it seems important that the romancing motive in Ford's work should be identified, and properly understood, if the work – both what is good and what is bad in it – is to be justly valued.

The original version was first published in *Modern Fiction Studies*, ix (spring 1963).

7

The Chesterbelloc

a Chesterton

'All reputations, except those of the utterly imbecile, dwindle and rise again; capable men are praised twice, first for the wrong reasons and then, after a cycle of obloquy, for the right.' Chesterton wrote that sentence in an early, amiable defence of Macaulay, and as a general theory of literary reputations it is true enough. But it will not do as an account of Chesterton's own history. He has had no cycle of obloquy, and the small praise that he has had has not varied much. One can scarcely call a writer neglected when nearly a third of his hundred-odd books are in print, but the public that apparently remains is a silent one, and in places where literary reputations are made and preserved his name is seldom mentioned.

Part of the fault for this state of affairs must fall upon Chesterton's fellow Catholics. Thirty years ago, when Belloc wrote his essay 'On the Place of Chesterton in English Letters', he concluded that his friend's reputation would ultimately depend upon 'that doubtful contingency – the conversion of England'. This absurd proposition assumes, as every other Catholic writing about Chesterton has assumed, that he was a 'Catholic Author', and that posterity would read him, if at all, for the same reason that it would read the *Spiritual Exercises*. Belloc neglected, as Chesterton's Catholic admirers have tended to neglect, those great merits in his work that do not appeal to doctrinal minds and are not to be explained in doctrinal terms. (He also neglected the fact that Chesterton was a Roman Catholic for only the last fourteen years of his life.) This parochial regard has given Chesterton's reputation a kind of parish-newspaper security, but it has not helped him with the larger literary audience. It is time that Chesterton was removed from the loving disservices of his co-religionists; above all, he needs secular attention.

Even so, the elevation of Chesterton will be uphill work. For one thing, he didn't work seriously in the right forms. He called himself a journalist and a man-of-letters (terms which could still be understood, in Edwardian times, as sometimes synonymous), and he practised his profession on whatever subject came to hand. He was a political pamphleteer, a religious polemicist, an informal essayist, a sociologist, a novelist, a poet – and all without ceasing to be a journalist. Of this mass of work he said, 'I have never taken my books seriously; but I take my opinions quite seriously'. In our own time, when critics are more likely to reverse that judgment, and take books more seriously than opinions, Chesterton has inevitably been underrated.

Certainly he has no present place, even an insecure one, in the history of English literature. He made no important contribution to any major literary form, and he has had no success in the academies; his novels are not taught in university courses in modern fiction, his poems are not anthologized, and scarcely anyone even remembers that he wrote plays. If there were such an academic subject as The History of Controversy, or if the casual weekly newspaper essay were susceptible to heavy scholarship, then Chesterton might figure importantly; but as it is, he is cast among Miscellaneous Authors, the writers-on-everything.

It is an interesting historical fact that the Edwardian years produced an extraordinary number of such writers, including men as gifted as Shaw and Wells. Surely there has never been a time, before or since, when controversy, in the press and in the lecture hall, was so intelligent and so entertaining. It was a time peculiarly suited to public cerebration, for everyone recognized that an age had died when the old queen died, and the new one had to be defined. Clearly changes had to be made in morals and in manners, in politics and religion, but the exact forms of change were still unclear. There were the rights of workers and employers to be settled, and the rights of women, Irishmen's rights and the rights of Peers, the right to be educated and the right to buy a drink. On all these subjects Chesterton had opinions: he believed in Christianity, Liberalism, Englishness, monogamy, drink, the family, and the right of every man to a modest possession of property; he was against Imperialists, Feminists, Capitalists, Pacifists, Teetotallers, Free Thinkers, Free Lovers, Liberals, and Jews. And he said so, week after week, with cheerful violence and gusto.

Most of the books in which those arguments were preserved are now as dead as Lamb's pig, and only the historian of Edwardian thought will disturb their graves. The same is true of Chesterton's uncontroversial essays, those weekly bursts of charm with titles like 'A Case for the Ephemeral' and 'The Domesticity of Detectives', that were regularly gathered together under titles – *Tremendous Trifles*, *The Uses of Diversity*, *All Things Considered* – that frankly confessed their unimportance. It is a fact to be noted about the Edwardians that they had apparently boundless appetites for such stuff, but that taste has passed: *Gusto*, one might say, has fallen out of fashion, and with it the status of Chesterton-the-essayist has quietly declined.

Chesterton's reputation as a man with Gusto was to a considerable degree his own doing, as it was his undoing. He did devote a good deal of attention, in his more ephemeral writings, to Beef-and-Beer heartiness, and when he wasn't being hearty, he nevertheless *looked* hearty. For most modern readers who know Chesterton at all, the visible image of the man is probably James Gunn's painting, 'Conversation Piece', in which Chesterton appears with his friends Baring and Belloc. In the picture Baring and Belloc seem to be watching in mute astonishment while Chesterton writes something. And no wonder, if one considers the figure that Gunn has made of Chesterton – a sort of monstrous Toby jug of a man, wrapped in a vast cape like a collapsed circus tent, and writing with a hand so corpulent that it seems to have swallowed the pencil. It is impossible to think that he is writing anything serious – he is writing a Tremendous Trifle – but he is obviously writing with Gusto.

Gunn's painting is a grotesque, but so was the man, and his appearance surely encouraged the common notion of Chesterton as a jolly journalist full of high, fermented spirits. But perhaps the figure also influenced Chesterton; perhaps he took up the role that his figure cast him in, and was sometimes guilty of more jollity and gusto than his true vision of the world confirmed. Perhaps within that jolly journalism there was a slender melancholy trying to get out.

What Chesterton's true vision was he explained often enough, though like his great antagonist, Shaw, he sometimes said it with too much wit to be taken seriously. For Chesterton, the time in which he lived was the decadence of a great revolutionary period, represented in his mind by the French Revolution and in England by Cobbett's 'rural republicanism'. He saw the nineteenth century as a time of moral compromise, in which ideals had been accommodated to industrial capitalism, with disastrous consequences for philosophy and religion. And since he considered that what men believed about ultimate things mattered, he could not help but view the Edwardian intellectual disarray as the ruined end of a dismal process. He was like a man who has inherited a bankrupt firm, or a farmer across whose field a battle has been fought; he acknowledged that the mess was his to deal with, but he regretted it.

In Chesterton's writings, the sense of disarray precedes the sense of a solution: *Heretics* comes before *Orthodoxy*. *Heretics* is Chesterton's account of the false prophets of the Edwardian intellectual world; Shaw and Wells, Kipling and Moore and Lowes Dickinson are attacked with wit and ingenuity for the unreason of their doctrines. But more than that, the book is a vision of the modern world, wrapped in its spiritual darkness. 'The human race, according to religion, fell once', Chesterton wrote, 'and in falling gained the knowledge of good and of evil. Now we have fallen a second time, and only the knowledge of evil remains to us. A great silent collapse, an enormous unspoken disappointment, has in our time fallen on our Northern civilization.'

This vision of lost good, and of impending dissolution, is a recognizable Edwardian state of mind; one finds it in the writings of Chesterton's friend Charles Masterman, in Kipling and Galsworthy, and even in the usually ebullient Wells. Perhaps it is the last consequence of the collapse of Victorian optimism, that the survivors of the fall should see their world darkly; perhaps only a man who had felt profound security once could respond to the insecure modern world with such dark distress. For Chesterton, the second fall, the fall from good, had loosened the world's restraints, and set free powerful and evil forces of disorder. His lifelong preoccupation with religion was a long effort to restore restraints, and reaffirm the power of good, and so to make life possible.

That sense of dark forces at large is what makes Chesterton's stories and novels disturbing and alive. He called his best novel, *The Man Who Was Thursday*, a 'nightmare', and it is as a writer of nightmares that he engages the modern imagination. Ostensibly *The Man Who Was Thursday* is about anarchists, but in fact it is not a political book at all; the force of evil in it is not anarchism, but *anarchy*, the total dissolution of order. For Chesterton, anarchy was the name of Christendom's antagonist, the opposite of sanity and faith, and between the two was an eternal struggle. One of the things he admired about *The Song of Roland*, he said, was its representation of this struggle: 'The poem ends as it were with a vision and vista of wars against the barbarians; and the vision is true. For that war is never ended which defends the sanity of the world against all the stark anarchies and rending negations which rage against it forever. That war is never finished in this world.'

Chesterton's novels and stories are representations of that war that is never finished, and of his deep fear that the barbarians' version of existence, as meaningless disorder, might be true. His hero, Thursday, has a vision of that possibility when he confronts the six men who have, he thinks, sworn to destroy the world:

> He knew that each one of these men stood at the extreme end, so to speak, of some wild road of reasoning. He could only fancy, as in some old-world fable, that if a man went westward to the end of the world he would find something – say a tree – that was more or less than a tree, a tree possessed of a spirit; and that if he went east to the end of the world he would find something else that was not wholly itself – a tower, perhaps, of which the very shape was wicked.

Chesterton had a genius for the shape of wickedness; that is to say, he had an allegorical imagination. All of *The Man Who Was Thursday* is a dark conceit, and so is *Manalive* and *The Ball and the Cross* and *The Napoleon of Notting Hill*. Even the Father Brown stories have something in them of allegory or parable: each offers an inscrutable, irrational, often obscurely unnatural event, and then explains it, through Father Brown's understanding, as an aspect of the intelligible order of existence. At the end of each story the sanity of the world has been defended against the stark anarchies, and we are reassured.

It is in his uses of his allegorical imagination that Chesterton seems most 'modern', for nightmare is the allegorical form for our time, an allegory of the unconscious by which our deepest anxieties and fears are revealed. When Chesterton dedicated *The Man Who Was Thursday* to his friend E. C. Bentley, he wrote:

> This is a tale of those old fears,
> Even of those emptied hells,
> And none but you shall understand
> The true thing that it tells . . .

But in fact we *do* understand that true thing, because we share it; we feel at home in his nightmares. And partly for literary reasons, for Chesterton shares this allegorical category with a number of other interesting and important modern writers – with Wells and Kafka and Orwell, Rex Warner and Charles Williams and Graham Greene.

And it is not surprising that a parabolical writer like Jorge Luis Borges should admire Chesterton, or that he should have written the best short appreciation of Chesterton's imagination.

The sense of the world as a moral battlefield is at the centre of Chesterton's thought: it underlies his allegorical fiction, and it informs his criticism. It made it possible for him to live in a world of anarchies and negations and yet preserve that moral energy that he called optimism. 'This world can be made beautiful again', he wrote in his *Charles Dickens*, 'by beholding it as a battlefield. When we have defined and isolated the evil thing, the colours come back into everything else. When evil things have become evil, good things, in a blazing apocalypse, become good.'

It is in part because he saw the world in this way that he was so excellent a critic of the Victorian period; for he understood the importance of religious struggle for the age, and emphasized it even at the peril, as he put it, of making the spiritual landscape too large for the figures. He was born into that landscape, and he sympathized with the Victorians in their High Seriousness. But he was also an Edwardian, removed enough from the past age so that he could see it whole, and thus become the first Victorianist. His *Victorian Age in Literature* is still the best single work on the subject, and his studies of Dickens and Browning remain valuable. If the criticism sometimes seems dated, that is because the personal voice of the critic is so clear in it: for Chesterton, criticism was an aspect of belief. Rereading the *Victorian Age* now, one cannot but be struck by how wise a book it is, and how superior to Strachey's mean-spirited version of the period – superior in sensitivity, superior in tact, but most of all superior in generosity of mind.

Perhaps because Chesterton was so good a Victorian, and so great an Edwardian, he made a poor Modern. Unlike Bennett (who was his elder by seven years) he did not change with the times. Bennett could appreciate Joyce and Lawrence, and was quick to receive and publicize the young. But for Chesterton, Joyce was a writer 'who manages to be very coarse in very esoteric language', Lawrence was a genius deformed by 'the moral chaos of his time', and Eliot was a wild maker of head-spinning verse. The difference is simply that Bennett was entirely a literary man, who could admire a man for writing well, while Chesterton, a man with a philosophy and a religion, founded his judgments on his beliefs. He believed in a way of ordering the world, and as he grew older he saw that way lost; and he judged the writers of those later days as symptoms of the universal decline. He used *modern* as a term of opprobrium, along with *sceptic, impressionist,* and *aesthete,* and so, though he could write pugnaciously and well about the failings of the modern world, he could not be just to its writers.

The same points could be made of Chesterton as a poet. He used verse as a traditional, public means of addressing a general audience, or, equally traditionally, as a way of talking to friends. He used it to praise the past and the values he found there, to celebrate the good things of life, and to condemn the follies and heresies that he saw around him. He was a skilful versifier, a good maker of ballads and ballades and sonnets, and a master of rhymed narrative, but his poems scarcely seem to belong to the century in which they were written. Of the poems in *Collected Poems,* only a few continue to have a life of their own: 'Lepanto', lodged permanently in many a middle-aged head since it was first learned in childhood; 'The Ballad of the White Horse', revived by inspiration-hunting patriots during the last war, and still a moving poem; 'O God of earth and altar', the best of modern hymns, which has found its way into *The English Hymnal,* and is sung in English churches. No doubt there are still Chestertonians here and there who continue to read the satirical verses, and who recognize that Chesterton was the cleverest of modern satirists, but most of those witty attacks have faded with the fading of their subjects, and no amount of wit will make the follies of F. E. Smith and Walter Long compelling reading. Which is a pity, for the skill and the wit are remarkable, and there has been no popular poet to match him since his day.

In his book on Stevenson, Chesterton observes: 'No man ever wrote so well . . . who cared only about writing.' This may not do as a generalization, but it points to a truth about Chesterton; he is one of the greatest of modern stylists, because he believed in something else. If he was witty and epigrammatic, it was in order that deep beliefs might be well and pungently expressed; and if he was illogical and paradoxical, it was because the world did not strike him as logical, but as a great Impossibility, a miracle. Because he believed, he was a controversialist; he could think of no better use of his marvellous style than the defence of his faith. Consequently his best writing is not concentrated in the most literary works, but is scattered carelessly over everything, even his most casual letters to editors. He wrote no perfect book, nor even any book on which he seems to have spent quite enough time; he was always hasty and prodigal, like a man for whom a merely literary immortality was unimportant. One is less

likely to admire a whole work by him than to cherish portions –
marvellous episodes, skilful arguments by paradoxical example,
turns of phrase that no one else could have written. Surely Chesterton
would approve of this, for he was, as he always maintained, a journalist
and not an artist, and he would rather be savoured than revered.

Chesterton's achievement, like his figure, was enormous, and in a
way all of it was typical, so that it is difficult to identify the essential
man in the work. But perhaps one comes closest in 'The Ballad of the
White Horse' – so English, so Christian, so dark – and within that
poem in the song of Elf the minstrel:

> There is always a thing forgotten
>   When all the world goes well;
> A thing forgotten, as long ago,
> When the gods forgot the mistletoe,
> And soundless as an arrow of snow
>   The arrow of anguish fell.
>
> The thing on the blind side of the heart,
>   On the wrong side of the door,
> The green plant groweth, menacing
> Almighty lovers in the spring;
> There is always a forgotten thing,
>   And love is not secure.

This is dark but not gloomy, emotional, a bit old-fashioned in style
and sentiment. It is the way the world looked to Chesterton, and the
basis of his faith; for it was *that* dark world that made faith necessary.
But it is also skilful and lyrical, and it reminds us of the obvious fact,
beyond journalism or art, that Chesterton was among modern writers
one of the most extraordinarily gifted.

The original version was first published in *The Times Literary Supplement*,
7 August 1970.

b   Belloc

If Chesterton is worth reviving, then surely Belloc ought to be,
for the two seem, in retrospect, to depend on one another. Chesterton
and Belloc, the Chesterbelloc of Shaw's shrewd essay – how could one
end of that comical monster reappear without the other? How, indeed,

could one end have existed without the other? They have become, for most literary people (the kind, that is, who don't read them much), a single entity, two ample bodies with one Catholic mind, twin missionaries to the English heathen.

In fact, the differences between the two are more striking than the similarities, a point that Shaw made most emphatically; and those differences bear on the wisdom of an anthology of Belloc's writings. Chesterton was jovial, with the urgent joviality of a melancholy man. But Belloc in his prose writings was neither jovial nor charming; he had the iron spirit of a regimental sergeant-major, and in his best work that spirit – vigorous, authoritarian, aggressive – drives the argument and the language (in another age he would have made an excellent inquisitor). Chesterton can be made entertaining, and treated as minor (although wrongly); but Belloc resists reduction. He *must* be taken seriously and whole, or not at all.

When Shaw constructed the Chesterbelloc he made Belloc the front end – the part of the creature that leads and bites – and Chesterton the rear – the part that follows and digests. Belloc himself said that the chief thing he had done for Chesterton was to open his eyes to reality, and there is no doubt that in public matters Belloc's influence was strong. Reality, for Belloc, meant politics and history, military actions and the French tradition, the English countryside, Europe, and the Church. In all these matters he led Chesterton, and not, one must conclude, to Chesterton's advantage as a writer. For Chesterton was by nature a man of private fancy, more at ease in the private world than the public, and his best writing is that in which he could indulge his imagination without too much restraint from principles and dogmas. Belloc's dogmatic mind embraced Chesterton's like an iron corset, supporting but confining, and the books by Chesterton in which the Belloc influence is most evident are his weakest books.

Belloc, on the other hand, worked best in his sergeant-major role. On soldiering and sailing he was often magnificent: *Hills and the Sea*, *The Cruise of the Nona*, *The Campaign of 1812*, all have fine writing in them, and some of Belloc's historical portraits – particularly those from French history – are vivid and compelling likenesses. His prose in these pieces has a plain directness that will never date – it is a model of the right way to treat narrative action. But Belloc was not always that good, and when one finds an acute critic like Mr Auden describing him as 'one of the great masters of straightforward English prose' one wants at once to qualify the praise. For when Belloc attempted a more deliberate, meditative style, when he turned to the familiar essays that were done, as he put it, 'because my children are howling for pearls and caviare' (but which he nevertheless collected and preserved), he fell into the dreary belletrism of his time, the Wardour Street whimsy that was Edwardian England's most distinctive contribution to English letters. Take, for example, this bit on mowing a field from *Hills and the Sea* (published in 1906):

> For what we get when we store our grass is not a harvest of something ripe, but a thing just caught in its prime before maturity: as witness that our corn and straw are best yellow, but our hay is best green. So also Death should be represented with a scythe and Time with a sickle; for Time can take only what is ripe, but Death comes always too soon. In a word, then, it is always much easier to cut grass too late than too early; and I, under that evening and come back to these pleasant fields, looked at the grass and knew that it was time. June was in full advance: it was the beginning of that season when the night has already lost her foothold on the earth and hovers over it, never quite descending but mixing sunset with the dawn.

This is a period piece, from a bad period – mannered, decorated, self-consciously cadenced; but it is nevertheless as typical of Belloc's prose as the splendid, rapid narrative of 'The First Day's March' (from the same volume) or 'The Death of Danton'.

If Mr Auden's praise of Belloc's prose seems a bit extravagant, one can only join him without qualification in his long admiration for Belloc's verse. It is now some thirty years since he identified Belloc and Chesterton as 'the two best light-verse writers of our time', and that judgment still seems sound (though one might wish to add the author of 'Letter to Lord Byron' to the list).

Belloc's bestiaries and cautionary tales are perfect examples of their kind, and belong with the best of Lewis Carroll and Edward Lear. Like all good light verses they are embodiments of ideas that are not at all trivial, and a serious student of social values would find much matter here, in Belloc's haughty peers and rude, rich children. Belloc's other light and satiric verses, those not designed for children – 'The Modern Traveller', for instance, and the epigrams – are considerably less distinguished; for a mind like his, lightness and adulthood did not suit well together. As for the non-light (perhaps the correct critical term is 'heavy') verse, it has neither particular merits nor gross faults.

Some of it has a certain familiarity – 'Tarantella' as an example of going too far in euphony, the drinking songs as rare modern examples of that genre – but the serious Belloc was, on the whole, an undistinguished versifier.

1970 was Belloc's centenary year and it is good to see that some of him has survived a century. Not all, though; no one will ever want to read the pages of *The New Witness* again, and it would be well if *The Jews* could crumble quietly away. Belloc had in his nature a streak of cruelty and blunt aggressiveness that comes out in his polemical work in a very ugly way. It was this side of Belloc that made this revealing judgment of Chesterton:

> He wounded none, but thus also he failed to provide weapons wherewith one may wound and kill folly. Now without wounding and killing, there is no battle; and thus, in this life, no victory; but also no peril to the soul through hatred.

No one can say what hatred did to Belloc's soul, but it did destructive things to his thought and to his work. Still, one may learn the lesson from Belloc's books, that hate ages faster than love. There are no benefits to be derived from reading the books in which he set out to wound and kill; but one can still share his deep feeling for the South Country, for France, for wine, and for plain prose and careful, ordered verse.

The original version was first published in *The Times Literary Supplement*, 15 January 1971.

8

Edward Thomas

Among British poets, Edward Thomas must surely be unique in that he took up poetry for the first time in his mid-thirties, lived his entire poetic life in less than three years, and died without seeing a single poem published under his name. 'Did anyone ever begin at thirty-six in the shade?' he asked his friend Eleanor Farjeon. Nobody did, except him, and one wonders at the forces in his nature, in his life, and in society that pressed him to that brief achievement, so personal, so solitary, and so sure.

The story up to the day in 1914 when Thomas became a poet is the dreariest Grub Street history. Married while still an undergraduate, and a father six months later, he came down to London without money or influence or even parental approval, to support his family as a writer. Inevitably he became a hack (and that *is* the right word), editing, compiling, reviewing whatever came along, meeting impossible deadlines, hating his work and himself for doing it. He wrote in all nearly sixty books, of which perhaps seven or eight – mainly the posthumously published poems – could be described as voluntary work. The others were written to order, and at rates that made extraordinary speed necessary (six books appeared in one year, 1911).

At the same time Thomas was reviewing constantly, whatever editors would send him: volumes of mediocre verse, books on books, and more and more, as he established a reputation, books on country life. In 1904 he wrote to Bottomley: 'Perhaps the "man & a landscape" plan has a future for me.' It did: a future of reviewing books called *Peeps into Nature's Ways*, *A Country Diary*, and *Travels round our Village*, and of adding his own titles to that vast Edwardian sub-genre, The English Countryside Book. His first book was *The Woodland Life*, and before his drudgery was done he had also written or edited *Beautiful Wales*, *The Heart of England*, *The Book of the Open Air*,

The South Country, The Country, and *In Pursuit of Spring,* and had written lives of Jefferies and Borrow.

Thomas's nature writing was good of its kind and time – it was accurate on flora and fauna, and made its nightingales sing at the proper season – but it was also decorated, literary, and a bit arch. It was to the great tradition of English natural history what Georgian poetry was to the Romantic tradition – the exhausted fag-end. Thomas himself described his *Heart of England* as 'pseudo-genial or purely rustic – Borrow & Jefferies sans testicles & guts', and his harsh judgment will do for more nature-writing of the time than his alone – will do for the *Peeps* and the *Diaries* and the *Travels,* and for most of the country poems in *Georgian Poetry.* The whole lot expresses that Edwardian desire to keep English traditions alive beyond their time that one finds in so many aspects of the prewar period (in the House of Lords, for example). Faith in England and faith in Nature had become conventions, charms to hold the twentieth century at bay.

Thomas's books on Jefferies and Borrow are still worth reading because he cared for his subjects, and to a degree identified with them, but the other literary studies – the books on Maeterlinck, Lafcadio Hearn, Swinburne, and Pater – are less worthy. Like his nature books, they were all done hastily and on commission; none of the subjects appealed to Thomas and some he actively disliked. Because he was a conscientious writer, and because he had a deep love of letters, his criticism was never worthless; but the work is essentially Edwardian literary journalism, and though it is better than most of its kind, it is not good enough to survive. Circumstances compelled him to take whatever work came his way, but he was too serious to write superficially, and too gifted to write badly, and so he made a poor hack. He spent his talents, and most of his life, in the manufacture of literary mediocrity that he could not even do well. Small wonder, one may think, that he was chronically melancholy, that he took opium, that he contemplated suicide.

Thomas's melancholia was more than a consequence of misfortune, though; it was a part of his nature. 'I suppose every man thinks that Hamlet was written for him', he told Eleanor Farjeon, 'but I *know* he was written for me.' He had, as he put it, a habit of introspection and self-contempt, and he brooded self-consciously upon his excessive self-consciousness. What he saw, when he examined his own existence, was a life of labour that was both endless and valueless: 'Think of the pain', he wrote to his friend Bottomley, 'going on living & not being

able to do anything but eat & drink & earn a living for 5 people.'
Many an industrial worker must have felt that pain before and after,
but it was a peculiar accomplishment of late Victorian and Edwardian
England that it made the life of letters a dark satanic mill for men as
gifted as Thomas and Gissing.

The cure for this state was clear: a decent income and a little leisure.
Lacking these, Thomas sought help from nerve specialists and medi-
cines and diets; he gave up butcher's meat and tobacco, and he sought
changes of climate and company. Most of all he sought out that stock
romantic dose against melancholy, communion with Nature. Alone,
or with his wife or a friend, he went on prodigious walks (often note-
taking as he went, since there was usually some nature book to be
written) until he had a footpath knowledge of most of southern
England and Wales. But all his walking seems only to have proved that
Nature *will* betray the heart that loves her, if that heart is troubled
enough and poor enough. Thomas remained a tormented man, hating
his life and himself, even hating his profile.

Thomas's private letters during those Grub Street years make bitter
reading: they are not so much communications as written groans. A
change came into his life, and into his letters, in 1914: 'I have given up
groaning', he wrote to Bottomley, 'since the war began.' What Nature
could not do, War had done. It may seem odd that so catastrophic an
event had raised his spirits, but anyone who was young and male in
1939 will recognize the experience; War had taken over, and had
liberated individuals from their drab responsibilities. In a nation at war,
Thomas's precarious life as a writer was impossible; there was almost
no work to be had. The only courses open, it seemed, were emigration
to America, or enlistment. For a time Thomas did neither, but simply
drifted, 'getting little scraps of work', he wrote, 'that prevent me
from quite seriously facing questions'. He wrote one substantial book,
a life of the Duke of Marlborough; and having finished it, he wrote to
Bottomley in June 1915: 'Now I am going to cycle & think of man &
nature & human life & decide between enlisting or going to America
before I enlisted.' The next month he enlisted. He served for a time as
an instructor of troops in England, was commissioned in the Artillery,
and volunteered for service in France. He was killed there in the Battle
of Arras, 9 April 1917.

The sense of relief that one finds in Thomas's letters after August
1914, is partly his response to the release from responsibility that war,
and especially service in a war, brings to men. But in Thomas's case

there was an additional factor: shortly before the war he had met Robert Frost, who had told him what perhaps anyone might have said, but Frost had to – that Thomas had been a poet all his life. 'You are a poet'. Frost said, 'or you are nothing', and the fact that this was so seems to have affected Thomas as another sort of enlistment: he had joined the armies of poetry.

The effect of Frost on his new friend was instantaneous and striking – the more so if one considers that Thomas had been consorting with poets all his adult life. He had been exchanging letters and visits with Gordon Bottomley for more than ten years, yet Bottomley had not made him into a poet; he knew many of the other Georgians – Abercrombie, Brooke, de la Mare, Freeman, Gibson, Trevelyan – but none had turned him from his prose life. In less than a year of talk and friendship, Frost undammed Thomas's poetic talent, and showed it how to flow.

What Frost did was simply to show Thomas how one might write verse about natural things without sounding like Thomas's own prose – without sounding, that is, like *Georgian Poetry*. Thomas recognized at once what he had been given; his review of *North of Boston*, written in June 1914, begins 'This is one of the most revolutionary books of modern times, but one of the quietest and least aggressive'. Farther along in the review he spelt out what he meant:

> These poems are revolutionary because they lack the exaggeration of rhetoric, and even at first sight appear to lack the poetic intensity of which rhetoric is an imitation. Their language is free from the poetical words and forms that are the chief material of secondary poets. The metre avoids not only the old-fashioned pomp and sweetness, but the later fashion also of discord and fuss. In fact, the medium is common speech and common decasyllables. . . . Yet almost all these poems are beautiful. They depend not at all on objects commonly admitted to be beautiful: neither have they merely a homely beauty, but are often grand, sometimes magical. Many, if not most, of the separate lines and separate sentences are plain and, in themselves, nothing. But they are bound together and made elements of beauty by a calm eagerness of emotion.

In praising Frost, Thomas was composing his own programme: there is nothing in that paragraph that could not be said of Thomas's own plain and lovely poems.

Though Thomas met Frost in 1913, and saw much of him in the first months of 1914, he did not begin to write poems until the autumn, when Frost had returned to America. Then, with war ahead and his journalistic sources drying up, he could write wryly to Eleanor Farjeon: 'One may as well write poems.' The poems, once he began, came freely, so freely that he worried whether his 'delight in the new freedom' might have led him to write too readily, to 'accept intimations merely'. In a little more than two years' time, of which most was spent on active, wartime service, he wrote the 141 poems that are in his *Collected Poems*.

Thomas's attitude towards his poems shows how different this new life of writing was for him: the poems were written out of private impulses, and he showed no interest in identifying them publicly with the Edward Thomas who wrote prose about nature. The drafts of poems that he sent to Eleanor Farjeon to be typed were often written out without line-divisions, as prose; Thomas explained that when he copied them out he was among his comrades, and he did not want the other soldiers to know him as a poet. Those few that he sent out to editors went under the name of 'Edward Eastaway', and he did not seem troubled when they were rejected. Only a few were published during his lifetime, all pseudonymously.

The pseudonym was necessary, Thomas explained, because people were likely to be prejudiced for or against Edward Thomas – that is, readers would associate the poems with what he had done in prose. By choosing the pseudonym, Thomas accepted the failure of his past, prose-writing self, and buried that self in his name; when he was a poet he was another person. Certainly his friends saw some such transformation take place: the war, Frost observed, 'has made some sort of new man and poet of Edward Thomas'.

The poems that this new man, 'Edward Eastaway', wrote were both new and old. They were new in that they were unlike the fashion of Georgian poetry, and a reaction against it: but they belonged to an old and strong English tradition of nature poetry, and they helped to extend that tradition into the twentieth century. An approximate way of making the distinction clear might be to say that Georgians like Brooke and Abercrombie were poetic 'insiders', and that Thomas belonged to the 'outsider' tradition. The insiders found their relations with Nature comfortable, and their sentiments appropriate and ready, because they wrote from a conventional intimacy with the natural world. The Georgians, one might say, were poetical rentiers, spending the capital that their Romantic ancestors had earned.

The outsider is the poet who approaches Nature directly and without assumptions. He will find there emotions that are colder and stronger than an insider would, and he will make cold, strong poems out of them ('a calm eagerness of emotion', Thomas said). Such poetry is solitary, sometimes fearful, never cosy; it is concerned with darkness and with death, sometimes with violence, and it can be tragic. (The poems of Hardy are full of examples: 'The Fallow Deer at the Lonely House' is a good one that resembles one of Thomas's best, 'Out in the Dark'.) In this poetry, Nature offers no assurances, and only the coldest of comforts; it says, what Georgian poetry never admitted, that man in a landscape is alone.

Thomas's proper poetic company is clear, then: it is that tradition of outsiders which descends in modern poetry from Hardy, through Frost to Thomas, and includes the early rhyming Lawrence, Edmund Blunden, Robert Graves, Andrew Young, and R. S. Thomas. Together these poets compose a major modern tradition, less noisy than the School of Pound, and without the convenience of a collective name (perhaps that is why this 'quiet tradition' has never been anthologized as a group), but important nevertheless, poets of fine achievement.

'Edward Eastaway' read only one review of his work, that in the *TLS* of 29 March 1917, of an anthology, *An Annual of New Poetry, 1917*, published by Constable, in which six of his poems appeared. The reviewer recognized that Thomas was 'a real poet, with the truth in him', but he also recognized, and was alarmed by, Thomas's 'outsider' quality. Comparing Thomas to Wordsworth, he wrote: 'Mr Eastaway makes his poem wholly out of the natural fact. Wordsworth passes from it at once to human things.' The point, as he realized, was whether one saw man and landscape as a consoling unity, or as two solitudes. Thomas read the review with approval, and observed, 'I don't mind now being called inhuman'. Reading through the *Collected Poems* one will scarcely think inhuman the right word, but Thomas and his reviewer were justly observing, each in his own terms, a true quality of the poetry – its austere comfortlessness. The natural world is there, in all its beauty, as fact: but in it man lives a mortal and solitary life. The whole attitude is summed up in the last line of one of Thomas's best poems:

There's nothing like the sun till we are dead.

That blunt, monosyllabic line will do as an example of Thomas's formal intentions, too. 'If I am consciously doing anything', he wrote to Eleanor Farjeon, 'I am trying to get rid of the last rags of rhetoric and formality which left my prose so often with a dead rhythm only.' In poetry, honesty has its own sound, and when conventional ideas go the formal conventions must follow. Thomas offended his Georgian friends with his 'everyday syntax', but it is that rough, blunter-than-conversation style that makes him seem more modern than they (in the same way that Hardy's harshness seems modern): even in his sentimental moods, Thomas's poems have a saving gracelessness.

Because Thomas came late to his poetic life, and left it early, his work has an unusual unity: there are no juvenilia, and no significant variations in matter or tone. The making of the man came first – and the letters record how painful that process was – and then the swift body of poetry that expressed his maturity. 'God bless us all', he wrote to Bottomley,

> what a thing it is to be nearing 40 & to know what one likes & know one makes mistakes & yet is right for oneself. How many things I have thought I ought to like & found reasons for liking. But now it is almost like eating apples. I don't pretend to know about pineapples & persimmons, but I know an apple when I smell it, when it makes me swallow my saliva before biting it.

He had come a long way to reach that confidence, where living was like eating apples. And he had brought his troubles, his melancholy nature with him. But he had found somehow the refining process by which melancholy becomes poetry, no longer personal and corroding, but creative.

The original version was first published in *The Times Literary Supplement*, 16 January 1969.

9

Harold Monro

During his lifetime Harold Monro played many roles on the English literary scene: he was a poet, a critic, an editor, an anthologist, and a publisher; he was a Patron of the Arts and a Man of Letters. But the role that he played best, and for which he was most cherished, was the role of shopkeeper. Other men did the other things better – wrote better poems, published livelier pamphlets, subsidized out of deeper pockets – but only Monro worked steadily at the actual business of selling books of verse. He opened his Poetry Bookshop in 1913, and for nearly twenty years kept it going, in the obstinate belief that a general market for modern poetry existed; his receipts refuted him, but he stayed in the shop until his death in 1932, a stubborn Shelleyan business-man in the unprofitable service of his art.

Monro's faith that a general audience existed for the best current verse marks him as an anachronism, or, to put it another way, as a Georgian, for Georgian refers not so much to a kind of poetry as to an idea about poetry and its audience. The Georgian faith has not been possible for any later generation, but in the years just before and during the First World War men did believe that poetry could be assimilated into the existing social structure, to the mutual benefit of poetry and society. Edward Marsh founded *Georgian Poetry* on that conviction, and the enormous sales of his anthologies seemed to prove him right. The Poetry Society flourished in the same belief, and published the *Poetry Review* to express it. Monro, who was the editor of the *Review* in its first year, wrote confidently in the first issue that 'good poetry is as much read now as at any time since the invention of printing'; it was only a matter of providing new poetry that would sound suffi-ciently like the good poetry of the past to be familiar.

In that sentence, 'the past' means, of course, the *English* past: to be a Georgian was to attach oneself self-consciously to the tradition of English poetry, and to be not simply a poet, but an *English* poet. For

Monro this was not difficult, for he was by nature, training and experience very much an Englishman. He had been to a public school and to Cambridge (at the same time as E. M. Forster); he married a girl who played hockey for England; he served as an officer in the Royal Artillery. According to John Drinkwater, he looked like a dejected Guards officer. And he believed, as an English poet should, that poetry was a native English characteristic, like British phlegm.

> Thought is difficult [he wrote]; it is wonderful when an Englishman achieves it. But poetry is far more native to the national genius. We have a strong capacity for enthusiasm; we have a calm obstinate persistence, and there is no one so inflexible as an Englishman who has finally set his eyes towards Beauty.

To be a Georgian was for Monro simply to be himself – obstinately idealistic and inflexibly English in the pursuit of Beauty.

But the years of Monro's greatest activity, the two decades between 1910 and 1930, were just the years when the English tradition in poetry seemed least vital, and when vigorous foreigners like Pound and Eliot were engaged in making English poetry European; Monro, for all his enthusiasm and dedication, was engaged in a rearguard action almost from the beginning. 'I know too much to go on writing the old sort of stuff', he wrote in 1911, 'and too little to write any new.' And what he could not write, he could not appreciate; he rejected 'The Love Song of J. Alfred Prufrock' when it was offered to him for *Poetry and Drama*, and he could not see the quiet merit of Edward Thomas. Monro's one critical book, *Some Contemporary Poets* (1920), is a stubborn defence of lost Georgian causes that places D. H. Lawrence beside Helen Parry Eden, and devotes a chapter to Abercrombie, Bottomley, Gibson, and Ronald Ross. And his anthology, *Twentieth Century Poetry*, which was published in 1929 and should have contained the final wise judgments of a life's experience in poetry, is a dismal and dated collection (Pound described it as 'an anthology in which every worst and most damnable poet in England is shown with his best foot forward').

One must conclude that however heroic and self-abnegating Monro's devotion to poetry was, he made no significant contribution to it in any role but that of poet. The course of English poetry was not altered by the shop or by what was published there. Monro encouraged poets according to his lights, but he was a cautious and traditional-minded man in a time of radical change, and the poets he backed were the safe and second-rate. He tried to bring poets together, he published their poems and sold their books, and all this at great personal sacrifice, but English poetry would be just where it is now if he had left shop-keeping to the shopkeepers.

If he had not been a martyr to poetry, he might have been a better and more prolific poet – how is one to say? The shop took his time and his energies and his money, but it also seems to have satisfied a need to serve, and by serving to demonstrate his own worth. And in spite of the demands that he made upon himself, he did manage to be a genuine poet, and to write some poems that are unique, and deserve to survive. There are not many, because he found his own poetic voice slowly and with great difficulty; most of his poems are undistinguished imitations that recapitulate the poetic fashions of his times. The models change – first Shelley, then Francis Thompson, later echoes of Yeats, Hardy, and de la Mare, some Imagist poems, some poems 'almost too Georgian even for *Georgian Poetry*', as he put it. They seem the poems of a man who wanted desperately to be a poet, and who rummaged for a subject and a style among the poems of the past (one can imagine Monro in his shop, pulling down volume after volume from his shelves). In a more stable time he might have found his model, and become a readable, derivative poet. But falling as he did between generations – too young to be Decadent, and too old to be influenced by Pound – he found no authority, and imitated in too many direc-tions. Most of his *Collected Poems* are of this sad kind – toneless and faceless, and altogether without poetic identity.

Monro's problem of poetic identity does not seem explicable entirely in literary terms, however. When a poet finds it difficult to utter his own voice, it is sometimes because he cannot allow himself to express the self that he knows is there. Monro was by nature intro-spective and individual, and his best poems are those in which he is least like other poets of his time, and most like himself. 'He does not express the spirit of an age', T. S. Eliot wrote of him; 'he expresses the spirit of one man, but that so faithfully that his poetry will remain as one variety of the infinite number of possible expressions of tortured human consciousness.' Eliot, who knew something about tortured human consciousness, recognized a fellow sufferer; but the poems he described are a small part of Monro's total work. For Monro, the expression of his torment was itself a torment. The most individual poems came with greatest difficulty, and are seldom entirely clear or formally finished; they are often rather mysterious and reticent, allegorical or dream-like (or nightmare-like) – for example the fragmentary 'Strange Companion', and 'Lament in 1915'. Evidently some part of his imagination resisted exposure, uttered itself in harsh, strained ways, and pulled his experience towards abstract and veiled expression. But why should a man who desired so passionately to be a poet feel this resistance to the realization in poetry of his own truest subject – himself?

The answer appears to lie in unresolved conflicts in Monro's nature. He was an alcoholic, and made some painful poems out of his addiction, but the roots of his unhappiness lay deeper than his need for drink. Conrad Aiken, in his *Ushant*, recalls what seems a significant incident in Monro's later life:

> never would D. forget that final dinner in London, over the bookshop, where . . . he found the unhappy man seated at the table, his head in his hands, all but speechless, or his speech reduced to four-letter words of imprecation, imprecation from the last depths of loathing and disgust and despair. Incapable of serving the cold collation which had been laid out on the sideboard, he rolled his head in his hands (while D. served himself) and cursed his existence, cursed everything, cursed everyone, but above all cursed the utterly meaningless caprices and bad jokes and filthy connivings of a destiny that would compel one to fall in love, for instance, with a dishonest little tailor's assistant, who was utterly incapable of fidelity; and thus to destroy all that one had believed in, or been faithful to, in one's life, all that was good. What was it for? What? And the muttered imprecations would begin again, round and round and over and over, in an ecstasy of self-loathing.

The self-loathing, whatever its sources in Monro's nature, was at once his subject and the basis of his mind's resistance to expression of it. Sometimes his poetic impulse overcame that resistance, and the painful poems that resulted are most of Monro's best work, but the price of his true voice was, it seems, a life of private misery, and what we hear in the best poems as the note of authenticity is the true accent of his wretchedness.

Even those poems are not often direct and explicit. Monro apparently found it necessary, in dealing with his personal problems, to mythologize them, or to transmute them into more acceptable themes – desire into loneliness, loathing into death, love into comradeship. Often the ellipsis is so private that the meaning can only be guessed at, or inferred from external evidence. Consider, for example, one of the poems in which Monro describes a dreamlike relationship with a mysterious man – 'The Garden'. In this poem a stranger tells the speaker of the poem of a ruined garden that only he knows. The two drink together, and then set out to visit it, but cannot find the entrance. A year later they meet and discover the garden, but meet in the gate an angel with a flaming sword, barring their way. In this private enactment of the Expulsion from Paradise, the two men are Adam and Eve; and what, then, is the Garden itself, which is forbidden them? The poem has the compelling near-meaning of a vivid dream, but it does not seem altogether under the poet's conscious control. If it is nevertheless moving, that is perhaps because, as Stephen Spender said of Monro's work, 'it has that kind of inevitable sincerity which cannot evade revealing the truth even when it seems to wish to do so'.

There was another side of Monro's poetic character from which the suffering introspective voice was excluded. It is expressed in good poems that simply celebrate the existence of things. 'Praise whatever is for being', Auden says, and Monro was sometimes capable of that kind of praise – of old houses and domestic wares, of animals and scenes, and of the earth itself. These are the things in a life that an unhappy man might hold on to – the things with which it is possible to have a guiltless relationship; and in this sense these poems of celebration are the affirming side of Monro's dark introspection. Some of the poems have seemed sentimental to Monro's detractors: 'Every Thing', for example, with its talking Kettle and Copper Basin, and 'Dog'; but a more sympathetic reader may find them touching and truth-telling, the expressions of a lonely man's need to love existence.

When these things were country things, Monro sometimes approached what was falsest in Georgian poetry – that commuter's pantheism that draws too easily on the poeticness of nature. His sonnet sequence, 'Week-end', appears to be this kind of performance, and it has been used as a model of Georgian 'week-end Romanticism'. But Monro was aware of the sentimentality inherent in the situation of the city man who retreats briefly to the country, and that is what the poem is about. It is an honest account of his feelings for the country, and his hatred of city life; and where sentiment is the conscious subject, it is surely a legitimate matter for poetry. Monro's country poems are full of awareness of the city, where the real life must be lived; similarly his city poems – and Monro wrote a number of very good ones – acknowledge the country outside (as for example 'City-Storm'). In both kinds, one feels the poet's scrupulous fidelity to the rest of reality, the sense that he would rather write an honest, comprehending poem than a well-made one. Aiken described this essential quality in Monro's writing in *Ushant*, in the character that he calls 'Arnault':

> Paul had once happily described Arnault's own poetry as an 'interesting fumble'; and nothing could have been truer. There was a kind of angry desperation in it, and in its dogged insistence on the literal truth, nothing less, and every inch of it, it tangled itself in the contingent, got helplessly in its own way, and suddenly came to an end exhausted.

It is this quality of dogged truthfulness that makes Monro's best poems sometimes seem abrupt, harsh, unfinished, obscurely private (when the literal truth is private), uncompromising. As he approached the end of his life, and sank into the illness from which he must have known he would not recover, he became most himself in his verse; imitativeness and reticence fell away, and he wrote a few last poems that are nakedly personal, powerful, and fine. There is something very moving about these poems of a dying man, so completely a poet that he took what strength he had to turn his own death into poetry.

Monro is not much anthologized these days, but there is always another anthologist coming, and for him one might leave this note: Please do not make your anthology out of other anthologies; if you do, you will represent Monro (if at all) with 'Milk for the Cat' and 'The Nightingale Near the House'. Instead, kindly read the following: 'Bitter Sanctuary', 'Living', 'Midnight Lamentation', 'Dream Exhibition of a Final World', 'In the Night', 'The Silent Pool', 'Underworld', 'Introspection', 'From an Old House', 'City-Storm', 'While we Sleep', 'Every Thing', 'Week-end', 'Aspidistra Street', 'London Interior'. If you do, you will not have read all of Monro's excellent and individual poems, but you will have read enough to know that this gifted, unhappy man merits a place – a minor, but a permanent place – in the canon of modern poetry.

The original version was first published in *The Times Literary Supplement*, 4 October 1970.

10

E. M. Forster

a   The Old Man at King's: Forster at 85

At eighty-five, E. M. Forster enjoys an odd and enviable status among living men of letters: he is a singularly well-loved man who appears to have made no enemies, acquired no detractors. It is not surprising that a good man should be well-liked; it is surprising, though, that an important novelist should have aroused no hostility, nor even serious reservations, among his literary critics.

Forster's novels came early, but serious criticism of them came late, and it is no doubt for this reason that his critics have treated him with that affectionate respect which one accords the very old, and especially those who have outlived their own era. Forster, the oldest living ex-novelist, the last of the Edwardian gentlemen, the incredibly surviving spirit of the English *belle-époque* – how else could one approach him but with deference? Even young and strenuous critics who would not for a moment subscribe to the morality of Forster's novels, nor admire his old-fashioned, didactic technique, lower their voices (and their standards) when they speak of the Old Man at King's.

One might conclude that his novels have survived into the present as they have, substantially untouched by hostile criticism, partly at least because *he* has survived, and survived so modestly and graciously. So admirable an old man – so kind, so self-deprecating, so steadily behind the best liberal causes (although, as he admits, at a considerable distance) – a man who like King Duncan hath borne his faculties so meek, can scarcely be criticized with that impersonal ruthlessness which we expend on the young and the dead. And so we regard him with affection and respect, as a lingering reminder of perished values, an intelligent, civilized, decent old man.

But though intelligence and decency are admirable, and perhaps even adequate human values, they are not enough to make a work of art excellent. (If they were, Santayana would have written a better novel than he did.) The terms do describe Forster's personal qualities, and they also describe qualities in his novels, but as literary values they are not sufficient to describe high merit. If Forster's work deserves the permanent-looking place that it currently enjoys in the hierarchy of English fiction, it must be for other reasons.

Part of the difficulty in judging Forster's novels lies in the fact that, though the man is in the present, the work is far in the past. Forster's career as a novelist ended forty years ago, and all but one of his novels were written in the reign of Edward VII. They are Edwardian, not in terms of publication dates alone, but in their atmosphere and in their values; they speak from that curious decade between the death of Victoria and the First World War, a time as remote from our present as the reign of William and Mary, and a good deal more remote than Victoria's age. If we look at Forster's career as an Edwardian one we will, I think, understand much about the novels – their excellences and their weaknesses – and perhaps we will also find the answer to the question of why the career ended when it did.

We should look first at Forster's stories, but they need not detain us long. With one or two exceptions they are not distinguished enough to survive without the support of the novels. They do, however, demonstrate certain of Forster's values and habits of mind – his Victorian Hellenism, his visionary romanticism, his habitual opposing of head and heart, and his intense feelings for 'the genius loci'. The stories are fantasies, full of improbable meetings of gods and men; fantasy was a popular Edwardian mode – *Peter Pan* is an Edwardian play – and no doubt it is in part because we have lost the taste for this sort of Pan-ridden goings on that Forster's stories seem dated and trivial.

Then there are the five novels. The first two are best described as social comedies, though this term does not quite do justice to *Where Angels Fear to Tread* (1905) and *A Room with a View* (published in 1908, but the first to be written). In these novels, Forster put aside the tiresome trappings of his stories, and revealed a gift for intricate, melodramatic plotting and comical-farcical satire which make these the best comic novels of the period. The object of Forster's satire is his own British middle-class; Englishmen, Forster later wrote, suffer from 'undeveloped hearts', and protect themselves from feeling by snobbery and respectability.

In these two novels, Forster exposes representatives of the British middle class to the abundant, anarchic vitality and emotion of Italy; head meets heart, and is transformed by the encounter. Though one novel ends in melodramatic disaster, the other in happy marriage, the two make substantially the same point, and in the same manner. The style is charming, the structure deft, and it is hard to see how either novel could be improved. But charm is a dangerous literary virtue – difficult to sustain, and likely to become intolerable if administered in too heavy doses. Perhaps Forster was aware of this danger; at any rate, in his next novel he assumed a different manner, and did worse.

The Longest Journey is generally regarded as Forster's least successful book, though he perversely prefers it above all the others. It is the most personal of the five novels, using details of Forster's own life at school and at Cambridge, where the first two novels used comic inventions; it is also the most overtly visionary, and in this respect approaches the manner of the stories. One can understand why a novel which includes so much of himself should have a special meaning for Forster, but for the rest of us, the general view seems the right one – it is a novel which doesn't succeed.

The last two novels, *Howards End* (1910) and *A Passage to India* (1924, but begun a decade earlier), are the most serious, the most didactic, the most symbolical, and altogether the most ambitious of Forster's books, and his critics agree that these are the best of the novels, though they differ as to which is the better of the two. Admirers of *Howards End* find *Passage to India* too mystical, and can't understand what the last part is doing there; admirers of *Passage to India* think *Howards End* is imperfectly resolved.

In *Howards End* Forster attempted to set head against heart without the help of an external term – without Italy or India or Pan. Perhaps as a consequence of this, it is the most overtly moralistic of the novels, and appeals to those who like their liberalism spelled out. *A Passage to India* is Forster's most nearly political novel, and attracts readers who like their writers to be 'engaged'; though, like most political novels, it has rather outlived its engagement, and its satirical treatment of the British Raj seems a bit quaint now.

After *A Passage to India* Forster started another novel – it was called *Arctic Summer* – but was unable to finish it, and, as he put it, 'just drifted out' of novel writing. But 'just drifted out' isn't very satisfactory; one wants to know why. We can find the answer, I think, in two ways; we can look at the novels themselves, and consider whether they propose values which would support an active artistic life in the modern world;

and we can examine his more recent occasional writings for statements of his sense of his relations to this modern world in which he is apparently unable to exercise his creative imagination.

Let us try the latter course first. Here is a longish quotation from a review which Forster wrote for the BBC a few years ago:

> Fifty years ago, when I was young, the idea of a Problem was exhilarating. The nineteenth century had emphasized Progress. The early twentieth century, while not rejecting Progress, felt itself to be more realistic if it approached progress through problems. The problems lay about like sheets torn out of Euclid, all waiting to be solved, and posed with impeccable clarity. 'Here is a completely new problem,' a statesman would enthusiastically exclaim. And though people occasionally remarked that one problem often led to another, no one realized how sinister the remark was. With proper attention and adequate commercial resourcefulness all problems would be solved and God's great Q.E.D. peal out.
>
> This attitude was scotched rather than killed by the first world war. . . . Disillusionment and distrust of problems began back in the 'twenties – the most clear-sighted decade of our own half-century. It realized that nothing had been solved, and that so-called solutions were hydras who produced more heads than had been decapitated. . . . Today more and more people realize that the world we are pleased to call 'ours' has passed out of our control, and that though the human race may not be destroyed, it is powerless to avert its own destruction.

The two worlds defined here – the worlds before and after the First World War – are offered as radically different, and based on diametrical ideas of life and value. But most important, Forster admits sadly that the pre-war world, *his* world, was wrong. His novels belong to that lost Edwardian Age of Problems, that age when men believed that they could, by being intelligent and decent, find ultimate solutions; they are Edwardian Problem Novels.

But to write Problem Novels you must believe in solutions – you must postulate 'God's great Q.E.D.' Time and History overtook Forster's solutions; war and violence, the overwhelming evidence of man's inhumanity and the failure of Love, dried up his creative gifts. D. H.

Lawrence, that perceptive man, saw this happening early in the war; in a letter to Bertrand Russell dated 1915 he wrote: 'Forster is not poor, but he *is* bound hand and foot bodily. Why? Because he does not believe that any beauty or any divine utterance is any good any more.' The personal values remained; but though they were good enough to live by, they were not good enough to create by. Forster accepted this fact with characteristically resigned good humor: 'I don't fret over the changes in the world I grew up in', he wrote. 'But I can't handle them. I would write atomically if I could.' We might therefore regard Forster as one more casualty of the War, though it would be more accurate to say that he was a casualty of the too-confident, complacent peace that preceded it.

The novels will tell us much the same story, if we read them in order. The early ones – the Italian comedies – make their value judgments confidently, affirm the life of head-and-heart, and condemn those who sin against that ideal. The values are clear enough, perhaps too clear: thinking and feeling, passion and truth, Eros and Pallas Athene are good. If one suppresses neither, one will be moral; and, we gather, one will also be happy. The only enemy that matters is the enemy within, and external restraints upon passion and truth are of no apparent concern. There is no such thing as guilty passion, and no obstacles to the discovery of truth. Man can be good and happy, if he will only try.

This, in all its nakedness, is Forster's liberal humanism. It is a faith which links him properly with the ninteenth century rather than with our own time. The moral strenuousness and the ready Hellenism remind one of Matthew Arnold; the individualism and the assumption that happiness is attainable to the good-hearted are very like Dickens. George Orwell once wrote of Dickens that 'his whole message is one that at first glance looks like an enormous platitude: If men would behave decently the world would be decent.' That enormous platitude spreads out to cover Forster with its vast and comforting shade; but it does not comfort us.

A more profound and more satisfactory representation of the humanistic position is *Howards End*, Forster's longest and to my mind his most impressive novel. The novel carries on its title page the enigmatic motto, 'Only connect . . .'; the action explains the enigma, by showing us characters in a complex of efforts to connect with each other, person-to-person, class-to-class, values-to-values. The most overt formulation of this moral core of meaning occurs in a meditation of the principal character, Margaret Schlegel, an aesthetical young woman who has become engaged to a rather elderly business man:

> Margaret greeted her lord with peculiar tenderness on the morrow. Mature as he was, she might yet be able to help him to the building of the rainbow bridge that should connect the prose in us with the passion. Without it we are meaningless fragments, half monks, half beasts, unconnected arches that have never joined into a man. With it love is born, and alights on the highest curve, glowing against the grey, sober against the fire. . . . Only connect! That was the whole of her sermon. Only connect the prose and the passion, and both will be exalted, and human love will be seen at its height. Live in fragments no longer. Only connect, and the beast and the monk, robbed of the isolation that is life to either, will die.

This is pretty rich stuff, with its rainbow bridges and loaded words like 'love' and 'salvation', and it may persuade us that something profound is being said. The message seems at first very like that in the earlier novels – an exhortation to live a whole life, and out of wholeness to create love. But there is one distinct change: the terms of the division are no longer Eros and Pallas Athene, individually valuable, though incomplete; here they are monk and beast, unpleasant and life-denying fragments. The 'enemy within' has become something more ominous, though the exact nature of salvation is as unclear as ever.

Howards End is a more serious novel than, say, *A Room with a View* because it acknowledges more of the disagreeable aspects of reality: the injustices of class, the need for money, the existence of evil, the potential destructiveness of passion – all these are present, as they are not in the earlier novels. But by acknowledging these divisive elements in life, Forster made 'connection' impossible. The novel ends with an innocent man dead, a strong man made weak, and the house which is the symbol of the good life threatened by the inevitable spread of the red rust of London. The two women who survive are both 'disconnected' from life: one cannot love a man, the other cannot love a child. The effort to connect has failed, no one is involved in living.

But then, the mind behind these novels is not involved in living, either. This is not a statement about Forster's personal life, but about the character of his writing – it remains always at a distance from its subject, observing, not participating. One finds this quality manifested in many ways: in the way, for example, that the most fully realized characters tend to be the least active ones, and in the number of scenes in which passion is observed from a position apart (the scene in *The Longest Journey*, in which Rickie learns about love by watching Agnes and Gerald kissing is a paradigmatic example, but there are many others). If characters fail to 'connect', one might also say that Forster fails to connect with the life of his fictional world.

Failure to connect is also a principal theme of Forster's last novel, *A Passage to India*. In the final scene Fielding, the moderate Englishman, rides through the Indian countryside with Aziz, the Indian with whom he wants to be friends. 'Why can't we be friends now?' Fielding asks, 'It's what I want. It's what you want.'

> But the horses didn't want it – they swerved apart; the earth didn't want it, sending up rocks through which riders must pass single file; the temples, the tank, the jail, the palace, the birds, the carrion, the Guest House that came into view as they issued from the gap and saw Mau beneath: they didn't want it, they said in their hundred voices, No, not yet, and the sky said, No, not there.

'Only connect. . . .' Yes, that would be nice. But Forster's novels are not about connecting, they are about failure to connect, and progressively more so as time carried him past the Edwardian age of problems and solutions. The marriages he contrived are unhappy, other personal relationships are partial and transient, and the novels customarily end on episodes which symbolize disconnectedness as an aspect of the human condition, supported even by earth and sky at the last. A more precise formulation of Forster's motto would be 'If only we *could* connect. . . .' But, say the novels bleakly, we can't. It is because Forster admitted to his world the probable failure of human communion, and the related possibility that in this unconnecting world life itself is without meaning, and because he could face that daily nightmare, which must for many men be a condition of existence, with grace and quiet irony, that he merits the admiration that he has received. Such negative honesty may not be the highest human achievement, but it is an honorable one, and we can only regret that it was not, apparently, enough to sustain Forster's creative imagination.

Still, there the five novels are, for us to go on reading. We do so, I think, partly because they express a personality which we find attractive and admirable; they reveal not only intelligence and decency, but a generous sense of humor, and a great capacity for affection, including an unashamed love of the English land which can be very moving. These are all human rather than literary qualities, and I think it true, though it may be contrary to the most austere critical precepts, to say that we really like the man, and read the books simply to get to know him. He is well worth knowing, the speaking voice of these novels: kinder than Joyce, wittier than Lawrence, a better stylist than Conrad. But to put his name in such company is to see at once how little he belongs there. His imagination is of a lesser kind – which may be one reason for our liking him (how could one like Joyce?).

The problem is, I suppose, a matter of head and heart: heart asserting that Love the Beloved Republic will prevail, head saying 'No, not yet, no, not there'. To my mind, head and heart remain unreconciled in even the best of Forster's books; perhaps they had to, in the world that Forster saw. But even without reconciliation, that world is worth knowing, and these five novels, with their wit, their intelligence, and their decency, will survive their failure to be more perfect than life has seemed to the Old Man at King's.

The original version was first published in *Commonweal*, 21 February 1964.

b   E. M. Forster. An Obituary

E. M. Forster is dead. Thinking of the event, one wonders how he would have recorded it. Not so bluntly, perhaps, as he did the death of Gerald, but with a calm directness, and without the crepe and sentiment of mourning. For he knew that death is too commonplace to be elevated, and that the death of the old is small loss to the living. Perhaps the death of Mrs Moore offers a model of the right Forsterian attitude. Hamidullah and Fielding, hearing the news, feel regret,

> but they were middle-aged men, who had invested their
> emotions elsewhere, and outbursts of grief could not be expected
> from them over a slight acquaintance. It's only one's own dead
> who matter. If for a moment the sense of communion in sorrow
> came to them, it passed.

This is the kind of honesty, so plain that his critics have called it irony, with which Forster saw life and death. For his admirers – and they amount to generations now – he may for a moment seem one of their own dead, but he would assure them that the moment will pass.

He would not wish to be eulogized. In his own words about dead friends he was above all things honest; he did not think that the dead deserve lies. So he wrote of Edward Carpenter, who had been his friend and teacher: 'He is not likely to have much earthly immortality . . . He will not figure in history.' Forster will fare better – no one can doubt that he will figure in the history of the English novel – but he will not be with the greatest. It does not seem wrong to say so at this time; certainly Forster was the first to refuse the attribute of greatness.

And indeed it was his steadfast refusal to be great that made him what he was. In a time that too often praised the superhuman while it practised the inhuman, Forster stood for truth and ordinariness, for the importance of plain individuals and the value of unheroic virtues – tolerance, good temper, sympathy, personal relationships, pleasure, love. These values define both his work and his life, and work and life are alike so filled with the personality of the man that no critical rigour can separate them. For Forster did not believe, as other influential writers of our time have believed, in the impersonality of art. Everything that is most personal and individual he celebrated, and in his own voice. In his novels the good characters have his own best qualities, and the wicked ones are wicked because they do not feel, or do not love. The essays say the same things, and in the same voice that speaks from novels and stories; Forster himself exists in all his writings more definitely than any character he invented. No other novelist of our time so exposed and committed himself, or moralized so freely upon his inventions.

Both the morality and the omniscient voice now seem old-fashioned; the faith in right feelings belongs to another, more trusting time. Forster thought it worse to be unfeeling than to be sentimental, and consequently came sometimes to the edge of sentimentality, but never close to callousness. (We have reversed his faith, and not, perhaps, to our own good.) And that quiet authorial voice in the novels, speaking up to remind us that what we are reading is a story with a moral, is also from the past. But though the morality and the technique are old-fashioned, they are also reassuring; because we can trust Forster to engage himself in his action, we can trust him in other things.

It is not, after all, surprising that they should be old-fashioned. The novels are a young man's books that grew old with him, and all but one belong to the Edwardian period of more than fifty years ago. No other novelist has had a career quite like Forster's; not because it was over at forty-five – many important writers have died earlier – but because in the few creative years so few books were written, and because those few Edwardian novels were carried, as it were, into the present by the long life of their author. It is difficult to imagine the state of Forster's reputation if he had died when Edward VII died, or even in 1924, after *A Passage to India*; but one can guess that the novels would have retained their period costumes, and would be read now for what they are – the best English novels, after Conrad's, of a remote decade.

Forster himself saw them as period pieces, out of a lost pre-war world. 'I have been accustomed to write about the old-fashioned world with its homes and its family life and its comparative peace. All that went, and though I can think about the new world I cannot put it into fiction.' It is perhaps partly because of their pastness that he was able to judge his novels with such objectivity. He placed his own work on the second level of novels, as good but not great, and he had his reasons.

> In no book [he said] have I got down more than the people I like, the person I think I am, and the people who irritate me. This puts me among the large body of authors who are not really novelists, and have got to get on as best they can with these three categories. We have not the power of observing the variety of life and describing it dispassionately.

But though he was critical of his own work, he was not self-denigrating. He was certain that he had written good, substantial fiction, and he was frank to admit that he re-read his novels with pleasure. His judgment seems, at this point in the record, just on the whole, but on one book it is surely too severe, and too modest: most of Forster's readers would agree that *A Passage to India* should be raised from this second level of achievement, for in that novel Forster did escape his Edwardian limitations and wrote a great book.

Forster's place in his time cannot be equated with the place of his novels, secure though that place is. One is likely to forget that though the novels ended after the war, Forster went on writing, and in fact wrote more books after *A Passage to India* than before it; and beyond the books there is the life, a long testimony to courage and integrity. In his later years Forster was many men, and in all his roles he spoke for his liberal values. As a Humanist, he spoke for the individual against authority; as an Edwardian Englishman he expressed his unembarrassed love of England in a simple, moving pageant; as a Man of Letters he encouraged younger writers; and tolerated the curiosity of his admirers. His criticism was disarmingly casual and apparently old-fashioned, but he nevertheless made his critical ideas current terminology; *Aspects of the Novel* is still attacked by academic critics, but his notions of flat and round characters and of the causality of plot are a part of the way those same critics discuss fiction.

Perhaps one should add one more role – Forster-the-realist, the man who could accept what could not be altered, and do it with dignity and honesty. He regretted the changes that had overtaken the world he grew up in; he would have preferred that the Edwardian Age should last. But he did not pretend that it had – he lived in the present, however bleak that present was. The end of the Edwardian peace had cost Forster his creative imagination, and he did not disguise his regret, but he accepted both the cost and the regret. He was saddened at the passing of the rural heritage of his childhood, but he accepted as inevitable the spreading red rust of cities; like the character in *Arctic Summer*, 'he knew that much of the earth must be dull and commercial, and that to revolt against her is ridiculous'. And when he considered the future of man in the post-atomic world he judged that the odds were against him.

Yet for all this he never lost his Humanist's faith, and never despaired. Though he thought that the human race might not survive, he still urged upon individual man 'his duty to create and to understand and to contact other individuals. A duty that may be and ought to be a delight.' All Forster's qualities are in that passage – the supremely valuable individual, the sense of duty, the sense of delight. It is this human voice that is silenced in his death, and it is his humanity that makes him one of our dead who matter.

Parts of this section were first used in 'E. M. Forster at 90', *The Times Literary Supplement*, 2 January 1969.

c   Forster's Cramp

In February 1915, Forster visited D. H. Lawrence at Greatham, and while he was there Lawrence wrote his impressions of his guest in a letter to a friend: 'He is very nice. I wonder if the grip has gone out of him. I get a feeling of acute misery from him – not that he does any-thing – but you know the acute, exquisite pain of cramp.' We may take that intuitive diagnosis as essentially accurate: what Forster was suffering from was homosexual cramp, the spiritual and imaginative restraints of a suppressed and guilty sexuality. At the time that he visited the Lawrences he had accepted his sexual nature, and had even written a novel about it, but he had no thought of publishing the book, or of revealing his condition to the world; and so, when Lawrence and Frieda began to analyse his problems, he responded first with reticence and finally with anger. His cramp might have been painful, but it was none the less necessary; it made his literary and social existence possible.

For Lawrence, Forster's cramp was a pain that could be cured: 'Why can't he take a woman', Lawrence wondered, 'and fight clear to his own basic, primal being?' But Post-Freudians know better than that, not only about the persistency of sexual drives, but also about the creative consequences of psychic wounds. The impulse that suppresses and distorts the sexual life may liberate the imagination, though at a price that only the artist can reckon. Forster may have disliked and resented his condition – it seems clear that he did – but it was as central to his art as to his sexual being; to say that he was homosexual is to define not only his private nature, but the nature of his imagination.

With the private nature the critic has no proper business, and it is easy to respect and continue Forster's life-long reticence. But the homosexuality of his imagination is a critical matter, for it explains both the qualities and the limitations of his work. It informs the essential properties of his novels – the voyeuristic distancing of the narration, the ironic tone, the self-deprecating humour, and it imposes the most serious limitations – the blind spots and imaginative failures.

Most obviously, Forster could not imagine any aspect of the range of experience between men and women – heterosexual attraction, hetero-sexual relations, marriage were mysterious to him. No wonder he resented having to write 'marriage novels' – the subject was quite beyond his range. If we consider the crucial marriages in his books – Lucy Honeychurch and George Emerson, Lilia and Gino, Margaret Schlegel and Mr Wilcox, Rickie and Agnes – they seem equally unreal and unrealized; and the one irregular union that he attempted – the one-night affair of Helen and Leonard Bast – is even worse, a case of conception as an Edwardian schoolboy might have imagined it, out of a few facts and a large ignorance.

No doubt this is why one feels in so many of Forster's novels a kind of transference at work, as though one were reading a different sort of story, but translated into socially acceptable terms. *The Longest Journey*, Forster's most personal novel, and the one he liked best, is a case in point. It is a 'marriage novel', but not in any ordinary sense; rather, it seems a kind of homosexual nightmare, in which the condition of marriage is imagined – cold, loveless, and degrading. The central relation is not that between husband and wife, Rickie and Agnes, at all, but between Rickie and Stephen Wonham. Forster confessed in an interview that he had 'had trouble with the junction of Rickie and Stephen. How to make them intimate . . .', and the difficulty is surely that he was writing a crypto-homosexual story, in which his protagonist is 'saved' by his intimacy with a young man of humble station (Forster himself favoured young men of the lower classes). Forster made the relationship acceptable by basing it on kinship, and by marrying Rickie to Agnes (his abnormality is transferred to his crippled foot), but the curious dissonance remains, that all the heat of the novel is concentrated on the man-man scenes, and the man-woman scenes have a chill repugnancy. Agnes, we are told, had a child, but the statement is incredible: how could a child possibly have been conceived in such a union?

In other novels there are other signs. In *A Room with a View*, for instance, no physical scene between the lovers is treated as vividly as the all-male bathing scene, so reminiscent of the pederastic bathing of Victorian homosexual writing and photography. In it, male nakedness liberates George and Mr Beebe from their conventionality, and the women, when they appear, are a confining and depressing end to the affair. Over the whole episode a vague spiritual-mythological presence hovers that is evoked in the purplish prose that Forster characteristically employed on such occasions: 'it had been a call to the blood and to the relaxed will, a passing benediction whose influence did not pass, a holiness, a spell, a momentary chalice for youth.' As an account of the effect of pond-bathing this seems rather fruity; but it works better if we take it as a veiled description of sexual feeling – physical and urgent, beneficial but temporary, a relaxation of the controlling and repressing will, outside the ordinary range of society's possibilities.

Pan is not quite present in that scene, though one can feel him, as elsewhere in the novels when feeling is released; he is Forster's presiding deity, the spirit of liberation from convention, the god of boys and bumpkins. He appears most overtly in the short stories, but he is also present in Stephen Wonham, and in Forster's passionate Italians. Pan may be identified with the force of Nature in Forster, but one must qualify that remark somewhat; for Forster was never really interested in Nature as such, and what Pan really represents is an idea of natural human behaviour – a complete life without conventional restraints, a life that acknowledges animality. Which is to say that Forster's Pan is the deity of a homosexual world, or a world in which homosexuality is natural. He is necessary to the stories and novels simply because, in Forster's Sawston-and-Cambridge world, homosexual love could not be a force in itself; it was only by supernatural intervention that direct emotion could find expression.

Looking back over the novels and stories, one must conclude that Forster was incapable of recording deep currents of feeling – sexual feeling most obviously, but other deep feeling as well. The occasions when feeling should flow – sexual love, birth, death – are treated distantly, with a cold casualness; we remember 'Gerald died that afternoon', in *The Longest Journey*, but forget from the same novel 'while he was out his brother died', and 'by the time they arrived Robert had been drowned' – three throw-away deaths of loved persons. Ordinary emotional states were beyond Forster, and perhaps the moments of melodrama so often remarked in the novels are there because they offered him his only means of indicating strong feeling; but how gross it always seems – the stabbed man in the piazza, the baby hurled from the carriage, death under a train, extreme stimuli for the feelings they express.

When the emotion is explicitly sexual, the failure is complete. *Howards End* is the weak novel it is because it has heterosexual relationships at its centre – an engagement, a marriage, and a fornication move the plot – and Forster could not handle any of them convincingly. And so the events that should be fully treated are either shuffled off-stage or are brought on so wrapped in rhetoric as to be quite meaningless (all that embarrassing stuff about 'rainbow bridges', for instance). *Where Angels Fear to Tread* is a better novel than *Howards End* partly because it does not attempt sexuality, or only indirectly: what it is really about is the difficulties that a homosexual has in understanding the behaviour of heterosexuals, and Forster knew a good deal about that.

The exception to these strictures is, of course, *A Passage to India*, which is more and more clearly Forster's one achievement. Perhaps Forster learned about love in India, or perhaps race did what sexual difference didn't do; at any rate, the relation between Fielding and Aziz is the one deeply moving intimacy in the novels, far more intimate than any marriage Forster attempted, or any love affair. It is the principal evidence that he did have a developed heart, for all his donnish reticence.

'How much time does love take?' Forster asks in *Aspects of the Novel*, and he concludes that two hours a day is a handsome allowance. And indeed in Forster's world that is more than enough; setting aside Aziz, one can scarcely find a character in the novel who spends as much time loving as he does in being ridiculous or nasty. This is in part a circumstance of the curious Forsterian tribe that inhabits his world, a tribe that seems designed to make loving, and especially sexual loving, unnecessary, or even impossible. Typically it has at its centre a fatherless family: a widowed mother, some daughters, and one – always just one – rather inadequate son. There are some variations (no daughters in *The Longest Journey*, Mrs Wilcox for the mother-figure in *Howards end*), but the tribal pattern is strikingly uniform through the novels up to *Passage to India*. The tribe represents restraints: convention, propriety, suburbanism, and the sexual restraints of widowhood and virginity. To escape the tribe is to free the imagination, to move from suburbs to country, from the rule of the C. of E. God to the rule of Pan, from control to freedom, from no-sex to sex. It is also, in the most personal books, to escape from a world of women to a world of men; women is the Mother, but man is the Comrade, the brother that Rickie wanted but did not have.

In each of Forster's tribes there is a Forster-like character, a boy or young man, ascetic and detached, imperfectly involved in life, and slightly ridiculous. These characters differ a good deal in particulars, and in the roles they play in the actions, but they are always in evidence – in Forster every mother has a son to devour, and every son has a slightly chewed look. Seen together – Freddie and Rickie, Tibby and Philip – they seem a common type without a common function. What they provided for Forster is a steady point of reference, a self in the novel, who can view the emotional lives of others with some ironic detachment, but, because he is a character, can also in turn be viewed ironically. If society disapproves of limp-wristed young men, then Forster will put one in each of his novels, and ridicule him. These are Forster's selves, but seen through the world's eyes, and denied and disinherited by their creator.

Though Forster was homosexual, he lived in a world that believed in marriage and in marriage-novels, and his desire to remain in that world was stronger than his desire to tell the truth about himself. Obviously his work was affected by this disharmony, and certainly his gifts were distorted by it, but it would be too simple to say that the repression of his sexual nature crippled his imagination, or was necessarily a factor in his 'drying up' as a novelist. One could more readily argue that in fact a *creative* tension existed between the impulse and the work, and that the effort to transform homosexuality into socially acceptable forms was an ordering force, that determined both his characteristic vision and his characteristic tone. He saw the world as emptied of absolutes, lonely, and threatening (the truest expression of this vision is in the concert scene in *Howards End*, when Helen hears 'Panic and Emptiness!' in Beethoven's Fifth Symphony); but he expressed this bleak vision with a self-deprecating irony that refused to be altogether serious, and never reached towards tragedy. If one says that tragedy and homo-sexuality do not sit well together, but irony and homosexuality do, this is not to be taken as a judgment of a sexual state, but as an observa-tion of social attitudes. Forster was a sensitive judge of such attitudes, and he wrote, one might say, defensively, to preserve his place in the society that would ostracize him if it knew. But cunning defensiveness suited his talent, and he made out of self-deprecation, transference, and evasion, a personal and functioning style.

One had always heard rumours that there was one exception: that there was an unpublished novel that eschewed evasion, and was too frank to be published. Now at last we have that novel, and some of the circumstances of its composition. It was written in 1913–14, and in a 'Terminal Note' Forster explains the initial impulse. He had been visiting Edward Carpenter, the Edwardian guru of sandals, the simple life, and 'homogenic love', and while he was there Carpenter's friend, George Merrill, had touched Forster fondly on the backside. 'The sensation', Forster writes, 'was unusual and I still remember it, as I remember the position of a long vanished tooth. It was as much psychological as physical. It seemed to go straight through the small of my back into my ideas, without involving my thoughts.' He returned to his mother, who was taking a cure at Harrogate, and began to write *Maurice*. The novel came to him easily – no doubt because he did not have to translate his feelings into other terms – and he seems to have written with a sense of private liberation. But having written, he recovered his instinctive cautiousness, and did not try to publish it (not that publication would have been easy in a decade that suppressed *The*

Rainbow). He showed it to friends from time to time, and he went on tinkering with it (most recently in 1960), but he was unwilling to endure the disturbance to his quiet life that publication would cause, and he left the manuscript at his death with the laconic Forsterian comment, 'Publishable – but worth it?'

Maurice is an example of a common twentieth-century kind of novel, the novel of growth and self-discovery; it belongs to the same category as *A Portrait of the Artist, Of Human Bondage,* and *The Longest Journey.* But it differs from those novels in what Maurice discovers – that he is homosexual, and that homosexual love is possible. In his personal circumstances Maurice is Tibby and Rickie and Philip all over again, the Weak Young Man with a widowed mother, sisters, a house in the Surrey suburbs, and a Cambridge education; and though Forster made some effort to make him un-Forsterian by giving him healthy good looks and a rather dull mind, this scarcely matters – he is in essentials true to type.

There is, however, one significant deviation from the tribal pattern; Maurice comes to a happy ending, in fulfilled love with a gamekeeper. Forster mistrusted and disliked happy endings; most novels, he thought, went off at the end as the author huddled resolutions together, and his own instinct was for dissonances. But in this case, he wrote, 'a happy ending was imperative. I shouldn't have bothered to write otherwise. I was determined that in fiction anyway two men should fall in love and remain in it for the ever and ever that fiction allows . . .' He was writing, this time, for the sake of homosexual love, and was willing to violate his own sensibility to assert that such love was possible. The ending of the novel is clumsy and improbable, and is altogether without the defences of irony that protect the other novels; but it is done that way by intention, to put a human principle above an aesthetic one. This is a very Forsterian thing to do, but it complicates the act of critical judgment, as it complicated the act of creation.

The crucial question about *Maurice* is, what happens when that creative tension between the homosexual imagination and society's restraints that informs Forster's other novels is abandoned for truth-telling? What happens when Forster tries to put 'the private lusts and aches' of his sexuality into fiction? How, in short, does he write without cramp? The answer, alas, is that he has written a novel of such uncharacteristic badness as not to be comparable to any other of his works, a novel almost as good, perhaps, as *The Well of Loneliness,* but certainly no better. He has sacrificed all of the qualities that make his work interesting – the ironic tone, the distance, the humour, the touches of shrewd wisdom, the style – and he has gained no commensurate values. The sentimentality that is always close to the surface in Forster (his liberalism was never much more than sentimental humanism) here oozes forth everywhere; indeed both the sentimentality and the prose style are so reminiscent of Edward Carpenter at his worst that one can only regret that trip to Milthorpe, and the pat on the bottom that started it all.

Most serious of all the novel's faults is what can only be described as the incompleteness of the imaginative act. *Maurice* is composed of many short chapters, more of them, and shorter, than in any other Forster novel. This is more than a statistic; it suggests what is indeed the case, that episodes are not fully realized, that the imagination has been imperfectly made verbal. Forster wrote the book rapidly because he was writing from experience, and no doubt for the same reason he did not succeed in turning experience into literary reality. If one examines, for example, the three pages that see Maurice through his public school, one finds a tissue of thin and general statements that might have been written by an Edwardian headmaster; 'Thoughts: he had a dirty little collection. Acts: he desisted from these after the novelty was over, finding that they brought him more fatigue than pleasure' – so much for the adolescent sex-life of our protagonist. One is surely not being prurient in suggesting that a novel about the Growth of a Homosexual ought to treat sex more frankly than that.

The heart of the matter is there, in the treatment of sex. Forster may have thought he wrote the book because he had come to terms with his own nature, but the book shows that this is not quite the case; *Maurice* is about homosexuality, but the attitudes it expresses are far from liberated. The language is the language of society – *morbidity*, *perversion* vs. *normality* – and the attitude is substantially guilty and regretful. Maurice accepts his condition, but he disapproves of it, and so, one gathers, does Forster, for at the end he turns from the real, social world, and sends his lovers off into a sentimental world of romance, like two Scholar Gypsies; there is to be no assimilation, no contact with society, but rather a sentimentalized form of ostracism.

Nor does Forster give to homosexual love any greater reality than he was able to evoke in his accounts of marriage. One had thought that he was vague and rhetorical with Lucy and George because he didn't and couldn't know anything about their relationship, but he is no better with Maurice and Alec – there is the same poverty of feeling here, the same lack of emotional complexity, the same cramped heart. The language is meticulously decent, but the treatment is as emotionally thin as pornography is. And this, too, must be a consequence of Forster's ambivalence and sense of sordidness; he could not imagine sex that was neither furtive nor repulsive. Love for him may have been a Beloved Republic, but it was never an innocent act.

Maurice is interesting as an Edwardian view of homosexuality, but it does not transcend that historical limit, and so, as a friend told Forster when he had read the manuscript, it can only have a period interest, plus, one might add, that morbid interest that one has in the unsuccessful work of a good writer. It adds nothing to his achievement as a novelist, and little to his reckoning as a man. If he had published it when he wrote it, it would have been a courageous act, as Carpenter's was when he published *Homogenic Love* and *The Intermediate Sex*; but now it appears as evidence of his fearful caution – the sort of thing that Sawston would have understood. Forster would probably not mind; he had a modest opinion of his place in the record, and did not worry about it, and in any case he would rather have had the kind of immortality that he ascribes to Carpenter, the sort that rests, not on words and deeds, but on the constancy and intensity of affections. But the critic can make no estimate of that achievement, and must be content to judge the book. And for that judgment, the words of Mrs Failing, upon reading Rickie's story, are perhaps the best. ' "It is bad", said Mrs. Failing. "But. But. But." Then she escaped, having told the truth, and yet leaving a pleasurable impression behind her.'

The original version was first published in *The Times Literary Supplement*, 8 October 1971.

11

T. E. Hulme:
The Intellectual Policeman

T. E. Hulme is the sort of writer whose reputation is based rather on what he was, or what he seemed to be, than on what he did; and that reputation is by now so firmly established that it is difficult to look beneath it to the actual facts of his achievement. Like many flamboyant people, he nourished in his own life a cult of personality; he flourished knuckle-dusters in philosophical discussions, and interrupted Café Royal conversations to seduce maidens in the Piccadilly Tube; he ran a celebrated salon in his mistress's drawing room, and from that salon he carried Wyndham Lewis out into Soho Square and hung him from the fence railings; he explained sculpture to Epstein and poetry to Pound. Wherever he went, he towered over disciples and adversaries alike. And now his reputation towers over him.

But beneath this massive poet-philosopher-lecher myth there is a figure of some importance; Hulme does deserve a place in the history of modern thought, not because he was original in any of his activities but because he was a highly articulate representative of his time, the spokesman of a new point of view though not the creator of it. Philosophers, he said, provide 'conceptual clothing' for new attitudes, and it is only in this rather special sense of the term that one can call him a philosopher at all (he was content to call himself a 'philosophic amateur'). In the transitional years before the 1914–18 war, the years when, as Yeats put it, 'everybody got down off his stilts', Hulme was able to dress a post-Victorian change of mood in conceptual clothing which seemed, at least for a time, to fit. His essays remain the best expression we have of the way that change felt to someone involved in it.

To many of his contemporaries Hulme seemed to have genius, but if he had it was a genius for simplifying complex social and intellectual processes so as to fit them into apparently ordered systems, rather than for original thought. He was one of the great simplifiers, the kind of writer who makes intellectual history look easy. He saw history as a road composed of alternate straight stretches and right-angle turns, and himself as a sort of intellectual policeman, posted at one of history's corners to direct traffic into the twentieth century.

Hulme's particular corner was the turn from Victorianism to what, for the time being, we may call 'modernism'. He chose, however, to see this turning in rather more grandiloquent terms, as a change from a continuous humanistic tradition stretching back to the Renaissance, to a revival of 'the religious attitude'. This humanist-religious antithesis was Hulme's first principle, and underlies virtually everything he wrote; he saw the changes of his own time – in philosophy, in art, in poetry, in politics – as constituting a single change, 'the break-up of the Renaissance'.

The Renaissance, in Hulme's version of history, was defined by a humanistic belief in human perfectibility, and the pressure under which it was breaking up was simply a revival of belief in the dogma of Original Sin. The results of this break-up would, Hulme believed, be a number of vast reactions: in philosophy from rationalism to anti-rationalism; in politics from liberalism to conservatism; in poetry from rhetoric to precise statement; in art from representationalism to abstraction. Original Sin would set man free.

These speculations must have seemed salutary and liberating to Hulme's auditors at 67, Frith Street and, to judge from the amount of current interest in Hulme, they are still attractive to many readers. This is not surprising, for in many ways Hulme is still very much alive; his anti-romanticism is still current, the visual arts continue in the general direction which he predicted for them, poetry and the criticism of poetry are still much concerned with the image, and the reactionary social and political ideas which he articulated have become a respectable tradition.

But while we can confirm Hulme's vision in some particulars, we can also, fifty years later, add some sobering details which he did not foresee. We can add that the breakdown of humanism in politics may bring totalitarianism and genocide, that 'non-vital' art may dissolve into sterile abstraction, and that a poetry of 'small, hard things' may exclude the great and moving human themes. The reactions that he wanted did occur, but they had their dark side – the side of authoritarianism, violence and unreason, which Hulme could view with equanimity but which we, on the other side of the reactions, cannot. Hulme's own Frith Street gang can provide us with sombre enough examples of the reactions he desired; in politics Ramiro de Maetzu, who died for Franco; Wyndham Lewis, who praised Hitler; and Ezra Pound, who broadcast for Mussolini; and in poetry *The Cantos*, that chaos of precise statements and repellent ideas.

It is idle, of course, as well as inaccurate, to call Hulme a Fascist, or to blame him for the actions of his followers. His political ideas were not that clear – like most of his ideas, they were developed mainly in negative terms. His rejection of liberal democracy is clear enough, but his 'Tory Philosophy' is a vague muddle of incomplete ideas about art and metaphysics.

The one political principle which we can deduce from Hulme's writings is that he was a convinced authoritarian. 'Nothing is bad in itself', he wrote, 'except disorder; all that is put in order in a hierarchy is good'; and one of the ideas that he found most attractive in Bergson was that 'man's primary need is not *knowledge* but *action*'. These two principles – order for its own sake and action for its own sake – are at the bottom of any authoritarian philosophy, but Hulme did not seem conscious of their uglier possibilities. Because he habitually reduced human choice to simple alternatives, he assumed that the only alternative to liberal humanism was a return to a religious view of existence. We know better now.

But even the religious view, as Hulme defined it, has little that is attractive (or for that matter religious) about it. Hulme employed certain religious terms because they were useful to him, but he showed no sign of the faith that should attend the terms. Thus he used the dogma of Original Sin as a support for his authoritarianism and as a weapon against humanism and romanticism; man's radical imperfection was the important thing, but humanists 'chatter about matters which are in comparision with this, quite secondary notions – God, Freedom, and Immortality'. Most religionists would surely reject this, as they would reject Hulme's cognate notion that religious values are anti-vital and opposed to life. Hulme's religion was a sanction for imposing discipline, but the discipline he urged was a secular, not a spiritual one.

'It is my aim', Hulme wrote in *A Tory Philosophy*, 'to explain in this article why I believe in original sin, why I can't stand romanticism, and why I am a certain kind of Tory.' The answer to all these questions was essentially the same: Hulme did not regard theology, literary criticism and politics as discinct disciplines, but as aspects of the single question of one's beliefs about the nature of man and his relation to the world. Starting from a belief in human perfectibility, one *must* arrive at humanism, romanticism, and liberalism. Starting from original sin, one must arrive at religion, classicism, and Toryism. Thus romanticism could alternately be regarded as bad politics or as 'spilt religion', and original sin as a 'sane classical dogma'.

The starting point in all Hulme's distinctions is metaphysics; in his best-known essay, 'Romanticism and Classicism', for example, the distinction is between 'a bad metaphysic of art' (romanticism) and a good one (classicism). 'Here is the root of all romanticism', he wrote,

> that man, the individual, is an infinite reservoir of possibilities;
> and if you can so rearrange society by the destruction of oppressive
> order then these possibilities will have a chance and you will get
> Progress.
>
> One can define the classical quite clearly as the exact opposite to
> this. Man is an extraordinarily fixed and limited animal whose
> nature is absolutely constant. It is only by tradition and organization
> that anything decent can be got out of him.

It is difficult to apply this distinction to either literary or intellectual history, and Hulme had a good deal of trouble in doing so himself. His romanticism, for example, stretches back to the Renaissance (though he saved Shakespeare for classicism by calling him 'dynamically' classic); and even classical Greek art seems to share in certain romantic qualities. On the other hand, Hulme's 'good' metaphysic of art has some profoundly romantic characteristics.

The point of 'Romanticism and Classicism', however, is that it is not so much philosophical as propagandist – it is the 'conceptual clothing' in which Hulme sought to dress the change of taste which he discerned in his own time. The standard critical terms were useful, just as the language of theology was useful, to give names to the change; but Hulme was primarily interested in the change itself rather than in its philosophical ancestry. He sensed a new spirit in the arts – a turn away from the romantic and the rhetorical, and toward the abstract, the geometrical, and the precise – and he described it in the terms that were at hand.

It was in poetry, however, that Hulme most directly influenced the course of the new spirit, through the Imagist movement. In retrospect Imagism seems at most a brief chapter in the history of modern poetry; but because it had a name and a manifesto it gained considerable attention in its time, and it has since been taken more seriously than it deserves by the professors and academic historians of literature. The exact origins of the movement are now too obscure to be sorted out, and in fact it is unhistorical to suppose that it had a single originator – individuals never invent changes of taste. Poets were reacting against nineteenth-century rhetoric before the Imagists appeared; Verlaine had said, 'Prends l'éloquence et tords-lui son cou' a long time before Hulme cried 'Smoothness. Hate it', and Yeats and Henley, each in his own way, had already wrung rhetoric's neck in English.

Hulme's contribution to Imagism was the authority and dignity of a philosophy, or rather the notes for a philosophy which are scattered through his 'Notes on Language and Style' and other essays – notes like the following:

> Thought is prior to language and consists in the simultaneous presentation to the mind of two different images.
> Language is only a more or less feeble way of doing this.
> Thought is the joining together of new analogies, and so inspiration is a matter of an accidentally seen analogy or unlooked-for resemblance.

Here we may apparently read *intuition* for *analogy* ('this is all worked out in Bergson', Hulme said); the essential poetic datum is unsought-for intuition, out of which the poet, by 'a deliberate choosing and working-up of analogies' makes literature. To express his intuition of reality, the poet must use visual images; plain speech is not precise enough for poets.

This is an acceptable enough account of the poetic process as far as it goes, but one can scarcely call it revolutionary, or even original. Hulme did not invent the poetic image, nor was he the first to observe its importance in poetic discourse. What he did do was to elevate the image to the level of a poetic principle, and thus to emphasize the power of imagery divorced from abstract emotive language.

Hulme's own poems are useful examples of his theories in action; they do juxtapose visual images, and they are unrhetorical, hard and dry. They also demonstrate what one might guess from Hulme's remarks on metre – that he had no ear at all for the sound of poetry, and regarded metre as simply a tiresome restraint on free expression. They are at best trivial pieces, and it comes as a bit of a shock to be reminded that Mr Eliot once described Hulme as 'the author of two or three of the most beautiful short poems in the language'. It is perhaps an indication of Mr Eliot's critical authority that Hulme has managed, on the basis of the five poems that Pound included in *The Complete Poetical Works of T. E. Hulme*, to find his way into a great many anthologies of modern poetry; surely no other poet has done so well with so little.

When *Speculations* appeared in 1924, Mr Eliot wrote:

> he appears as the forerunner of a new attitude of mind, which should be the twentieth-century mind, if the twentieth century is to have a mind of its own. Hulme is classical, reactionary, and revolutionary; he is the antipodes of the eclectic, tolerant, and democratic mind of the end of the century.

We can see now that the twentieth century does not have a mind of its own; where it is not mindless, it is uncertain. The eclectic, tolerant, and democratic values have not faded away as Mr Eliot expected, though they have had some hard times; nor have Hulme's antipodal attitudes yet come to dominate our thoughts. Liberalism and reaction still exist uneasily together, abusing each other; a rancorous dialectic between the two is our customary modern discourse. As long as this is true, Hulme will have his importance.

The original version was first published in *The Times Literary Supplement*, 24 June 1960.

12

Pound and the Prose Tradition

Every theory of poetry is a defense of poetry; every poet in his theorizing deals with, because he must deal with, the question, 'What is your poem good for?' Among modern poets, there have been two principal answers to this question: either poetry supplies 'the satisfactions of belief', or it provides a peculiar knowledge of the world's particulars. The first answer (which is Wallace Stevens's) leads us toward religion, or at least toward a surrogate for religion in the mystery and magic of *words*; the second (which is William Carlos Williams's) often seems to be a surrogate for science, and offers us the quiddities of *things*. Both are serious attempts to reassert the authority of poetry, and to preserve it from the abrogations of art-for-art's-sake, but it is important to see that these two answers to the question of poetic value describe two very different modern traditions, and in fact point in opposite directions.

We may get at the essence of the first tradition by recalling that conversation between Degas and Mallarmé, in which Degas complained that he had plenty of ideas, but couldn't finish his sonnet, and Mallarmé replied that poems are not made out of ideas, but out of words. The conversation is memorable because Mallarmé's answer contains the core of an important modern theory, the theory that the essence of a poem – what the estheticians call its ontological existence – is linguistic. This is, of course, a principle of the symbolists, but it has entered generally into the way we think about poetry.

We may approach the other tradition through another conversation, this one between Ezra Pound and T. E. Hulme. Pound's version of the exchange goes like this: 'I spoke to him [Hulme] one day of the difference between Guido's precise interpretive metaphor, and the Petrarchan fustian and ornament, pointing out that Guido thought in accurate terms; that the phrases correspond to definite sensations undergone . . . Hulme took some time over it in silence, and then finally said: "That is very interesting"; and after a pause: "That is more interesting than anything anyone ever said to me. It is more interesting than anything I ever read in a book".'

I don't suppose many present readers find Pound's remark more interesting than anything they ever read in a book. And I don't really think Hulme found it so, either – the anecdote seems a clear case of the American innocent having his leg pulled. But the point that *is* interesting is that Pound thought his idea of precise phrases corresponding to definite sensations both valuable and original – valuable and original enough, in fact, to build a theory of poetry on. The theory that he constructed began, as Mallarmé's did, with a desire to purify the language of the tribe, and to restore poetry to a place of value in human experience; but Pound moved in a direction opposite to the symbolist's. While Mallarmé put his faith in words, Pound committed himself more and more to the principle that ultimate reality lies in *things*, and that the essential poetic act must therefore be an exact rendering of things. This theory he called 'the prose tradition', acknowledging thus his debt to Flaubert and realist esthetics.

The phrase 'prose tradition' first occurs in Pound's writings just before the First World War, and his most elaborate definitions of the tradition are from the same period. But there is nothing in his later work which contradicts, or even alters significantly, those early statements; Pound's poetic theory was fixed by the time he was thirty, and his theoretical remarks in the *Money Pamphlets*, the later *Cantos*, and the *Letters* merely repeat what he had said before. His most important statements date from the years 1913–16 – the years immediately preceding the first *Cantos*. In the prose writings of this period we can see the process by which Pound formulated the esthetic which underlies his epic; and it seems reasonable to say that the esthetic had to be defined before the major work could proceed.

Pound first used the phrase 'prose tradition' in one of his 'Approach to Paris' essays in the *New Age* in 1913. Because this is both the first and the most detailed statement of his theory, it is worth quoting at some length. In the essay Pound has been discussing a French poet called Laurent Tailhade, and comparing him to Heine and Gautier. He then continues:

> I think this sort of clear presentation is of the noblest traditions of our craft. . . . It is what may be called the 'prose tradition' of poetry, and by this I mean that it is a practice of speech common

to good prose and to good verse alike. It is to modern verse what the method of Flaubert is to modern prose, and by that I do not mean that it is not equally common to the best work of the ancients. It means constatation of fact. It presents. It does not comment. It is irrefutable because it does not present a personal predilection for any particular fraction of the truth. It is as communicative as Nature. It is as uncommunicative as Nature. It is not a criticism of life, I mean it does not deal in opinion. It washes its hands of theories. It does not attempt to justify anybody's ways to anybody or anything else. . . . It is open to all facts and to all impressions. . . .

The presentative method does not attempt to 'array the ox with trappings.' It does not attempt to give dignity to that which is without dignity, which last is 'rhetoric,' that is, an attempt to make important the unimportant, to make more important the less important. . . .

The presentative method is equity. It is powerless to make the noble seem ignoble. It fights for a sane valuation. . . .

Most of the familiar Poundian attitudes are here – the emphasis on plain speech and the presentation of facts, the anti-rhetorical bias, the hostility to didacticism and to personality in poetry (with a passing shot at his favorite antagonist, 'the donkey-eared Milton'). It may not be all quite as Flaubert would have put it, but Pound is not far off when he says that he is applying Flaubert's methods to poetry.

It is not surprising, then, that Pound selected Ford Madox Hueffer as the occasion for his next 'prose tradition' essay, 'Mr. Hueffer and the Prose Tradition in Verse'. Hueffer was the most vocal disciple of Flaubert writing in England at the time, and from him Pound got a good deal of his esthetic theory, and some of his favorite aphorisms (it was Hueffer who first remarked that poetry should be written at least as well as prose). As a poet Hueffer was at best a minor talent, better than F. S. Flint, perhaps, and not quite as good as Aldington. Nevertheless, he was for Pound a 'significant and revolutionary' poet, because Pound could see in Hueffer's *Collected Poems* what he was looking for, an 'insistence upon clarity and precision, upon the prose tradition; in brief, upon efficient writing – even in verse'.

He could also see that the prose tradition of which he had (rather inaccurately) made Hueffer the representative figure was antithetical to another current mode of poetry, the kind represented by Yeats;

that is to say, he recognized in 1913 the two directions in which modern poetry was moving. 'Mr. Hueffer's beliefs about the art', Pound wrote then,

> may be best explained by saying that they are in diametric opposition to those of Mr. Yeats. Mr. Yeats has been subjective; believes in the glamour and associations which hang near the words. 'Works of art beget works of art.' He has much in common with the French symbolists. Mr. Hueffer believes in an exact rendering of things. He would strip words of all 'association' for the sake of getting a precise meaning. He professes to prefer prose to verse. You would find his origins in Gautier or in Flaubert. He is objective.

Not only did Pound recognize the two traditions; he also saw the poetic dangers implicit in each – that the prose tradition 'tends to lapse into description', while the symbolist 'tends to lapse into sentiment'. But between description and sentiment, the former was obviously the lesser sin. Pound felt, as most of his contemporaries did, that sentiment had dominated English verse of the past century, and that it had dulled the tools of poetry with vague emotionalism, high-minded moralizing, and rhetorical decoration. The role that Pound set for himself was to resharpen poetry's cutting edge.

The strategies by which Pound set about this resharpening process are familiar enough to students of modern poetry; the 'Few Don'ts by an Imagiste'; the note on Imagism written by Flint, but at Pound's dictation, for *Poetry*; the anthologies *Des Imagistes* and the *Catholic Anthology*; Vorticism; the publicizing of Fenellosa's work. What these propaganda moves had in common was a theory of language, which Pound put most succinctly in a letter to Harriet Monroe: 'Language is made out of concrete things.' Imagism starts here; *The Cantos* start here, on this concrete foundation.

In the general tenor of his linguistic theory Pound is not, of course, by any means unique; his mistrust of the conventional cognitive properties of language is characteristic of a great deal of twentieth-century thought. A kind of 'neonominalism' is part of the intellectual climate of our time. Numerous literary and philosophical examples come to mind: J. Alfred Prufrock, who cannot tell us what he means; Frederick Henry, who will not use words like *honor* and *glory* because they have been made meaningless; Stephen Daedalus and Bloom conversing without communicating in the cabman's shelter. The theme of failure

of communication, the preoccupation with inarticulateness, are part
of the same pattern, and so are some of the most quoted remarks
of our literary heroes: the objective correlative, 'no ideas but in
things', 'it was before all to make you see'. This emphasis on the
physical and the non-discursive, this direct and immediate appeal to
sensory response, is so much a part of what we call modern literature
that words like *didactic*, and even *intellectual*, have become terms of
opprobrium when applied to imaginative writing. A similar mistrust
is evident in much of twentieth-century philosophy – in Logical Posi-
tivism, in General Semantics, in the current Oxford school, in Ogden
and Richards, in Wittgenstein. (I suppose one might argue that it
has its correlative also in non-representational painting.)

But if Pound's nominalism has been in a main current of his time,
he has gone farther with it than most of his contemporaries have.
Starting with the Flaubertian ideals of economy, precision, and objectivity, he took a further theoretical step which separated him
ontologically from his source – he argued the idea of an exact rendering of *things* with a literalness which language cannot sustain. Pound's
letters to Iris Barry in 1916 are the most detailed record of this conclusion, although, typically, the theoretical points are squeezed in
between reading lists, comments on literary reputations, and gossip.
Here is a passage from a letter of 27 July 1916; as usual, Pound has
been drawing up reading lists for the education of the young.

> Shifting from Stendhal to Flaubert suddenly you will see how
> much better Flaubert writes. AND YET there is a lot in Stendhal, a
> sort of solidity which Flaubert hasn't. A trust in the thing more than
> the word. Which is the solid basis, i.e. the thing is the basis. . . .

Now how can this be made to make sense? How *can* a writer,
whose medium is necessarily words, put his trust in *things*? Perhaps
by carrying a sack of things around on his back, like the projector in
Gulliver's Travels, but surely in no more reasonable way. Pound is
here indulging in his favorite false antithesis. The quoted passage
assumes that, to the question 'What is literature made of?' there are
two possible answers – *words* and *things* – and that these answers are
antithetical. But it should be obvious to the most casual consideration
that *both* answers are right. Poems are of course made of words –
what else? But since words are referential, poems can also be said to
be made of the referents of their words – of Penelopes, Flauberts,
obstinate isles, and Muses' diadems. No contradiction is involved in

asserting that both statements are true. We may, of course, say that poems with more exact sensory referents are better poems, but this doesn't seem to be what Pound is saying.

Pound goes farther out on his limb in another passage in the same letter:

> The whole art is divided into:
> *a* concision, or style, or saying what you mean in the fewest and clearest words.
> *b* the actual necessity for creating or constructing something; of presenting an image, or enough images of concrete things arranged to stir the reader.
> Beyond these concrete objects named, one can make simple emotional statements of fact, such as 'I am tired,' or simple credos like 'After death there comes no other calamity.'
> I think there must be more, predominantly more, objects than statements and conclusions, which latter are purely optional, not essential, often superfluous and therefore bad.

This strikes me as an extraordinary statement for a poet to make. As advice to a young girl writing poetry in 1916 it no doubt has its practical value; but still, the size of the baby that Pound throws out with the bath is startling.

There are two antitheses implied in the quotation: words vs. things, and general words vs. particular, concrete words. The first is specious, as I have already argued; poems are both words and things. The second is perfectly legitimate, so long as it is not confused with the first. But Pound does confuse the two here, in order to suggest that there is a greater degree of reality, a closer relation to the actual, in words which name concrete objects than there is in 'credos'. He does so by using words like *construct*, *concrete*, *object*, *things* – words which suggest a more than verbal existence in the poetic creation. Perhaps he draws back slightly from this extreme position when he allows that his concrete objects are in fact only *named* (names are, after all, as abstract as credos), but the general impression he gives is that things are only 'called by their right names' when they are presented in images. The passage, taken as a whole, is a fallacious argument for a poetry of things, by which the discursive efficacy of words is minimized, and poems become relationships among arranged objects – or rather, perhaps, among the images of objects.

When Pound identifies imagery with the naming of concrete objects, he exposes one of the weakest and most crucial points in his whole theoretical position. It is curious, but true, that though Pound is generally regarded as the Prime Minister of Imagism, his theoretical remarks reveal a view of the nature and function of poetic imagery which is both limited and naive, even when glorified with terms like *phanopoeia*. *Phanopoeia* is defined in *How to Read* as 'a casting of images upon the visual imagination', a process in which, Pound adds, 'we find the greatest drive toward utter precision of word'. Both parts of this definition are inadequate: the first (as F. R. Leavis pointed out long ago) because it restricts the range of imagery to a single sense, and postulates a visualizing process in the poetic experience which may not, in fact, be there; the second because, while imagery may be precise, it may also be elusive, ambiguous, and indirect, and these may all be excellent qualities in a poem. Pound's concern with the concreteness of things seems to have led him to exaggerate the pictorial dimension of imagery, making a poem a kind of stereopticon performance, and neglecting other, less overtly visual qualities.

We find the same motive behind the sleight-of-hand by which Pound applies the term *ideogram* to English poetic practice. In Chinese orthography (if Fenellosa is right) it is possible to speak with some accuracy of the 'presentation' of images, since the symbol for *horse*, for example, has four visible legs. But the assertion that the symbols of the English alphabet, however arranged, can do the same thing is obviously false, and *ideogrammatic* is at best a remotely figurative way of talking about poetry in English. One can see, though, how it might be a necessary figure in Pound's theory. For if you accept the principle that meaning resides in things, then you are forced to the following principle that that poem means most which is the most precise presentation of things, and the closer imagery can be brought to actual representation, the better.

The rules for writing such poetry will go something like this: (1) Direct treatment of the 'thing' whether subjective or objective. (2) To use absolutely no word that does not contribute to the presentation. These are, of course, the ground rules for Imagism, as laid down by Pound, H. D., and Richard Aldington in 1912. But they describe equally well the method of *The Cantos*, for Pound's briefest lyrics and his vast epic have a common root in the theories of the prose tradition – they all belong to one class of poetry, the poetry of things.

Let us consider what a thorough-going adherence to the prose tradition might be expected to produce in verse. One might look, first of all, for what Josephine Miles calls 'phrasal poetry', a poetry, that is, in which substantives and their modifiers outnumber verbs and verbals. And indeed this does seem to be the case with Pound. For example, two well-known Cantos – the fourteenth (the first of the Hell Cantos) and the forty-fifth ('With *Usura*') – though they differ in mood, are the same in this respect, that both are essentially catalogues, XIV a series of incomplete sentences without main verbs, XLV a series of parallel examples. Each in its way is extremely forceful, but the force comes from the weight of the substantives, and not from the pressure of verbal action. And if we look at Pound's most anthologized Imagist poem, 'In a Station of the Metro', we will find that it goes right off Miss Miles's scale: she describes her poetic types in terms of the relation of the number of nouns and adjectives to the number of verbs, but 'In a Station of the Metro' has no verbs at all.

It seems rather odd that a student of Fenellosa should be so indifferent to the power of verbs, for the main point of Fenellosa's theory, as described in 'The Chinese Written Character as a Medium for Poetry', is that the essence of poetry is in its verbal action, in its power to represent 'things in motion'. Pound picked up the representation of things, but he seems to have overlooked the motion. Perhaps such an oversight is to be expected in a poetry of things.

We might also expect, though it is certainly not necessary, that a poetry of things should minimize, or even abandon, syntactical forms. Syntax demands some non-substantive, and therefore insubstantial, language, and it imposes a form upon experience which is not *in* experience. In *The Cantos*, Pound has employed three kinds of syntax-substitutes: the catalogue (as in Cantos XIV and XLV mentioned above), the associative juxtaposition, and the pattern of recurrences. These three verbal constructions come as close as one can come in words to the representation of physical relationships – either one-after-the-other, or side-by-side, or again-and-again. Like Hamlet to his mother, Pound tells us to 'look here upon this picture and on this'; but unlike Hamlet, he expects that the relationship will do the job alone. This structural mannerism has become more pronounced in the later *Cantos*. The argument for the defense is that by now the readers who are left are used to the method, and can recognize allusions to earlier matter; but though this may justify increasing condensation, it does not affect the essential problem of establishing conceptual and progressive relationships within the limitations of a purely substantive ordering.

Juxtaposed images have some of the properties of metaphor, but they do not compose metaphors, and Pound has generally been wary of endorsing actual metaphorical constructions. 'Art deals with certitude', he once wrote. 'There is no "certitude" about a thing which is pretending to be something else.' And he advised young poets: 'Don't mess up the perception of one sense by trying to define it in terms of another.' Thus in his theorizing he emphasizes the emotional power of the thing in itself, the 'natural object', and condemns ornamental metaphors as 'arraying the ox with trappings', and his enthusiasms are for writers like Joyce (the Joyce of *Dubliners* and the *Portrait*), in whom he found 'a hardness and gauntness, "like the side of an engine", efficient; clear statement, no shadow of comment, and behind it a sense of beauty that never relapses into ornament'. (Pound put Joyce with Hueffer, diametrically opposite to 'the softness and mushiness of the neo-symbolist movement'.)

In his principal remarks on imagery – the 'Retrospect' notes, 'How to Read', and 'As for Imagisme' – Pound has much to say about economy and precision in presenting the image, but nothing to say about the figurative use of language. He does, to be sure, quote Aristotle on the apt use of metaphor in his 'Note on Dante', but the remarks that follow make only elementary distinctions among varieties of epithets, and don't take us very far toward understanding why Aristotle should think that 'the apt use of metaphor . . . is the hall-mark of genius'.

Pound's mistrust of metaphor has, of course, a historical dimension: he was reacting against the conventional figures of speech – the 'dim lands of peace' and 'dove gray hills' of his nineteenth-century predecessors – and against what he called 'the abominable dog-biscuit of Milton's rhetoric'. This line of attack was necessary, and Pound deserves all honor for the beneficial operation that he performed on poetic style. But there is also, I think, an ontological point here. If reality inheres in things in flux, and the best poem is the 'direct treatment of the thing', then figurative language is bad because it is an abstraction from reality, an imposition of intellectualized order upon the actual flux, which only offers us object beside object, event after event.

But it is impossible that a poet should altogether avoid metaphor, and Pound has ignored his own advice again and again in his best verse. In 'Mauberley', for example,

> There died a myriad,
> And of the best, among them,
> For an old bitch gone in the teeth,
> For a botched civilization,
>
> Charm, smiling at the good mouth,
> Quick eyes gone under earth's lid,
>
> For two gross of broken statues,
> For a few thousand battered books.

Here the old bitch and earth's lid are metaphorical, but one can see how Pound's mistrust of ornament has lead him to use brief rather than developed figures, and to wind up the passage with non-metaphorical substantives.

In *The Cantos*, Pound's determination to imitate the flux of experience carried him further toward pure juxtaposition of things, though the necessities of scale and theme required that he expand his notion of what a poetic 'thing' was. *The Cantos*, like the little imagist poems, are commonly constructed on a paratactic, building-block principle – this substantive mass is set on top of that one, and so on until a complex unit has been built. Sometimes this is done in a simple, imagist way, with a series of pictorial images. In other Cantos the building blocks are made of less directly imagistic material – of quotations, anecdotes, bits of history, personal reminiscences, scraps of conversation. It should be clear, however, that these all have the same relation to reality that the simple visual images have – they are all particular and substantive, manifest and not abstract. And like the elements of an imagist poem, they are related to each other, not by the artificial links of logic or of syntax or of metaphor, but simply by contiguity.

Metaphor and syntax are not the only traditional poetic resources that a thorough-going prose-tradition poet might be expected to suppress. 'Go in fear of abstractions', Pound advised would-be poets, and he has on the whole practiced his own preaching; in *Personae* the abstractions are as rare as the rhymes. But *The Cantos* would seem to raise serious problems; one can hardly expect that a long poem concerned with Justice, Good Government, Law, Equity, and Order could get along altogether without abstract terms. And of course it doesn't. But such abstractions as do turn up in *The Cantos* are particularized, either by putting them in the mouth of a persona (as when Kung 'gave the words "order" and "brotherly deference"') or by representing them visually in Chinese ideograms (as for example 'metamorphosis' in Canto LVII). Even Usury, Pound's most obsessive abstraction, is given an historical particularity by calling it *usura*. Abstractions are bird's-eye-views of experience, and Pound's view is sea-level – the periplum, the level of *things*. As for the vaster human speculations,

> Of heaven, earth and of things without shadows,
> Cut the cackle and do not believe 'em.

Let's pause here to gather together the assertions I have made about the nature of the prose tradition as Pound has practiced it. The hypothesis on which the whole theory rests is a simple one, a kind of naive phenomenalism. Reality consists in things. Poetry is the representation of reality, and therefore concerns itself with the presentation of things, and avoids any subject which cannot be embodied in an expressed image (Kung, one recalls, 'said nothing of "the life after death" '). Starting from this view of the nature of reality, Pound has created a poetry of things, a poetry, that is, which is essentially (1) particular, not abstract; (2) substantive, rather than verbal; (3) non-metaphorical; (4) non-syntactical.

The problems which such a poetic method raises should be obvious enough, particularly when applied to a 'poem of some length'. They can be divided into two general categories: problems of poetic action; and problems of poetic authority.

It seems to me axiomatic that a poem of any length must be the embodiment of change, the record of a significant process. 'Life', says Aristotle, 'consists in action, and its end is a mode of action, not a quality.' Literature gives form to modes of action; literary form is therefore always a *from-to* form – that is, it is a model of a process of significant change. Hence Aristotle wisely concluded that action is the primary constituent of tragedy, and I think we may add of epic and other major forms as well.

Now as far as I can see, there is no action in *The Cantos*. The various juxtapositional patterns are there – scene is set against scene, person against person, the transitory against the eternal, the present against the past – and usually one can conclude that some sort of tension exists between the terms. But what one cannot conclude is that the poem advances, out of tensions to resolutions. Literally nothing happens in the poem; there are allusions, to be sure, to other works in which things happen (e.g. the Homeric business in the first Canto and the Ovid in the second) but these allusions take their place as *things*, as artifacts in the total pattern. And though there are changes of subject – frequent and often baffling changes – the agency of change, and the direction of change, are not evident, so that the poem cannot be said to realize a 'mode of action'.

Both *The Odyssey* and *The Divine Comedy* are invoked in *The Cantos*, but it doesn't seem to me that there is any fundamental similarity between Pound's epic and either of the others; they are built upon one of the most basic models of significant change – the Symbolic Journey, from initial problem, through discovery, to resolution, from departure to arrival. *The Cantos* neither departs nor arrives; it begins with a conjunction in the eleventh book of *The Odyssey*, and 109 cantos later shows no sign of ending. Nor is there any discernible voyager to do the discovering. The poem *cannot* embody action, since there is no continuing figure to be acted upon, and no temporal frame in which action might occur; this is surely a crippling, if not a fatal limitation in an epic. It is significant, I think, that the title of the poem does not identify either its theme or its action; it is neither a Divine Comedy nor an Odyssey, and indeed one is not sure whether the title *The Cantos* should be treated as a singular collective noun or as a simple plural.

By poetic authority I mean two things. A poem has authority if one, on reading it, is conscious of direction in interpretation offered by the poem itself. This may derive from the authority of an ordered system of symbolism, whether traditional or coined; or it may derive from the authority of a clear and definite point of view, an authoritative speaking voice (what Henry James calls 'the primary author'). *Paradise Lost*, for example, draws its authority from both sources: the symbolism is Christian, the voice is a consistent first person. *The Waste Land* depends on the ordering force of symbolism alone – in spite of Eliot's footnote on Tiresias, the poem cannot be read as the utterance of a single, embracing consciousness.

The prose tradition raises an initial difficulty in that an ordered symbolism does not seem possible in terms of things which remain things. The papers of Sigismundo Malatesta, the records of John Adams's administration, details of life in the Pisan prison camp – all these are potentially the materials of symbolism, but they cannot become fully symbolic while they remain discrete. They do, of course, incline toward symbolism, as any emotionally weighted elements in a discourse tend to, but the form in which they exist prevents their entering into a significant order.

Two of Pound's critics provide a useful example of the difficulties involved in interpreting an unordered symbolism in their discussions of Canto XVII. This canto has three principal sections: first a lyric passage of goddesses, landscape and sea; then a passage describing Venice; and finally a recapitulation of the two. This is the Venice passage:

A boat came,

> One man holding her sail,
> Guiding her with oar caught over gunwale, saying:
> "   There, in the forest of marble,
> "   the stone trees – out of water –
> "   the arbours of stone –
> "   Marble leaf, over leaf,
> "   silver, steel over steel,
> "   silver beaks rising and crossing,
> "   prow set against prow,
> "   stone, ply over ply,
> "   the gilt beams flare of an evening"
> Borso, Carmagnola, the men of craft, *i vitrei*,
> Thither, at one time, time after time,
> And the waters richer than glass,
> Bronze gold, the blaze over the silver,
> Dye-pots in the torch-light,
> The flash of wave under prows,
> And the silver beaks rising and crossing,
>   Stone trees, white and rose-white in the darkness.
>
> Cypress there by the towers,
>   Drift under hulls in the night.
>
>   'In the gloom the gold
> Gathers the light about it' . . .

Of this passage, Mr Clark Emery remarks: 'That Pound recognized the Republic's earlier glory is made evident in Canto XVII, where, ascending from hell and purgatory under the guidance of Plotinus, Pound comes to an earthly paradise described in terms of Venice's architectural remains.' Mr Hugh Kenner, while conceding the beauty of the lines, finds in them an image of 'a perversion of nature' which he relates to usury, and concludes that 'they apotheosize the arrest of living processes'. Obviously they can't both be right; if the passage describes an earthly pradise, then it cannot be a perversion of nature. But I can find no reason in the poem for choosing one reading rather than the other.

The lines are beautiful – the sound of the passage demonstrates, as so much of *The Cantos* does, that Pound has a marvelous ear, and the images are richly and vividly sensuous. But in the gloom of the poem they have not gathered sufficient light about them; they do not enter a significant order.

But if the poem does not have the authority of an ordered symbolism, it might still have the authority of a single speaking voice. It is fairly common in modern writing that this second kind of authority becomes prominent as the more conventional mode of ordering is abandoned: hence, I think, the development of subjective forms like the stream-of-consciousness technique, in which mind does the ordering work, and may in fact compose the only order in an otherwise chaotic reality. Pound tells us in the *Pisan Cantos* that 'the drama is wholly subjective', and in that group, at least, one is aware of an experiencing personality (as one is also in the 'Hell' Cantos). But *The Cantos* as a whole do not assume a single, continuous speaker, or if there is one the continuity of the things he utters is not such as to define either his personality or his role in the poem. There is an 'I', for example, in Canto XII, who met someone called Baldy at 24 East 47th Street, but what reasons have we for assuming that this is the same person as the 'I' who came to Venice in his young youth in Canto XXVI, or the 'I' in Canto XLVIII who thinks that Viennese coffee houses were established in 1600? None, so far as I can see. And there are large sections of the poem – notably the China Cantos – from which even this uncertain voice is missing.

If we refer back to Pound's definition of the prose tradition, we can see that the elimination of personality from the poem logically follows from his propositions: 'It presents. It does not comment. It is irrefutable because it does not present a personal predilection for any particular fraction of the truth.' It is, as I have been saying, essentially phenomenal, and since it is characteristic of phenomena that they are discontinuous, the poem is discontinuous, too. But while experience may present itself to us as a series of discontinuous phenomena, a recreation of such a series does not in itself define the experiencing personality – for definition, we require an impression of ordering. This we do not have; the form of *The Cantos* does not define its speaker.

To my mind, then, *The Cantos* is a poem lacking in significant action, lacking in order, and lacking in authority; and all these failings derive from the theories of language, of knowledge, and of reality upon which the poem is built. It is a success in so far as it demonstrates the far extremities of a poetic method; but it is a failure in that the method is inadequate to a discourse on such a scale. In any case it is an important poem, and the prose tradition of which it is certainly the most expansive monument is something which we, as critics, must deal with. In recent criticism there has been a tendency to deplore the twentieth-century poetic revolution as an unfortunate departure from the main road of poetry, an aberration of a few perverse poets, which would better not have happened. Such pinings strike me as both idle and unhistorical. Literary history, like any other kind of history, is causally determined and non-reversible; it is the product of a complex of many forces, and not of individual poetic perversities. *The Cantos* has its place in the history of modern poetry, and it is the critic's duty to try to understand that place, not to regret it. In this effort toward understanding, a knowledge of the tradition – the prose tradition – in which the poem exists should be of some critical value.

The original version was first published in the *Yale Review*, summer 1962.

13

Rupert Brooke

Rupert Brooke belongs, not to a generation, and certainly not to posterity, but to a date: in so far as his name survives, it does so in inevitable connection with 1914. Although it was his generation – the generation of Pound and Eliot, of Joyce and Lawrence, of Epstein and Picasso and Stravinsky – that made the modern world of art, Brooke has no place among them, and consequently no living contact with the present moment. He is a poet of his time, but his time was those few first months of the First World War, when Englishmen still believed that it was sweet and proper to die for one's country, and when Brooke's war sonnets could be read without bitterness or irony.

We think of Brooke, then, as a War Poet. But quite inaccurately. In the first place, it would be more precise to call him an On-the-way-to-the-war Poet, for, with ironic appropriateness, he died of natural causes en route to the Dardanelles campaign, and the emotions that his war sonnets express are not those of a combatant, but of a recruit. The *real* War Poets – Owen and Sassoon and Graves and Blunden and Rosenberg – came along later, out of the trenches, and spoke with a different tone; indeed, one might say that their poems exist to contradict the ignorant nobilities of Brooke. Sassoon recalled[1] that

> while learning to be a second-lieutenant I was unable to write anything at all, with the exception of a short poem called 'Absolution', manifestly influenced by Rupert Brooke's famous sonnet-sequence. The significance of my too nobly worded lines was that they expressed the typical self-glorifying feelings of a young man about to go to the Front for the first time. The poem subsequently found favour with middle-aged reviewers, but the more I saw of the war the less noble-minded I felt about it.

Poor Brooke never got past the self-glorifying stage, because he did not get to the war.

But Brooke was a would-be War Poet for only the length of those last five sonnets. Until then, through nearly a hundred poems, he had been a lyric poet of Youth, Love and Death, who developed from a Late Decadent to an Early Georgian. Most of these poems are hard going now, not because they are particularly bad, and certainly not because they are difficult, but because they are uniformly and conventionally dull; they are poems that might have been written by any of a number of mediocre pre-war poets, or by a committee of Georgians. They have no distinguishable individual voice, and this is no doubt one reason for Brooke's popularity among people who don't ordinarily read verse; his poetry sounds the way poetry *should* sound, because it sounds like so many poems that have already been written. Echoes of Marvell and Donne, of Shakespeare, Blake, Housman, Dowson and Yeats haunt the *Collected Poems*; the only ghost that is not there is Brooke's.

Almost any poem from *Poems 1911* (the only book that Brooke published during his lifetime) will confirm these strictures. Take, for example, this sonnet:

> Oh! Death will find me, long before I tire
>   Of watching you; and swing me suddenly
> Into the shade of loneliness and mire
>   Of the last land! There, waiting patiently,
> One day, I think, I'll feel a cool wind blowing,
>   See a slow light across the Stygian tide,
> And hear the Dead about me stir, unknowing,
>   And tremble. And *I* shall know that you have died.
>
> And watch you, a broad-browed and smiling dream,
>   Pass, light as ever, through the lightless host
> Quietly ponder, start, and sway, and gleam –
>   Most individual and bewildering ghost! –
> And turn, and toss your brown delightful head
> Amusedly, among the ancient Dead.

Not exactly a bad poem, and far from Brooke's worst, but a poem without any distinguishable merit – the diction abstract and conventional, the images the worn poetical coinage of the past, the theme Death, the most poetical subject that Brooke knew. Out of poems like this one a list of favourite words and gestures could be made that would constitute Brooke's sense of what was poetic, and that turn up again and again, rearranged, but essentially the same: dream and gleam, heart, tears, sorrow, grey, yearning, and weary cries and sighs, and of course, everywhere, Love and Death. In a rare moment of self-criticism Brooke composed a table of contents for an imaginary anthology, to which his own contribution was to be 'Oh, Dear! oh, Dear! A Sonnet'. This is very perceptive, for nearly half of his poems are conventional sonnets, and most of them, like 'Oh! Death will find me', say little more than 'Oh Dear!'

This body of boring verse suggests not so much a man who wanted to write a poem as a man who wanted to be a poet; or perhaps in Brooke's case a man who took poeticalness as his destiny. For if the poems are in the most conventional sense *poetic*, so was Brooke. No one ever looked so much like a poet as he did – not a *poète maudit*, but an ideal English poet, a gentleman poet, a Rugby-and-Cambridge poet, a healthy, pink-cheeked, blond, games-playing poet. He was, as Henry Nevinson said, almost ludicrously beautiful, and with his long hair and his flowing ties he made his own beauty poetical. (Even Beatrice Webb, who was deaf to poetry and immune to a pretty face, called Brooke 'a poetic beauty', though she thought him otherwise a commonplace, conceited young man.[2]) With such looks, great personal charm, and a modest talent, no wonder that he had such friends, that he dined with the Prime Minister and called Winston Churchill by his first name and never worked for a living. He was a Doomed Youth from the beginning, but his doom was his extravagant good fortune; as Henry James said, felicity dogged his steps.

More than any of his other admirers it was James who understood the expense of Brooke's beauty. 'Rupert expressed us all', James wrote after his death, 'at the highest tide of our actuality, and was the creature of a freedom restricted only by that condition of his blinding youth, which we accept on the whole with gratitude and relief – given that I qualify the condition as dazzling even to himself'.[3] The expressive self, the 'blinding youth' became a myth in his own time. Brooke was twenty-three and scarcely known when Frances Cornford published her epigram about him:[4]

> A young Apollo, golden-haired,
>   Stands dreaming on the verge of strife
> Magnificently unprepared
>   For the long littleness of life.

And he remained mythical in his life and in his death. Even D. H. Lawrence – a man not given to classical allusion – wrote[5] of Brooke's death that

> he was slain by bright Phoebus' shaft – it was in keeping with his general sunniness – it was the real climax of his pose. I first heard of him as a Greek god under a Japanese sunshade, reading poetry in his pyjamas, at Grantchester, – at Grantchester upon the lawns where the river goes. Bright Phoebus smote him down. It is all in the saga.

But as James perceived, the myth dazzled Brooke, too. He confessed to Ka Cox that he had 'always enjoyed that healthy, serene, Apollo-golden-haired, business'[6] and in most of his poems he allowed himself to be absorbed in it, so that the personal role and the poetic role were the same, and there is no creative tension between them. If one asks who wrote 'The Funeral of Youth' or 'The Great Lover' or 'Tiare Tahiti', the answer can only be, 'Apollo-Brooke did'.

A few poems suggest, however, that Brooke did recognize the danger of the myth to him as a poet, and that he was trying to destroy, or at least modify it by writing poems that were aggressively anti-Apollonian. His five so-called 'ugly poems' are all attempts to get beyond conventional poetic subject matter and language, to a more acrid reality. 'Channel Passage', the most noticed of these, is about seasickness and lovesickness; 'Dead Men's Love' is a vision of dead lovers kissing; 'Dawn' describes snoring Germans on a train; 'Wagner' shows a fat man at a concert; and 'Lust' is an anti-erotic love poem. I don't think it is only the changes of modern taste that make these poems seem better and more realized than most of Brooke's other work; they do manage to suggest that they were written out of actual life, and not out of the postures of poetry.

The motive that Brooke offered for including 'Lust' in his first book of poems is the motive for all of the ugly poems:[7]

> My own feeling is that to remove it would be to overbalance the book still more in the direction of unimportant prettiness. There's plenty of that sort of wash in the other pages for the readers who like it. They needn't read the parts which are new and serious. About a lot of the book I occasionally feel like Ophelia, that I've turned 'Thought and affliction, passion, hell itself . . . to favour and to prettiness'.

The poems were Brooke's effort to shake off the felicity at his heels. But they were also 'new and serious' – that is, they were his principal attempts at 'modernism'. Brooke was a very up-to-date young Edwardian, who went to 'Hello Ragtime' and the Post-Impressionist Show, and read Pound and Bennett and Forster, but his 'ugly poems' are a demonstration of the fact that you can't be modern simply by knowing what *is* modern. The five poems are very traditionally imagined (three are sonnets), and none shows the slightest affinity with the work that was then being done by his most advanced contemporaries – by Pound, for example, and Hulme.

But even though the poems seem tame, they were opposed bitterly by Brooke's editors and friends. Edward Marsh complained that he preferred poems he could read at meals (which seems an odd place to read serious poetry), and particularly objected to one line in 'Lust': 'And your remembered smell most agony'. 'There are some things', he wrote, 'too disgusting to write about, especially in one's own language.'[8] The editor of the *Nation* wanted one of the poems (probably 'Channel Passage') changed before he would consider it, and Brooke's publishers, Sidgwick & Jackson, urged him to omit both 'Lust' and 'Channel Passage' from *Poems 1911*, on the grounds that reviewers would single them out for criticism. The poems were kept in the book, but only after the title of 'Lust' had been changed to 'Libido'; and the reviewers did indeed attack these poems.

One may explain the opposition of editors and publishers as expression of a cautious Edwardian regard for propriety; but in the case of Brooke's friends I think the Apollo-myth enters, too; that is, poems like these tarnished the image of the 'blinding youth'. Would Apollo vomit? Would he feel Lust? Would he bend his gaze upon snoring Germans and fat music-lovers? Henry James, noting the inclination of all men to spoil Brooke, took the 'ugly poems' as 'a declaration of the idea that he might himself prevent the spoiling so far as possible'.[9] But in fact it wasn't possible. None of these poems went into Marsh's *Georgian Poetry* anthologies, which spread Brooke's reputation with their enormous sales; none appears in any anthology that I have seen. The Brooke canon remains pretty much what Marsh chose, the poems of 'unimportant prettiness' that Brooke worried about, the songs of Apollo.

There is only one poem of Brooke's in which a self speaks in what one can believe are the accents of an actual man. In 'The Old Vicarage, Grantchester', Brooke looked at his own posturing and sentimentalizing with a mild ironic eye. Perhaps because he was writing about Englishness from a café in Berlin, perhaps because he used a verse form that encourages a pointed facility, Brooke managed in this poem to sustain a tension of attitudes that is missing from his other work. England is both loved and laughed at, and he himself, though he confesses his sentimental homesickness, is also an object of amusement, a half-romantic, half-comic bard-in-exile. He intended to make the irony unmistakable by calling the poem 'The Sentimental Exile', but Marsh chose the present title instead – no doubt because the other seemed self-denigrating. He also asked for revision, which happily Brooke declined to make; and so it remains what he called it, 'a long lanky lax-limbed set of verses'[10] which is nevertheless his most sustained, most richly felt poem. It is also the least Apollonian, the least self-consciously posed: the self in the poem is 'sweating, sick, and hot', as well as sentimental, and this self, one must infer, comes close to the Brooke whom his friends so cherished.

One other poem by Brooke that shows something like the same attractive wit is not included among his *Collected Poems* (though Edward Marsh quotes it in his Memoir).[11] It is his rendering of Shakespeare's first twenty sonnets in the 'short, simple, naive' style of his friend Frances Cornford:

Triolet

If you would only have a son,
   William, the day would be a glad one.
It *would* be nice for everyone,
   If you would only have a son.
And William, what would *you* have done
   If Lady Pembroke hadn't had one?
If you would only have a son,
   William, the day *would* be a glad one!

This little joke demonstrates a number of Brooke's more attractive qualities – his cleverness, his good ear, his technical skill, his geniality. It is perhaps still the work of a clever undergraduate, but it is very well done, nevertheless, and in a manner very far removed from the Apollo myth.

Wit is perhaps the first human quality to go when a war is declared, and it is not surprising that Brooke's war poems show no sign of his natural wittiness. It is at first glance surprising, though, that they also completely lack that ugliness that he had been at such pains to insert into his 'ugly poems'. One might surely expect ugliness from a War Poet. But the point of poems like 'Channel Passage', Brooke had said, was that 'there are common and sordid things – situations or details – that may suddenly bring all tragedy, or at least the brutality of actual emotions, to you'.[12] In his war poems there are no actual emotions, no situations, no details; there are only the clichés of imagined heroism, 'the typical self-glorifying feelings', as Sassoon put it, 'of a young man about to go to the Front for the first time'. For this reason Brooke's poems have no proper place among the genuine poems of the First World War, all of which are about real ugliness. Still, they have a value which one would not want to lose, for they tell us with a terrible accuracy of the delusions of nobility which Brooke's generation carried into the war. It seems impossible that any young man should feel that way again; but the delusions were nevertheless historically real, a part of that dreadful time, and it is well to have them set down in these, the last poems by a serious English poet that treat war as romantic. It is also worth recognizing how, in a poem like 'The Soldier', Brooke had to fill an empty rhetoric with too-easily weighted words – *England* four times and *English* twice in fourteen lines, *heart, dreams, heaven, eternal mind,* and the vaguely comforting *somewhere* – to falsify the truth of dying, and glorify death by calling it sacrifice. It is no wonder that Winston Churchill should have responded to Brooke's death with the same plaster rhetoric. 'During the last few months of his life', Churchill wrote in *The Times,*[13]

months of preparation in gallant comradeship and open air, the poet-soldier told with all the simple force of genius the sorrows of youth about to die; he was willing to die for the dear England whose beauty and majesty he knew; and he advanced towards the brink with perfect serenity, with absolute conviction of the rightness of his country's cause and a heart devoid of hate for fellow-men.

The thoughts to which he gave expression in the very few incomparable war sonnets which he has left behind will be shared by many thousands of young men moving resolutely and blithely forward into this, the hardest, the cruellest, and the least-rewarded of all the wars that men have fought. They are a whole history and revelation of Rupert Brooke himself. Joyous, fearless, versatile, deeply instructed, with classic symmetry of mind and body, ruled by high undoubting purpose, he was all that one would wish

England's noblest sons to be in days when no sacrifice but the most precious is acceptable, and the most precious is that which is most freely offered.

The eulogy is as false to reality as the poem, but both are true to the time; neither Brooke nor Churchill was exploiting false emotions, they were simply sharing them. As D. H. Lawrence said when he heard of Brooke's death, 'Even Rupert Brooke's sonnet, which I repudiate for myself, I know now it is true for him, for them'.[14]

It is *that* truth, the true delusions of the ignorant young man on the way to war, that has survived, and has become Rupert Brooke. It is in a way only an extrapolation of the old Apollo myth, the beautiful young man in uniform, and when Churchill wrote his eulogy, three days after Brooke's death, that myth was already fixed. Brooke was the dream of English Youth, as an older generation might dream it, and his death became at once the symbol of England's sacrifice, the perfection of English manhood self-immolated on the altar of the war. Brooke-the-man, what there was of him beneath the fatal felicities, could scarcely survive such swift mythologizing.

The making of the myth continued after his death, at the hands of his mother and Edward Marsh, his executor. Friends did their part by withholding compromising records, and even now, nearly sixty years after his death, there are still letters – the correspondence between Brooke and his friend James Strachey – that are not to be made available for several years. Nevertheless, we do now know a good deal about Brooke's private life, thanks to the careful biography of Christopher Hassall, and he begins to emerge as a man who was both less and more than the Apollo myth – an attractive, troubled young man – immature (his favourite play was *Peter Pan*), provincial, puritanical, frightened by sex and harassed by a tyrannical mother who could end a typical letter, 'Why are you so unsatisfactory?'

That this young man wrote poems is interesting, but it is not of central importance: what is important is the way the story of his life and death becomes an obituary of a class and a generation that was destroyed in the war. The more we know about Brooke, and the more carefully we read his poems, the more he will be diminished as an important literary figure, and as a hero. And this is only proper: he has been Apollo too long. But myths are rarely killed by facts, and no doubt Brooke will remain the bard-like spirit to sentimental and immature minds like his own.

Poor Brooke: it is his destiny to live as a supremely poetical figure, shirt open and hair too long and profile perfect – a figure that appeals to that vast majority that doesn't read poetry, but knows what a poet should look like. But as a poet he is not immortal – he is only dead.

Notes

1 Siegfried Sassoon, *Siegfried's Journey* (London: Faber, 1945), p. 17.
2 Beatrice Webb, *Our Partnership* (London: Longmans, 1948), p. 415.
3 Preface to Rupert Brooke, *Letters from America* (London: Sidgwick & Jackson, 1916), p. xiii.
4 Frances Cornford, *Collected Poems* (London: Cresset Press, 1954), p. 19.
5 *Letters*, ed. Aldous Huxley (London: Heinemann, 1932), p. 226.
6 Geoffrey Keynes, ed., *The Letters of Rupert Brooke* (London: Faber, 1968), p. 341.
7 *Letters*, pp. 315–16.
8 Quoted in Christopher Hassall, *Rupert Brooke* (London: Faber, 1964), p. 294.
9 *Letters from America*, p. xxviii.
10 *Letters*, p. 394.
11 *Rupert Brooke: The Collected Poems*, with a Memoir by Edward Marsh, 3rd ed. (London: Sidgwick & Jackson, 1942), p. lxvii.
12 *Letters*, p. 328.
13 *The Times*, 26 April 1915, p. 5.
14 Huxley, ed., *Letters*, p. 379.

This essay is based on a short item in *Commonweal*, 18 September 1964.

The Art of Beatrice Webb

'This last month or so', Beatrice Webb wrote in her diary in 1889, 'I have been haunted by a longing to create characters and to move them to and fro among fictitious circumstances. To put the matter plainly – by the vulgar wish to write a novel.'[1] There would seem to be no reason why a wealthy, intelligent spinster of thirty-one shouldn't indulge her wish, and write a novel, but for this spinster it was more than a wish, it was a temptation: she had a gift for descriptive writing and the analysis of character; she was widely read in both English and Continental fiction; and she had, as she later put it, 'intellectual curiosity and an overpowering impulse towards self-expression';[2] but she also felt a strong contrary pull, the imperative to Duty, which made mere self-expression seem unworthy.

The diary passage continues:[3]

There is an intense attractiveness in the comparative ease of descriptive writing. Compare it with work in which movements of commodities, percentages, depreciations, averages, and all the ugly horrors of commercial facts are in the dominant place, and must remain so if the work is to be worthful . . . The whole multitude of novels I have read pass before me; the genius, the talent, the clever mechanism or the popularity-hunting of mediocrities – what have the whole lot of them, from the work of genius to the penny-a-liner, accomplished for the advancement of society on the one and only basis that can bring with it virtue and happiness – the scientific method? This supreme ambition to present some clear and helpful idea of the forces we must subdue and the forces we must liberate in order to bring about reformation may be absurdly out of proportion to my ability. But it alone is the faith, the enthusiasm of my life, the work which I feel called upon to do. Other work would mean vanity and vexation of spirit: would begin in self-indulgence and end in a craving for popularity – for a day's fame!

The conflicts set down here, between Self and Service, and between Art and Science, were deep in Victorian life and thought, and Beatrice Webb was, as she recognized, a representative Victorian. She was beautiful, wealthy, and well-born, and might have been a leader of society. She was an imaginative writer of some promise, and might have become a novelist. But she rejected both society and art and chose instead the most uncreative, self-abnegating course – to give her life over to social research and to the writing, with her husband Sidney, of those 'solid but unreadable books' that are in their way symbols of the life of Duty – admirable, but unappealing. In Mrs Webb's public life Service and Science won; but self-expression, like Religion, if thrust out by the front door will come in by the scullery window, and the novels that Beatrice Webb would not write found a kind of private existence in her diaries.

Her private writings, from the first jottings to the last diary entries, reveal her divided sensibility, in which one side created while the other suppressed the creative for the sake of some larger good. Consider, for instance, the two earliest examples. This paragraph, from a letter to her mother, was written when Beatrice Webb was about eight:[4]

> The two Conservative Candidates were here yesterday, one of them is very short and finely dressed; he had his top coat trimmed with sealskin; he had also silver buckles on his boots and his hands were covered with rings, with a very stylish blue tye which covered his vastcoat; He also saied he spoke Italian and French perfectly. He played on the piano and sung; he seemed not to now what mony words ment, for he asked papa what was the meaning of Demonstration and Major Lees aksed the meaning of Hustings and Nomination. Major Lees is very tall and very fat, with a great beard, mustache and whiskers, with an eye glass which he satisfied his curiosity in staring at everybody.

This sharp bit of observation, so like a fragment of a political scene in Dickens, is extraordinary from so young a child. But even more striking than the sheer descriptive power is the sense the passage gives of an acute perception of social nuance. This was a sense that Beatrice Webb had all her life; like Proust, whom she admired, she knew all the rules of the society to which she did not quite belong. Though she became a socialist, she retained the manners of an upper-class London matron, and the acute class-consciousness of her social station, and she was always quick to register and interpret the smallest social lapse. She had what one might call a 'social imagination'; she observed men in their social relationships (she was not much interested in men alone), and her judgments of men, even when ostensibly political judgments, were usually set in social terms. This sort of imagination is essentially comic – men in their social gestures are more likely to be ridiculous than tragic – and Mrs Webb was capable of a fine, disdainful ridicule, as the eight-year-old example above shows.

Two or three years later young Beatrice wrote this note:[5]

I am quite confident that the education of girls is very much neglected in the way of their private reading. Take, for instance, a girl of nine or ten years old, she is either forbidden to read any but child's books, or she is let loose on a good library; Sir Walter Scott's novels recommended to her as charming and interesting stories, 'books that cannot do any possible harm', her adviser declares. But the object in reading is to gain knowledge. A novel now and then is a wise recreation to be offered to a growing mind, it cultivates the imagination, but taken as the continual nourishment, it destroys many a young mind . . . The whole of their thought (for a child of nine or ten spends little or no thought on her lessons) is wasted on making up love scenes, or building castles in the air, where she is always the charming heroine without a fault. I have found it a serious stumbling-block myself; whenever I get alone I always find myself building castles in the air of some kind; it is a habit that is so thoroughly immured in me that I cannot make a good resolution without making a castle in the air about it.

This is an equally characteristic passage – expressing the strong pull of imaginative life, yet severely censorious of that impulse, setting art against discipline, and choosing discipline. Both passages are true revelations of Beatrice Webb's nature, and together they define the contrary impulses of her life: on the one hand the puritanical conscience, distrusting the powers of the imagination, and on the other the vivid imagination working nevertheless.

One can discover the same ambivalence in Beatrice Webb's private writings about imaginative literature. It is clear that in her earlier years fiction, and especially nineteenth-century fiction, was an important part of her intellectual life; she read novels in French and German as well as in English, and she read them with sympathetic intelligence, like an artist. But when she judged them, it was in severe, moralistic terms. 'Les Miserables', she wrote in 1878, 'is a glorious drama . . . And then he is such a pure writer – there is no hidden sensuality.'[6] On the other hand,[7]

> though I have hardly read Jane Eyre carefully enough to be able to judge of it fairly, I must say it impresses me disagreeably. I do not think it a pure book. The author's conception of love is a feverish almost lustful passion. Her hero is frankly speaking a bad and immoral man, whom she endeavours to render attractive by giving him a certain force of character and much physical and intellectual power.

It is obvious, if one reads her sensitive appreciations of Balzac,[8] that Mrs Webb responded to imaginative writing in more subtle ways than this 'pure vs impure' kind of judgment suggests; but she could not separate her appreciations from her sense of moral values. In her maturity her criticisms became more sophisticated, but they did not become less moral; she was nearly seventy when she wrote of Virginia Woolf, for example,[9]

> I do not find her work interesting outside its craftsmanship which is excellent but 'precieuse'. Her men and women do not interest me – they don't seem worth describing in such detail – the mental climate in which they live seems strangely lacking in light, heat, visibility and variety – it is a dank mist of insignificant and monotonous thoughts and feelings – no predominant aims, no powerful reactions from the mental environment – a curious impression of automatic existence when one state of mind follows another without any particular reason.

She recognized that this point of view was old-fashioned, the view of an 'aged Victorian', but she never relinquished it, never ceased to look in literature, as in life, for a Purpose.[10]

The novelist who was most important to Beatrice Webb was, as one might expect, George Eliot. The two women were much alike, as Herbert Spencer, who knew them both, remarked; they shared a severe sense of duty, philosophical habits of mind, religious questionings, and unusual intelligence. It is clear that Mrs Webb knew George

Eliot's novels well; she turned to them naturally when she wanted a comparison (in a self-critical mood she was like Rosamund, and Spencer was 'a true Casaubon'), and she re-read them when she was ill to become better acquainted with George Eliot's mind, and thought that 'perhaps it was her noble influence which made me feel happier and more contented'.[11] If Mrs Webb had written novels they would surely have been more like *Middlemarch* than like any other model, for judged by the standards by which *Jane Eyre* failed, *Middlemarch* succeeds; it is a novel that both the artist and the moralist in Beatrice Webb could approve.

In spite of the noble influence of George Eliot, Mrs Webb did not write a novel. Instead, she spent her twenties debating with herself whether or not she should. For a person of her abilities, it seemed natural: 'Novel writing', she told herself in 1883,[12]

is the usual ambition of the individual with a vague hankering after literary work. Apparently, exhausting study is not required. But apart from the creation or adaptation from life of a dramatic plot, a talent not always requisite to good work in novel writing (George Eliot's longer novels are pages bound together by a series of coincidences) living pictures of persons in word and act demand not only a most accurate observation but considerable analytical imagination.

Observation and analytical imagination were qualities that Mrs Webb had, and knew she had (and, interestingly, saw as a resemblance between herself and George Eliot). But the debate that follows this entry in the diary, a debate between the study of literature and the study of science, is inconclusive; she could neither exploit her talent nor abandon it. Even at times of depression, when she had convinced herself that her talent was a delusion, she did not reject the idea of literary work flatly, and the indecision continued for more than five years before she at last suppressed the 'vulgar wish', and turned to socialism and social research.

The 'vulgar wish' came in September 1889. In October, she was sent a copy of the recently published *Fabian Essays*, and read it straight through. In January 1890 she met Sidney Webb, and on February 1 she wrote in her diary: 'At last I am a socialist!' From this time on there are no more yearnings toward literary work. The causes of the conversion, then, seem clear: Fabianism and Sidney Webb had entered her life, and driven out the novel and George Eliot.

But why in fact had she made her decision against the imagination? Certainly not because she had fallen in love with a socialist; one might rather say that her decision to marry Sidney was simply another expression of the same self-abnegating will, a part of the bargain: it was, she wrote in the diary, 'an act of renunciation of self'.[13] One might propose two explanations of her choice: one historical, and one personal. Historically, the authority of science was never greater than it was in the latter decades of the nineteenth century – in the years, that is, between Darwin and Rutherford. It was a time, in particular, of science turned toward mankind, when sociology and psychology developed, and science seemed an instrument for the improvement of man's state. What Beatrice Webb sought, as she said repeatedly throughout her life, was a view of existence that would combine Process (the scientific understanding of reality) and Purpose (the existence of moral values and imperatives). This combination she thought she found in the scientific study of society.

For such a person, a late Victorian searching for a life of Duty and high moral value, it must have seemed inevitable that life should be ruled by science, and not by imagination; for science was factual, serviceable, disinterested, and impersonal (was in fact very like Sidney), whereas the imagination was unverifiable, private, and self-indulgent (like the side of Beatrice's mind that she distrusted). Being a Victorian scientist, she would go on to the end of her life thinking about Purpose, and trying to make natural processes teleological (and would thus seem, almost from the beginning, an old-fashioned thinker), but she would never deny the authority of science. She needed that authority to sustain her choice, and to verify her life.

In personal terms, Mrs Webb's decision may be explained as the willed suppression of the whole realm of feelings. Her early emotional life had been lonely and unhappy; she had loved her mother, but had felt rejected by her; she had loved Joseph Chamberlain, but had felt his personality as a threat to her identity and had refused him (though perhaps he had not proposed to her – the story is not clear, but her fear of masculine love is); she had struggled with her powerful religious feelings, but had neither calmed nor satisfied them. She seems to me, as I read the diaries, to have been an emotional woman whose emotional life had failed her, and who felt, at the age of thirty, that she had been denied the love of mother, lover, and God; and so she chose a life, a career, and a husband that would be passionless (thirty years later she wrote in her diary, 'Physical appetites are to me the devil').[14]

The historical explanation will account for Mrs Webb's decision to be a social researcher (rather than, say, a missionary), but it takes more than the *Zeitgeist* to explain why she rejected imaginative writing so fiercely as vanity and vexation of spirit. Perhaps it was because her spirit was already vexed beyond endurance by her own imagination. Like many converts, she committed herself in part at least because she was tired.

The diaries before the 'conversion' of 1890 are several kinds of book: in part a spiritual and intellectual record, in part a novelist's notebook, in part a set of literary exercises. Religious meditations and summaries of philosophical and scientific studies are mixed among vignettes of town and country life, fragmentary dramatic scenes, and long characters of acquaintances – the whole expressing the uncertainty of direction that Mrs Webb was feeling as she groped toward her true vocation. One is aware on the one hand of the industrious and high-minded researcher that Mrs Webb was to become, and on the other of a writer who took pleasure in observation, and had a considerable talent for it. Take, for example, this portrait of a clergyman's wife, whom Mrs Webb met on a holiday in Switzerland in 1882:[15]

Just as I was meditating bed, father came up, with Mrs. Robeson, wife of the rector of Tewkesbury. This lady was a comely clerical-looking dame, with decided aquiline features, pallid face, large cold grey eyes, which with the mouth were slightly turned down at the corners, giving an air of piety; cap and dress of solid respectability, and general look of satisfaction with this world, and firm conviction as to her place in the next.

'It *is* such a pity we did not make your acquaintance before,' she was kind enough to remark, with a tiresome emphasis on particular words. 'There are such a *queer* set of people here. Last night I was talking to one of the *nic*est-looking men here, really quite a pre*sent*able man, and what *do* you think he turned out to be?' 'No! what?' 'A dis*sent*ing minister! Of course I *had* to stop my conversation; those dis*sent*ers have such *queer* notions and are so touchy about their social position and of course as a church-woman, as the wife of a clergyman of the es*tab*lished church, I could not talk to him, without probably off*end*ing him.' 'Of course not,' say I, tho' inwardly wondering why offence need be given. 'Then this morning I sat down on a bench near quite a *lady*like-looking girl; where *do* you think she came from?' 'No! where?' 'From *Bir*mingham.'

This is well-observed and well-heard; it demonstrates that Mrs Webb had a good ear for speech (a useful gift in a novelist) as well as a social satirist's eye for the nuances of social awfulness. One might perhaps add that it is rather self-consciously literary, the young author playing at being The Victorian Lady Novelist; and certainly at this point in her life she did play that role, though in her severer moments she condemned it as 'romancing'. On the whole one would have to call it a promising novelistic exercise.

Mrs Webb's first sociological writings, which began to appear in the late '80s, show the same mixture of gifts and styles, the promising novelist concealed in the factual researcher. The two essays on dock workers and on the tailoring trade (both in Charles Booth's *Life and Labour of the London Poor*) are flat and colourless, but 'The Jewish Community' (also in Booth) is full of vivid writing and imagined scenes, and 'Pages from a Work-girl's Diary', a fictionalized version of an adventure in the East End of London as a seamstress, is excellent narrative prose. Mrs Webb later dismissed the 'Work-girl's Diary' as 'a dramatized version of but a few of the facts',[16] but it is nevertheless her best writing of the early years, and one cannot doubt, on the basis of this example, that she could have been a novelist if she had wished to be one. (Even Sidney recognized that Beatrice was the only contributor to *Life and Labour* who had any literary talent.)

Still, it is the researcher, and the researcher's style, that dominate these essays; the factual overpowers the fictive, and makes what is imaginative seem irrelevant. Apparently a similar process was taking place in Beatrice Webb's diaries. 'Now that observation is my work', she noted in 1887, 'I find it is necessary to keep two books. . . . Otherwise the autobiography is eaten up by statistics of wages, hours of work, interviews with employers and workpeople – no space for the history of a woman's life.'[17] The decision that she finally made two years later – to put away the life of the imagination, to devote herself to social research, and to marry Sidney – was a kind of solution to this problem. She took the life of observation and statistics as her public role; for the other life, a woman's life, she would have her diary.

With the public role came a public style – a joint style for the books that were the products of her 'partnership' with her husband. It was a style that at first she disliked: 'it is a horrid grind, this analysis', she wrote in her diary in 1894, 'one sentence is exactly like another, the same words, the same construction – no relief in narrative.'[18] But she persevered, and came to feel that her own style had disappeared from her public writing: 'in writing I am parasitic on Sidney', she observed in 1913; 'I never write, except in this diary, in my own style, always in a hybrid of his and mine'.[19] There is no evident regret in this statement, and indeed the implied loss of individuality seems to have been something that she desired. She liked to pretend that she and her husband were two of a kind – 'slow-minded prigs like Sidney and me' is a phrase that she uses – and when she noted the differences that obviously did exist between their natures, she chastised herself for not being more Sidney-like: Sidney could work at statistics with single-hearted devotion, but 'with me it is always a struggle to keep my mind from wandering off into foolish romancings'.[20] She couldn't prevent the novelist in her nature from surfacing from time to time, but she could – and did – disapprove of her.

And so did Sidney. One of the saddest things in the diaries is Mrs Webb's sense of her husband's distaste for her private writing; 'I foresee the sort of kindly indulgence, or tolerant boredom, with which Sidney would decipher this last entry!' she wrote in 1899, and tolerant boredom seems to have remained his attitude toward the contents of the diary. It was no doubt because of his disapproval – or at least her expectation of it – that she continued to record her 'woman's life' privately. Nevertheless, she did go on with it, and some of her best writing is to be found in the diaries of the years when the Partnership was writing its heaviest hybrid prose. With one side of her nature she faced towards Sidney and 'the Work'; but the other side went on living in the prose that she addressed to herself. It is there, in the diary, that the personal view is set down – ironic, detached, ridiculing and judging – and there one finds the woman whom Spencer had called 'a born metaphysician', and compared to George Eliot.

The private side became public for the first time in 1926, and then only by a kind of accident. Mrs Webb had considered for some time writing an autobiography that would draw on the diaries, but it was only when politics separated her from her husband that she felt able to do so. In 1922 Sidney was elected to Parliament for the first time, and in the years that followed Beatrice was often alone in their house in the country while he was in London. It was there that she began to compose *My Apprenticeship*. But even then she was intimidated by Sidney's attitude towards the project:[21]

he does his best to approve, still more to help me; but there is something about it that he – not exactly resents – but which is unsympathetic. In his heart he fears that I am over-valuing it, especially the extracts from the diaries – the whole thing is far too subjective, and all that part which deals with 'my creed' as distinguished from 'my craft' seems to him the sentimental scribblings of a woman, only interesting just because they are feminine.

But Sidney was often away, and so the book proceeded, and with obvious pleasure to its author.

'I am absorbed in creative writing in which he has no part', she wrote in 1924, and there seems an anxious excitement in the remark. She and Sidney were both, in their old age, living new, and for the first time *separate* lives, he in politics and she, as she put it, in 'literature'.[22] It is interesting that she should call this new book 'creative writing' and 'literature'; clearly she did not think of it as simply a record of the facts, nor as a supplement to the serious work of the Partnership, but as a personal imaginative work. *My Apprenticeship* is the book that the statistics had crowded out, the 'history of a woman's life' that she preserved in secret over so many years. It is a book of remarkable, though uneven quality, one that will stand comparison with the best of Victorian autobiographical writing – with Mill, Ruskin, Newman, George Sturt, Gosse.

To my mind the best writing in the book is in the extracts from the diaries, where Mrs Webb was freest from the intimidation of Sidney's 'tolerant boredom'. There would be more of these extracts, but Sidney disliked them (recognizing, perhaps, that they recorded a Beatrice over whom he had little influence), and on his advice his wife cut a number of passages from the final text. The connecting matter is sometimes less sharply imagined, less alive. This is not, I think, a distinction of subject matter, but rather a matter of *which* Beatrice Webb was writing: the diaries are in the private style of the suppressed novelist, but the narrative connections sometimes slide towards the flat, hybrid prose of the Partnership. A reading of the unpublished diaries at the London School of Economics confirms the sense that one gets from *My Apprenticeship*, that there is an even finer book to come, and that when the full text is published Mrs Webb will take her place among the great diarists (her only modern rival will be Virginia Woolf).

A great diarist gives us, first of all, an observed world, in which he himself is one of the objects of observation; that is to say, it may be self-examining, but it cannot be self-regarding. For it is an historical world that the diarist observes; no other literary form is so intimately fixed in time, and if he and his scenes and figures and ideas do not emerge as of their time, the diary can have no permanent and public value. But because it moves *through* time at a nearly day-to-day pace, it offers its history in a peculiarly immediate way; in a great diary, the past is always *now*. Paradoxically, one might also say that in a great diary the now is always past; the figures belong to their time, and one does not tend to generalize from them (there is no such thing as a Pepys-like man – Pepys is always and only himself, locked into his own dates).

The world that Beatrice Webb observed was above all the world of a class – the governing class of England. There are some striking exceptions, some finely drawn working-class scenes, for example, but on the whole it was the governors – the political thinkers and doers – who engaged her attention, and got into the record. Over the nearly seventy years of her adult life, the governing class changed, and the dramatis personae of her diaries reflect that change (Sidney himself is the best example, a little tadpole-shaped man who turns up in an 1890 entry and becomes at the last a Cabinet Minister and a peer); but whatever their qualities and origins, the characters are public men, men from the corridors of power.

Her descriptions of these men are the best of her writing. She rarely deals with them in physical terms, except where she can treat physical details as significant of mental or moral qualities; it was the minds of men that mattered, and the ways in which their intellectual and moral natures impelled their public behaviour. (Private behaviour and scandal did not interest her as such; it was only when scandal became public, and thus a basis of public behaviour, as in the case of H. G. Wells, that she recorded it.) Her characterizations therefore tend to stand as examples or representatives of types – not because they are generalized over, but because they are analysed and explained. This was a habit of mind of which Mrs Webb was entirely aware from early maturity; in 1884, at the end of her diary account of her relationship with Joseph Chamberlain, she wrote: 'I cannot feel, or think, or see, without a desire to formulate; and then desire is not satisfied unless the formula is as complete as I can make it and expressive of the whole experience.'[23] This seems an odd way to emerge from an unhappy love affair, but it is a true perception of her intellectual nature, and the formulating process is evident wherever she considered character (including her own). This does not prevent her portraits from being vivid and novelistic, but it does mean that they suggest a certain kind of novel, more philosophical than particular.

Here, for example, is her portrait of T. H. Huxley as she observed him in 1887:[24]

> Throughout the interview, what interested me was not Huxley's opinion of Spencer, but Huxley's account of himself. . . . How as a young man, though he had no definite purpose in life, he felt power; was convinced that in his own line he would be a leader. That expresses Huxley: he is a leader of men. I doubt whether science was pre-eminently the bent of his mind. He is truth-loving, his love of truth finding more satisfaction in demolition than in construction. He throws the full weight of thought, feeling, will into anything that he takes up. He does not register his thoughts and feelings: his early life was supremely sad, and he controlled the tendency to look back on the past or forward into the future. When he talks to man, woman or child he seems all attention and he has, or rather had, the power of throwing himself into the thoughts and feelings of others and responding to them. And yet they are all shadows to him: he thinks no more of them and drops back into the ideal world he lives in. For Huxley, when not working, dreams strange things: carries on lengthy conversations between unknown persons living within his brain. There is a strain of madness in him; melancholy has haunted his whole life. 'I always knew that success was so much dust and ashes. I have never been satisfied with achievement.' None of the enthusiasm for what is, or the silent persistency in discovering facts; more the eager rush of the conquering mind, loving the fact of conquest more than the land conquered. And consequently his achievement has fallen far short of his capacity.

There is no single physical attribute here described – Huxley has no body and no face. But he has a mind, a moral and intellectual nature, and a particular melancholy that makes him an individual. The description moves from straightforward reportage to the fine image of intellectual conquest – an image that is more striking because the passage is on the whole so un-metaphorical – but it ends, as Mrs Webb so often ended, on a relentless judgment. It reveals a good deal about the mind of the observer, as well as of the mind observed.

More than thirty years later Mrs Webb observed another 'leader of men', and drew this portrait of the young Oswald Moseley:[25]

'Here is the perfect politician who is also a perfect gentleman', said I to myself as he entered the room. . . . If there were a word for the direct opposite of a caricature, for something which is almost absurdly a *perfect type*, I should apply it to him. Tall and slim, his features not too handsome to be strikingly peculiar to himself; modest yet dignified in manner, with a pleasant voice and unegotistical conversation, this young person would make his way in the world without his adventitious advantages which are many – birth, wealth, and a beautiful aristocratic wife. He is also an accomplished orator in the old grand style; an assiduous worker in the modern manner – keeps two secretaries at work supplying him with information but realises that he himself has to do the thinking! So much perfection argues rottenness some-where. . . . Is there in him some weak spot which will be revealed in a time of stress – exactly at the very time when you need support – by letting you down or your cause down or sweeping it out of the way?

Here physical appearances are used, but only for their suggested moral significance, as though Moseley were an allegorical figure, fair without and foul within; the portrait deals exclusively with *political* qualities – what would go to make the perfect politician – yet it retains particular-ity and a kind of flavour, the impress of a strong and individual intelligence.

These two descriptions are set pieces of the kind that the young Beatrice did as exercises; but she could deal with character in other ways as well. She could caricature with a single trenchant phrase, as when she described Ramsay MacDonald as 'a magnificent substitute for a leader'; and she could, with persons most dear to her, go on adding to a portrait so that it became a lifelong process. This is true of her account of Shaw, from her first meeting with him in the '80s through fifty years of observation. Shaw represented for her the route that she did not take – he was the artist, the humorous man of genius, the philanderer, with all the vanity and capacity for self-indulgence that she had suppressed in herself. She worked with him, cycled with him, argued with him, and probably spent more time with him than with any other man except her husband. She valued most highly his opinion of her own prose, and sought it whenever she could; but she did not like most of his plays, and had no great regard for his intellectual powers. It was Shaw-as-Shaw that she really admired: 'Bernard Shaw's personality is a work of art', she wrote in 1933, 'and grows more attractive with age – almost mythical!'[26] Her running record of that work of art is one of the valuable things in the diaries.

Even more interesting, though, is the oblique and reticent portrait of Sidney Webb that the diaries both conceal and reveal, like one of those children's puzzles with a face in a tree. Sidney is described most elaborately in the introduction to *Our Partnership*, a tender and affectionate, if somewhat stiff tribute to 'the Other One'. But the portrait that emerges from the sum of diary entries about Sidney is rather different, and a good deal less attractive. He appears, in the end, as the opposite of Shaw, a man without a personality – a cheerful, unruffled, and single-minded bureaucrat who had never known insomnia or indigestion, or anger, or passion, or despair. One feels that his overwhelming efficiency was a failure of ordinary humanity, something that removed him from the company of common, feeling men. It can hardly have been a part of Mrs Webb's intention to portray her husband in this inhuman way; on the contrary, she professed her continuing affection for him in terms that cannot be doubted. Still, the novelist in her created another character, who is credible but repellent. She did so principally by a large number of small strokes – a kind of literary pointillism, as for example in the two sentences at the end of this passage describing the muddle-headedness of trade union members:[27]

> they enjoy the vicarious glory of the Labour Cabinet Minister being among the rulers of the earth – a man whom they address by his Christian name and who sits and smokes with them. They cannot see that their representative may be a mere tool in the hands of men who have been hardened oppressors of their class. 'They are a hopeless lot', sighed Sidney as he turned with a contented smile to his morning's work. 'We are in for some strange events this coming year – let us get on with our work while we can.'

That preference for work over people was Sidney Webb's essential quality, but it's the contented smile that makes it so unpleasant. Beatrice notes it with detachment, as one datum in the range of her observation, but it seems nevertheless a kind of judgment, coming as it does from a woman who sometimes found research nauseating, and people fascinating.

Just as physical description is rarely a part of Beatrice Webb's 'characters', so the description of places does not enter much into her narrative. Nature was a place to take exercise in, not a subject for careful observation, and though Mrs Webb sometimes recorded the length of a walk, and the subjects of the walkers' conversation, she rarely noted what she had seen. One might say that she lacked a visual imagination, or one might argue that she had chosen a life in which physical experience could not play an important part, and that her avoidance of physical phenomena was deliberate. All accounts of the physical content of her life – the clothes she wore, the house she lived in, the meals she served – suggest extreme indifference, whether deliberate or not: 'we sit in two lodging house rooms', Virginia Woolf noted with distaste '(the dining room had a brass bedstead behind a screen) eat hunks of red beef; and are offered whisky.'[28] Mrs Webb is the only woman writer I can think of who pays no attention to other women's clothes or to the furnishings of their houses. Her world was composed of men's (and women's) minds and actions, not of appearances or of places.

The one important exception to this last point is in her descriptions of the lives of the poor. In her early accounts of life in the East End of London, and among her poor relations in Bacup, Lancashire, and in her later descriptions of Seaham, her husband's constituency in County Durham, she wrote with unusual and moving particularity. No doubt this is partly because description under these circumstances was an indictment of poverty, but the quality of the writing suggests more than this, suggests that there was a depth of feeling in Mrs Webb that she did not find it easy to express, but that the lives of the poor brought it to consciousness.

Though she was not usually very good at visual scenes, she had an instinctive gift for the dramatic. Both her awareness of class and her concern for moral values led her to see men's relations to each other in dramatic, conflicting terms. There are many strong scenes built on such conflicts, of which the following is a good example. The setting is a Trades Union Congress at Dundee in 1889.[29]

Another scene. Breakfast table. On my right Broadhurst, [General Secretary of the Stonemasons' Union] beaming over his ham and eggs and the delightful memories of yesterday's triumph over his enemies. 'Yes, we are now going to take our stand against the intrusion of strangers into our body on false pretences. They blame us for being exclusive; they have made us ten times more exclusive. We have cleared the platform of outsiders, we will now clear the press table from intriguers.'

All this muttered loud enough for my neighbour on the left to hear. Cunninghame Graham is pouring over the *Labour Elector*. (Cunninghame Graham is a cross between an aristocrat and a barber's block. He is a *poseur*, but also an enthusiast, an un-mitigated fool in politics, I think.) 'I have a letter from Kropotkin', Cunninghame Graham whispers to me; 'he says, and I agree with him, if Burns with 80,000 men behind him does not make a revolution, it is because he is afraid of having his head cut off. Burns is a grand fellow though, different from these miserable slaves of bourgeois trade unionists', he adds, with a wave of his hand towards Broadhurst, a wave of the hand which gradually settles down upon a loaf of brown bread which C.G. believes to be common property, but which, unfortunately, happens to be specially prepared for her great man's over-taxed digestion by Mrs. Broadhurst. The bourgeois slave watches with indignation the delicately tapering fingers of the anarchist clutch hold of his personal property, and with a large perspiring palm of the outstretched hand grasps the whole thing in his fingers. 'No, no, Sir, not that', he roars; 'this is my *own* bread, made by my *own* wife, in my *own* house, and carried here in my *own* portmanteau, that you cannot have.' Cunninghame Graham withdraws with the apologies of a gentleman. 'Not my bread; I'd rather he destroyed my reputation than took my bread', roared the dyspeptic but somewhat gluttonous Broadhurst. Cunninghame Graham looks unutterably disgusted, and wipes his aristocratic hand with soft cambric . . .

Here differences of class, of politics, of manners, and of intelligence all combine to make the appropriation of the bread a complex comic gesture. Mrs Webb's relation to the scene is that of the satiric observer – removed, superior, and amused, but nevertheless close enough to take note of details, and to insert into her account those particulars that make the scene real: the *brown* bread, the *cambric* handkerchief, the tapering fingers versus the perspiring palm.

As she grew older, Mrs Webb's diaries lost some of their novelistic qualities. The later entries are longer and less frequent, and lack the sharp immediacy that the greatest diaries give us, the sense of present life. There are fewer scenes and dialogues, and an increasing inwardness, a turn to longer meditations that are often like informal essays; one could easily extract from the later diaries whole essays, and give them the sort of titles that Chesterton gave to his informal pieces: 'On the Ethics of Friendship', and 'Why Englishmen Hate Science'. The intelligence is still there, and the fluent style, and occasionally a fine gossipy portrait emerges – of J. B. Priestley, Annie Besant, or Mrs Webb's nephew-in-law, Malcolm Muggeridge; but the narrative is slacker and more trivial, begins to take note of the hot-water bottle and the nine o'clock news, and has an old woman's preoccupation with failing health, pain, and medicine. These diaries of old age are still good social history, but they sometimes read like letters that one might get from a very intelligent but elderly maiden aunt. Mrs Webb was aware of this, and worried about it, not for stylistic reasons, but because she feared that she might be misusing her energies: 'If I am to get on with the work', she wrote in 1934, 'I must stop this drivelling in the diary at 3 o'clock in the morning. This scribbling has become what Benson termed "logorrhea" – a symptom of senility?'[30] Even at seventy-six, the conflict between 'the history of a woman's life' and the chosen work went on.

If there is one dominant theme in the later diaries, it is Old Age. The subject turns up before one expects it, in entries written when Mrs Webb was in her mid-fifties; as though she were hurrying towards old age, and out of life. She refers to Sidney and herself as 'old people', 'ancients', and thinks about how they should withdraw gracefully from the world. Reading *A Passage to India* in 1924, she was struck by the character of the old woman, Mrs Moore, and especially by the passage (in chapter 23) in which Forster describes Mrs Moore's feelings about the universe just before she dies.[31]

> In this description of an old woman's mind [she wrote in the diary], what appeals to me are the phrases 'the twilight of the double vision', 'a spiritual muddledom is set up'. Certainly with me there is a strange consciousness of standing on a bare and bleak watershed of thought and feeling – in itself a place without thoughts or feelings, but with countless thoughts and feelings streaming out of the past and into the future in directions so various and manifold that I can no longer estimate their relative

value. And the concrete questions which I have investigated –
trade unionism, local government, co-operation, political organization, no longer interest me. I dislike reading about them,
thinking about them, talking or writing about them.

In my present state of mind they seem stale and unprofitable.
It is states of mind that interest me.

This mood was by no means constant in Mrs Webb's last years, but
there is a good deal of the Mrs Moore state of mind in the diaries – the
doubt about absolutes, the questioning of meaning and value, the
sense of emotional exhaustion, and above all the desire to withdraw
from the world's muddle. Like most old people, she thought of herself
as belonging to a world that was past; she was an 'aged Victorian',
whose mind had been shaped by Victorian ideas, and she disliked and
disapproved of much that she saw around her; the young Fabians were
frightful, Bloomsbury was decadent, party leaders were weak and
stupid. It was not a world that she belonged to; *her* world remained
Victorian. 'Looking back from the standpoint of today', she wrote in
1926,[32]

it seems to me that two outstanding tenets, some would say two
idols of the mind, were united in this mid-Victorian trend of
thought and feeling. There was the current belief in the scientific
method, in that intellectual synthesis of observation and experiment, hypothesis and verification, by means of which alone all
mundane problems were to be solved. And added to this belief in
science was the consciousness of a new motive: the transference
of the emotion of self-sacrificing service from God to man.

This is a just account of the motives that formed Beatrice Webb's life –
the belief in science, and the belief in human obligation. It explains
her work, her marriage, and the contents of her diary. (It also explains
why, in her seventies, she became a devoted admirer of Soviet Russia,
for in her terms Russia was the last Victorian society.)

Beatrice Webb was an artist who never wrote a work of art; for a
diary is not really art, and can't be – it is too subject to accident, as life
is, as history is. A diary is rather a kind of account rendered, the debits
and credits of a self and a world. 'I want to brood over the past and
reflect on men and their affairs', Mrs Webb wrote; 'I want to summar-
ise my life and see what it all amounts to.' That is the true diarist's
motive – to see what it all amounts to. In her case, the diary served two

other functions: it allowed expression to the suppressed artist in herself, and it helped her to hold herself to the course that she had chosen, by re-defining her choice.

I am persuaded that if she had made the other choice, and had committed herself to art, she might have been a considerable novelist, a sort of latter-day George Eliot. But I see no reason to regret that she did not. It is surely only literary sentimentality to think that it is more worthy to be a novelist than to be a diarist, or a social researcher, and I am content that we have what we have, one George Eliot and one Beatrice Webb.

Notes

1 *My Apprenticeship* (London: Longmans, 1926), p. 398. Until 1889 Beatrice Webb was, of course, Beatrice Potter. However, all her major writings were published under her married name, and it is by that name that she is known. I shall call her Beatrice Webb throughout this chapter.

2 *My Apprenticeship*, p. 109.

3 *My Apprenticeship*, p. 398. The last sentence is from the typescript in the library of the London School of Economics (hereafter LSE).

4 From a letter to her mother, written perhaps as early as 1866; quoted in Kitty Muggeridge and Ruth Adam, *Beatrice Webb: A Life* (London: Secker & Warburg, 1967), pp. 34–5.

5 *My Apprenticeship*, p. 62.

6 LSE, June 1878.

7 LSE, 6 September 1875.

8 In particular the long passage on *Eugénie Grandet* in the diary for 27 August 1882 (LSE).

9 LSE, 5 February 1927.

10 In the early twenties, when she was nearly seventy, she observed in herself 'the faint beginning of a liking for exquisite literature irrespective of its subject-matter' (*My Apprenticeship*, p. 96).

11 LSE, February 1881.

12 LSE, 2 January 1883.

13 LSE, 22 May 1891.

14 Margaret I. Cole, ed., *Beatrice Webb's Diaries 1912–1924* (London: Longmans, 1952), p. 50.

15 *My Apprenticeship*, p. 112. I have, however, used the LSE diary version, which differs in some small details from the published text.

16 *My Apprenticeship*, p. 322.

17 *My Apprenticeship*, p. 280 n.

18 *Our Partnership* (London: Longmans, 1948), p. 170.
19 *Diaries 1912–1924*, p. 16.
20 *Our Partnership*, p. 170.
21 Margaret I. Cole, ed., *Beatrice Webb's Diaries 1924–1932* (London: Longmans, 1956) p. 58.
22 *Diaries 1924–1932*, pp. 33 and 78.
23 LSE, 16 March 1884.
24 *My Apprenticeship*, p. 28 n.
25 *Diaries 1912–1924*, pp. 242–3.
26 LSE, 24 May 1933.
27 *Diaries 1912–1924*, p. 74.
28 Virginia Woolf, *A Writer's Diary* (London: Hogarth Press, 1953), p. 149.
29 *Our Partnership*, pp. 22–3.
30 LSE, 3 June 1934.
31 *Diaries 1912–1924*, pp. 34–5.
32 *My Apprenticeship*, p. 130.

15

Maurice Hewlett:
An Edwardian Career

Maurice Hewlett kept a diary all of his adult life, and during the years of his greatest success he recorded there his astonishment and delight at the growth of his reputation. At the end of 1903 he observed that he and Barrie were commonly said to be at the top of Literature, and though he added that he didn't like to confess it, even to himself, yet he nevertheless wrote it down.[1] A study of Hewlett's career might best begin there, at the top of Literature (with a capital L), and lead downward; the decline of fortunes is usually more interesting than the ascent, as well as more instructive, and in Hewlett's case it will also tell us a good deal about the Edwardian literary situation.

Hewlett's decline was a long, slow one, and is now complete: he is out of print and out of mind. Yet at his peak, in the Edwardian years, he was the Complete Man of Letters, and his station in the literary world must have seemed secure. His historical romances were both popular and respected: he sold like Marie Corelli, but he was reviewed like Meredith. His poems were published in respectable journals, and admired by respectable readers. Shaw sought him out for a Royal Court play. He was elected a Fellow of the Royal Historical Society, and of the Royal Society of Literature, and he was for a time Chairman of the governing committee of the Society of Authors. He owned a house in town and another in the country – the beautiful Old Rectory at Broad Chalke, Wiltshire. Where, one might ask, could such a career go but down?

And down it went. But the decline of Hewlett's fortunes should not be taken as simply an oscillation of taste, or the operation of some natural law of popularity. His career records rather a conflict in the Edwardian period between two incompatible ideas of the literary life – the writer-as-gentleman, and the writer-as-professional (the same opposition that one finds among Edwardian cricketers). If Hewlett had been born earlier or later, or into another class, his literary ambitions might have taken other and more adequate forms; but he was what he was, the son of a middle-class professional man, born in the 1860s, who began to write in his spare time in the '90s, while holding a secure post in the government. Thus he joined that class of poetical civil servants that included Edmund Gosse, Austin Dobson, and Laurence Binyon – men who, because they were not dependent on their writings for their livelihoods, could go on writing villanelles and ballades and literary essays without any evident sense of the passage of time or the change of taste.

Hewlett's first ten years as a writer were of this belletristic kind. He tried his hand, in a vaguely classical way, at the traditional forms – lyric poems, a pastoral, tragedies – and he thought of himself as a Poet in an elevated, Romantic way; during those years he tended to write about his dedication to Poetry, and the necessity of being faithful to the Image of Beauty and Immortal Truth (the taste for capitalized abstractions never abated). But in the diary for that year one also finds another kind of entry: dickerings with publishers, records of poems and articles sent out and returned, and complaints at the grind of lecturing that create quite another image – of a man writing hard for money, and exhausted by the struggle.

Still he stuck to his double life, and in 1897 succeeded his father as Keeper of Land Revenue Records, a post that assured him of a comfortable career and a pension at the end of it. But that year he also wrote his first novel, *The Forest Lovers*, and its instant success changed his life. In his diary at the end of 1898 he noted that he was getting known, and could command a price, and that all the magazines of England and America were open to him. Two years later *Richard Yea and Nay* confirmed his position, and he confessed that he thought of himself as a force, known to anyone who knew about literary things, and classed with the literary elect. He also noted with satisfaction that that year he had been able to write a cheque for £2,500 to buy a London house.

He had his station, and he had his income; and he did not seem to feel that these two modes of measuring literary success might conflict. His diary entry at the end of the next year shows the same double standard – commercial success (he had earned nearly £3,000 during 1901), and a reputation that had by then extended beyond the literary world. He had stayed in great houses with persons of high social position; he had visited Arthur Balfour; he had been elected to the Committee of the Royal Literary Fund, and had been made a Fellow of the Royal Historical Society (apparently because of his historical fiction, and particularly *Richard Yea and Nay*). On the strength of this success, he resigned his civil service post and became a professional writer, though characteristically he thought of his new profession as Literature with a capital L. He does not seem to have anticipated that any change would follow in either his literary style or his style of life; he would continue to maintain his two houses, and his two children, without any infidelity to the Image of Beauty and Immortal Truth.

For a time he seemed to have achieved this improbable goal, and to have reached and stayed at 'the top of Literature'. Reading his early novels and then reading the reviews, one must feel some astonishment that they were so ardently admired, but they were, and Hewlett's reputation really was as high as he thought it was. But it is worth considering what it was that Hewlett was at the top of. In 1903 the best of the Edwardian novelists had scarcely begun to establish themselves: Bennett had written only *A Man from the North* and *Anna of the Five Towns*, Wells was a popular writer of scientific romances, and Galsworthy had begun to publish under a pseudonym; the novels that we think of as their best and most Edwardian work – *The Old Wives' Tale*, *The Man of Property*, *Tono-Bungay* – were still to come, and so were the reputations that went with them. In a few years these writers would define Edwardian fiction, so firmly that when Virginia Woolf launched her attack on their generation she would take these three as standing for the whole. (It would not occur to her to attack Hewlett.) But in 1903 it was not absurd to think of Literature in terms of *The Forest Lovers*, or to see Hewlett as a successor to Meredith.

Hewlett's early success continued for a time, but he found the profession of Literature more and more difficult. *The Queen's Quair*, an ambitious historical novel about Mary Queen of Scots, would not come right, and the diaries are full of gloom. This was not altogether new – Hewlett had always been subject to depression and nervous ailments, and the earliest of the surviving diaries record suffering and despair, but these early miseries had been balanced by a sense of achievement and recognition as an artist, and that sense was fading. What was left was a bleak awareness of the expense of success, and the end of inspiration. Thus at the end of 1904 he complained that he felt old and out of ideas, but that he had to write nevertheless to support his country house at Broad Chalke, and his wife's motor car. And at the end of 1905 he regretted that he had raised his standard of living to the point that he had to write novels, and that he was consequently not doing them well. The two writers in Hewlett – the belletrist and the professional – had come into open conflict, and like many another man before him he had found that he had mortgaged himself to his own success.

But the conflict in Hewlett was deeper than financial necessity; the belletrist in him had always been ill at ease with the professional. He was, for example, a leading figure in the professional Society of Authors, but his relation to that group was always an awkward one. He first went to the Society in 1906, not for help, but to report a dispute with a publisher that he thought might benefit other writers; the Society promptly invited him to join so that his case might be fought, and he in time became a member of the Committee of Management, and a vigorous champion of authors' rights. But he was less vigorous and single-minded in defence of his own professional advantage. On the one hand he could write to *The Times* complaining that the Times Book Club was reducing his royalties by selling second-hand copies of his book, but on the other hand he could announce, also in *The Times*, that his publisher had overpriced a short novel, against his wishes and in spite of his protests. Good commercial practice favoured a good price, but the honour of an Artist clearly came first.

This conflict in Hewlett's sense of his writing self led to a divided and conflicting public life. At the same time (1909–10) that he was responsible, as Chairman of the Committee of Management of the Society of Authors, for the rights of professional writers, he was concerned, as a Fellow of the Royal Society of Literature, that literature should be protected from professional debasement. Many serious writers of the time felt that popular writing threatened the purity and dignity of English letters, but Hewlett was an unusual case in that he seemed to be publicly committed to both sides.[2]

As Hewlett's public life increased, so also did his dislike and resentment of his own work. In 1906, working on *The Stooping Lady* because he had to meet expenses, he wrote in his diary that writing was a miserable struggle, and the book a bore. Writing fiction was by this time a torment, but a torment that he had to endure, for the sake of Broad Chalke and his wife's motor car. He had come to doubt his own talents as a novelist: 'I am not – and never can be – a novel-writer', he told one friend, and to another he confessed, 'I can't make characters that live';[3] and he resented being typed as a writer of romances who was expected to go on repeating *The Forest Lovers*. His popularity continued, but he hated it.

And the more he hated his work, the more he resented the standard of living that made it necessary. 'If comfort weren't so essential to us', he wrote to Henry Newbolt in 1912, 'if we were content to go back to lodgings in Hampstead, or empty palaces in Pisa – we should write our novels in verse – both of us. But – blast it, I'm writing a novel in prose . . .'[4] He went on writing, but he began to dream of escape; and at the end of 1912 he made a public gesture that made escape more than a fantasy: he resigned from the Committee of Management of the Society of Authors, and he made a farewell speech in which, while acknowledging the Society's service to the profession of authorship, he dissociated himself from it. 'It came to this', he said,[5]

> that between them the committee, chairman, and secretary, had
> made the status of an author a respectable thing, in the trade
> sense of the word, and were now proceeding to make it a com-
> fortable thing as well.
>
> He himself, however, shared the anarchical essence at the bottom
> of all authorship. He was against the extension of trade union
> ideas to their profession. Such ideas could not make him write a
> good book or sell a bad one. There was a pride of literature,
> which could be seen notably in the cases of Byron and Dr.
> Johnson. Authors had a right, when they chose, to 'poverty,
> total idleness, and the pride of literature.' The Society of Authors
> could not conflict with or abolish this pride. . . .

Hewlett's audience may not have known it, but he was bidding fare-well, not only to the Committee of Management, but to the respect-ability and comfort of the profession. He had given up his house at Broad Chalke, and over the next four years he would live in various more humble country places, in an effort to escape 'the degrading occupation of writing bad novels – novels in which I don't myself for one moment believe'.[6] It was undoubtedly a sound financial move, but more than that it was a romantic, poetical gesture, by which Hewlett joined the ranks of the poor poets, impoverished for the sake of their art (though in fact he always lived comfortably, and his income, though diminished, continued to support him).

But if Hewlett did not want the comforts that went with popular romances, what did he want? There are two answers. First, he wanted, and had always wanted, to be a poet. His earliest writings were in verse, and he thought of himself as having a poetical imagination in his fiction, though he often doubted his poetic gifts: 'I shall never be a poet', he wrote to Laurence Binyon in 1909, 'though I have never wanted to be anything else . . .'[7] His flight from success was in part a last effort, by a fifty-year-old man, to make this desire actual.

Another ambition grew out of the tradition of the romantic novel, in which Hewlett had been such an immediate success – or, to be more precise, out of Hewlett's dissatisfaction with that tradition. He had begun by working entirely within the established conventions of the popular romance. Critics who found imitations of this writer or that, of Stevenson or Meredith, in *The Forest Lovers* had been too clever, for Hewlett was not so precise a borrower: his debts were to the whole body of costume-fiction of the nineteenth century, from Scott to Ouida and Marie Corelli. His achievement was to add nothing at all except a frank authorial voice that confessed at once its own conventions. *The Forest Lovers* begins:[8]

My story will take you into times and spaces alike rude and uncivil. Blood will be spilt, virgins suffer distresses, the horn will sound through woodland glades; dogs, wolves, deer and men, Beauty and the Beasts, will tumble each other, seeking life or death with their proper tools. There should be mad work, not devoid of entertainment. When you read the word *Explicit*, if you have laboured so far, you will know something of Morgaunt Forest and the Countess Isabel; the Abbot of Holy Thorn will have postured and schemed (with you behind the arras); you will have wandered with Isoult and will know why she was called La Desirous, with Prosper le Gai, and will understand how a man may fall in love with his own wife. Finally, of Galors and his affairs, of the great difference there may be between a Christian and the brutes, of love and hate, grudging and open humour, faith and works, cloisters and thoughts uncloistered – all in a green wood – you will know as much as I do if you have cared to follow the argument. I hope you will not ask me what it all means, or what the moral is. I rank myself with the historian in this business of tale-telling, and consider that my sole affair is to hunt the argument dispassionately. Your romancer must be neither a lover of his heroine nor (as the fashion now sets) of his chief rascal. He must affect a genial height, that of a jigger of strings; and his attitude should be that of the Pulpiteer: – Heaven help you, gentlemen, but I know what is best for you! Leave everything to me.

This is the decadence of a genre, when its conventions are no longer believed in, but are used nevertheless, like worn coins that no longer bear a likeness of a king, but can still be spent. The teller promises a spectacle, but with all of the machinery showing, and with no connections to reality. In so far as *The Forest Lovers* refers to anything, it refers back to romantic medievalism, and ultimately to Malory; that is to say, its referents are entirely literary.

Hewlett quickly became dissatisfied with this kind of romance – as a form it was neither challenging enough nor serious enough – and one finds in his letters and diary after about 1900 a growing desire to do something more ambitious, something that he called subjective history, or imaginative history. The books that he wrote continued to be romances in manner, but they began to deal with historical subjects, and to show the signs of historical research (one, *Richard Yea and Nay*, made him a fellow of the Royal Historical Society).

Hewlett's historical romances do not in fact express a very sophisticated sense of what history is. The romantic conventions obviously dictate their own theory of history – that it is made of royal lovers, intrigues, betrayals, and battles against odds – and in his earlier fiction Hewlett accepted these limitations, so that his history is to serious history what romance is to novel – a falsified, simplified, emotionally heightened substitute. He paid little attention to political motives, or to economic motives, or to diplomacy, and the general populations of nations scarcely appear. (The world of romance is necessarily emptied of whatever is common, including the common people.)

Richard Yea and Nay, *The Queen's Quair*, and *The Stooping Lady* are scarcely adequate as history, even 'subjective history', but they do express an admirable quality in Hewlett, as a writer and as a man – his restless impulse to move on from what he could do easily to what was difficult. In better writers this impulse produces formal experiment, but Hewlett had no experimental streak, and went on to the end of his life using the prose style and the construction of *The Forest Lovers*. For him, difficulty meant subject-matter, the assimilation of historical reality into romance forms. He began in the distant past, with medieval history, and moved gradually forward in time, until by the end of the Edwardian decade he was writing a trilogy set in the 1890s, and stuffed with contemporary issues. He suggested to friends that this movement in time had been intentional, a gradual escape from the past and thus from romance; perhaps it was, but the chronological order of his books seems less important than the emergence, in the later ones, of more elaborate and explicit ideas of history and politics, and of characters who speak those ideas for their author.

Hewlett's interest in politics seems to have developed at about the time he finished *The Queen's Quair*, in 1904. He was active as a political speaker in the General Election of 1906, and from that time the public role that he played included a political element that gradually found its way into his writing. Between 1907 and 1909 he wrote a trilogy of novels – *Halfway House, Open Country*, and *Rest Harrow* – that are his most contemporary in setting and in themes. It is tempting to conclude that there must be some relation between the political history of the time and Hewlett's turn towards political writing, to propose that 'the fascination of what's difficult' takes particular form from the circumstances of society. Certainly the last years of Edward's reign were a time when the new Liberal Government promised fundamental reforms, and artists and intellectuals seemed to be part of the process. There were writers in Parliament, playwrights testifying before a Commission on Censorship, poets meeting with politicians in societies like the Royal Society of Literature. Hewlett must have shared with many fellow-writers the conviction that this was the time to demonstrate the importance of Literature by acting in the public world. His 'history as I see it' was this sort of public gesture, so was his work for the Academic Committee, and so was his activity as a political speaker. It was all an old romantic dream, that the poetic imagination might indeed play a more active role in the intellectual business of states, but for a brief time it seemed a dream that might become reality. At the same time it was a counter-attack against a new enemy, the corrupting, debasing influence of commercial journalism. The dignity of letters would be demonstrated if the influence of writers could be felt at the highest public level. And so Hewlett wrote his series of contemporary romances, to set before his large popular audience his personal opinions of the modern situation.

Hewlett was not a writer who could make fiction out of ideas, and his political opinions are thrust into the trilogy in the most obvious and unassimilated ways. The principal character, a romantically wandering philosopher named John Senhouse, is Hewlett's own image of himself, 'more like what I should like to be than what I am', Hewlett said. He loves the heroine, Sanchia, and it is through his conversations and correspondence with her that the ideas enter the novels. There are many long, didactic passages like this one, as Senhouse educates his beloved in his own turn-of-the-century romantic philosophy:9

Now, money, I say, is the one cause of slavery, and work the one hope of salvation. Therefore our civilisation, as they disastrously term it, is a condition of acquiring slavery easily, and of obliterating the hope of salvation. Pretty, isn't it, when you take the clothes off? Happy state of things! Noble ideals, shared by the Great Unionist Party and the Great Liberal Party, turn and turn about. There'll be a Great Labour Party, one of these days, bickering with the others for a share in these splendid endeavours. It really might seem to you as if I was joking; but I write with tears in my eyes – that these things should be!

Hewlett so fancied these philosophical musings that he extracted them from the novel and published them separately as *Letters to Sanchia upon Things as They Are.*

Hewlett thought that his views on things as they are were shockingly advanced; indeed he saw himself, in these years, as an extreme iconoclast, and expected to be ostracized for his opinions. Henry Newbolt tells a touching story of Hewlett's decision to testify before the Royal Commission on Divorce in 1910. At this time he had just been elected to the Academic Committee of the Royal Society of Literature, he was active in politics and in the Society of Authors, and he enjoyed a secure position as a respectable man of letters. He expected to lose that position by stating his opinions in public, yet he thought it his duty to testify. 'No moral cause can be successful until a leader has been crucified', he told Newbolt; 'someone must go, and it will be me.'[10] And so, like a knight in one of his romances, he went out to battle for his faith. He urged upon the Commission the view 'that marriage should be voidable by agreement of the parties and evidence from one of them that desire or intention were absent or elsewhere engaged, saving always the interests of children'.[11] The Commission heard him out, thanked him for his interest, and proceeded to do nothing, either about Hewlett or about divorce. Hewlett was not martyred, unless for such a man it is martyrdom to be ignored.

The ideas of the trilogy met a similar fate. The reviewers simply regarded him as a strayed romancer, and scolded him mildly for meddling with ideas. *The Times Literary Supplement* review of *Rest Harrow* is typical:[12]

Mr. Hewlett, in short, is entirely at sea when he drops below (or climbs above) the level of romance. Senhouse himself, the philosophic genius of the Wiltshire Downs, is a case in point.

So long as he is kept away from actuality he is excellent; but when he is made to paint impressionistic water-colours and to write to Sanchia letters about the religion and politics of the day, about Anglo-Catholics and Fabians, his ingenuous doctrines, offered us apparently in all seriousness, put a speedy end to his romantic mysteriousness. If he talks like that, we know his sort!

And indeed the reviewers were quite right in seeing that, though set in modern times, the trilogy is no less a romance than *The Forest Lovers*, that it is in fact an imperfect return to the unhistorical manner of Hewlett's first success. The setting, though ostensibly contemporary England, and fitted with railway trains and channel steamers, is empty of historical reality. Senhouse is simply Prosper le Gai, the errant knight, dressed up in flannel trousers and a white sweater; and in that costume he bored an audience that might have accepted him in surcoat and baldrick.

The critical failure of the trilogy must have hurt Hewlett particularly because in those books he had exposed his views of the personal life so frankly. Indeed, he may have exposed himself more fully than he knew, for there are strands, not only of Senhouse's situation, but of his feelings, that seem to have come directly out of Hewlett's own odd and wretched personal life. It is difficult, and perhaps impertinent, to speculate about another man's marriage, but in Hewlett's case there does seem to be sufficient evidence for some valid conclusions about the relations between his life and his writings.

When he wrote the trilogy, Hewlett had been married for twenty years, but for much of that time the marriage had apparently existed in only a legal sense. After the birth of her two children, Hilda Hewlett seems to have lived a life increasingly separate from her husband, though they remained married and on good terms until his death. She became interested first in automobiles (her 'beloved motor' was costing Hewlett too much by the end of 1904), was one of the first women in England to drive, and participated in European road-races until they were stopped because of frequent accidents. She then went on to flying, and became the first woman in England to qualify for the pilot's certificate of the Royal Aero Club, in 1911. She ran a flying school at Brooklands, and it was said that she trained the first six British Army officers to become pilots. She also taught her son to fly; he became a naval pilot, and led the British raid on Cuxhaven on Christmas Day, 1914. The personal expense of all this, she said in a speech in 1911, was that she had given up society for the sake of aviation; she had also, it seems, given up marriage.

'To my mind', Mrs Belloc Lowndes wrote, 'Mrs. Hewlett ought to have been a man, for though she was feminine in appearance and manner, and a devoted mother to her son and daughter, her only interest in life appeared to be centred in what can only be called machinery.'[14] Hewlett nevertheless was devoted to her during the first years of the marriage; his early letters are full of affection, and the annual summarizing diary entries during the 1890s record his sense of his indebtedness to her. But even then there are occasional unexplained shadows; for example, on his tenth wedding anniversary, in 1897, he wrote that he could hardly bear to think about the interval since his marriage. And from about this point on, Mrs Hewlett virtually disappears from both diary and letters, and one finds instead, 'I am sick of being alone'.[15]

I would suggest, then, that Hewlett's testimony before the Divorce Commission came from the heart, that he knew from experience what a marriage was like when 'desire or intention was absent', and that this colours and distorts his treatment of love in his novels. 'He had', said his friend John Freeman, 'a curious mind – very pure, yet (not a word against him) permitting a sort of prurience of imagination. I mean that he slipped his puppets into such queer, unnatural and unhealthy relations – with would and would-notting all through.'[16] The would and would-notting begins in *The Forest Lovers*, with a marriage of necessity without desire, and continues through the trilogy (Senhouse loves Sanchia, but encourages her to live with another man), to *Bendish*, in which the passive observer Heniker stands by while the girl he loves is betrayed by a peer, and only then wins her. These are all, in their ways, romances, but the feeling is not of romantic love, but of frustration, denial, temptation, and sexual torment. Desire, when it appears, is generally unilateral, marriages are made without love, and instead of sexual gratification there is often its surrogate, physical cruelty (as in the brutal treatment of Isoult La Desirous in *The Forest Lovers*). Where love is strongest – as in Senhouse's love for Sanchia – it is made spiritual, a selfless substitute for physical pleasure.

The same motive is present in Hewlett's poems. 'There is a poem called "Hypsipyle" in the "Helen Redeemed" volume', Hewlett wrote to an admirer, 'which I myself believed to be good, though I have never dared read it in public. It has an inner meaning, of course, which is, as they say, "neither here nor there". Apart from that, it has passion, and a good deal of art too.'[17] The poem is a classical imitation, about a maid who loves a goddess, is carried off by a demonic god, and in the end is loved – apparently to her satisfaction – by a poetic shade. If this tale is to be taken as a myth, with an 'inner meaning', then it is an anti-physical myth, of spiritual love relieved of its physical urgencies.

Across this theme of denial in Hewlett runs what seems a contrary theme, of liberation. Hewlett's most attractive characters violate conventions, defy society, marry one way but love another. Senhouse is a self-proclaimed Anarchist (as Hewlett sometimes claimed to be), who in some ways seems like a character out of D. H. Lawrence: he lives close to nature, sheds material things, is opposed to marriage contracts, and dislikes the modern world. Like Lawrence's Mellors, he is tired and worn down by life, and, also like Mellors, he loves someone he can't – or at least shouldn't – have. But, unlike Mellors, he is most passionate when alone; he is no kind of a lover, and when, after three volumes of separation, he at last loves Sanchia physically, the scene is hurried over – pages for a love letter, but not a paragraph for a consummation. This extreme restraint cannot be put down to the inhibitions of the time – after all, Elinor Glyn was a contemporary of Hewlett, and *Three Weeks* was published in the year that Hewlett began his trilogy. One must simply conclude that Hewlett was better at scenes of separation and renunciation and death than he was at scenes of consummation, that he knew more about the lineaments of ungratified desire than he did about gratification. And one may add the observation that Hewlett's particular talent – his would and would-notting – was enormously popular in 1898, but by 1910 had lost its audience; Ann Veronica had made Isoult la Desirous obsolete.

Nevertheless, Hewlett went on writing romances, and trying to thrust into them his subjective notions of history. In the fall of 1912 he wrote, very rapidly and without apparent difficulty, *Bendish: A Study of Prodigality*. The setting is England at the time of the First Reform Bill, and the characters are concerned, in various ways, with the question of Reform. Lord Bendish, the title character, is a false reformer, a false poet, and a false lover (in romance these sins are related), and his antagonist, Gervase Poore, is true in all these activities. Bendish, whose life and works somewhat resemble Byron's, sets out to be England's Mirabeau, to scourge the Tories with satirical verse, and to win Poore's wife; he is rejected and defeated, and Poore, a Shelleyan figure, survives. The political content of the novel is fairly insistent, as the historical circumstances of the subject would seem to require, but it is not always clear in particulars, and tends to concern itself with political emotions rather than with political ideas. Like the other novels, it is romance, not history.

The most interesting passage in *Bendish* is that in which Hewlett describes Gervase Poore's great poem, *The Vision of Revolt*.[18]

His hero is Hodge, the Englishman, and he tracks him from the Conquest up the ages, past the present and into the future. History sweeps by like a series of crimson dreams; Hodge is always in the foreground, bending to his fieldwork, on the down with his sheep, munching his bacon under the hedge while the withering north-easter screams through the thorns, and earth and air are a parched drab – all this while Norman squadrons and Plantagenet bowmen, Tudor and Stuart Cavaliers, Round-heads, Hanoverian levies, conscripts from his own stock march and counter-march across the scene. It is so far an Epic of Endurance, a dumb agony. Lurid lights play about this earth-born Prometheus – Black Death, Civil War, Lollardry, witch-burning; Chaucer sings and passes; Spenser, Marlowe, Shakespeare strut their hours. One Cromwell kills a god, another kills a king; Hodge remains bound to his glebe, eating bacon, working all day, sleeping like a log, loving his wife on Sunday afternoons, begetting and burying children. Masters drive him to the furrows, kings drive him into battle, priests bicker over his soul, the parish deals with his body. But he remains doggedly in touch with the eternal things – in a way not possible to any more glittering co-tenant of his – Love, Work, and God; and because of his foot-hold there he is immovable by those other transient phantoms, and remains the same while they change and pass.

The significance of this description is that it summarizes Hewlett's last major book, and his most ambitious effort to write a lasting poem. He called it first 'The Hodgiad' (and he makes a scornful critic apply the same title to Poore's *Vision*), and first referred to it by that name in his diary in August 1913, some nine months after he had finished *Bendish*. He was half-way through it when war was declared, and went on with it through the early war years until he finished it in March 1916. It had occupied his imagination at full-stretch for nearly three years (he wrote *Bendish* in two months).

It is touching, now that the poem is forgotten, to read Hewlett's high hopes for it. At the beginning he wrote to E. V. Lucas, 'I've done the Prelude to "The Hodgiad", and feel dimly that it may make me immortal, if I can keep it up.'[19] And he confessed to Newbolt 'a kind of deeply fundamental conviction that I've done it this time.'[20] At the end he still believed that *The Song of the Plow*, as he finally called it, was the one work that his reputation would stand or fall by; by then he was aware of the weaknesses of the poem – '19th Century sociology, legislation, Corn Laws, Ballot Acts and so on beat me'[21] – and he observed ruefully that perhaps what he had produced was 'a shot at an Epic rather than an Epic',[22] but he still wrote Epic with a capital E, and one might conclude that he thought of his poem as the completion of the classically-shaped poetic career that had begun with those first lyrics.

The Song of the Plow is very nearly what Hewlett said that Poore's *Vision* was – an epic of the dumb but enduring English peasant. As such it implies a theory of history that is very different from the history of Hewlett's romances. Hodge is not a hero – he is too passive, too victimized to be heroic – but he is something more, he is a source of what Hewlett took to be the most lasting and valuable element in English life. Hewlett called the poem 'the English Chronicle' and 'a history of the governed race', and he put all his political feelings into it – his radical trust in the English people, and his hopes for an egalitarian society. 'The Argument' of the poem he summarized in this way in his preface:[23]

A certain man, being in bondage to a proud Conqueror, maintained his customs, nourisht his virtues, obeyed his tyrants, and at the end of a thousand years found himself worse off than he was in the beginning of his servitude. He then lifted his head, lookt his master in the face, and his chains fell off him.

Not, perhaps, a political idea so much as a political faith, but it sustains a poem of nearly five thousand lines and twelve books. It allows for an odd mixture of opinions – anti-royalist, anti-mercantile, anti-Church of England (but approving of Franciscans, Quakers, and Methodists for their attentions to the poor), radical yet favouring the customs of the country, egalitarian but conservative. One might find similar opinions in the minds of literate English countrymen from Cobbett's time to at least the First World War – times when political faith could be founded on two fundamental values, the English people and the English land. Hewlett is perhaps the last writer to stand in that tradition, and *The Song of the Plow* would be worth preserving for that reason, if for no other.

It is, however, more than a relic of the past; it is a rapid, fluent narrative poem, surely one of the best *terza rima* poems in English. Perhaps it was the short line and the vast extent of the historical subject that held Hewlett this time to a plainer style; perhaps it was that the absence of romance subjects inhibited his florid inclinations. At any rate, the language does not luxuriate and sprawl, as it does in his romances and his earlier poems, but moves along – a bit literary, a bit archaic, but spare and efficient. Some of the descriptive passages are fine and moving (for example the account of the Black Death in Book IV, and almost any bit of simple natural description), and the satirical attacks are often witty and pointed. If the poem has a serious flaw, it stems from the unfortunate fact that the First World War began while Hewlett was writing, and that war-time emotions skewed and coarsened his thought. He was not the sort of man who could separate his own goals and feelings from the feelings of the time; he loved England, he loved heroics and brave soldiers, and his only son was fighting, and he swung with all his heart to the national cause. And so parts of his best poem – especially the 'Dedication to England' and the 'Envoy: New Domesday' – are written from a war-time patriot's point of view, and clash badly with the sombre tone of the rest of the poem. But if one reads it with Dedication and Epilogue removed, the whole work emerges, and is, I think, impressive.

The countryman of *Song of the Plow* became more and more Hewlett's persona in his last years. In 1917 he moved back to the Old Rectory at Broad Chalke, a house for which he said he felt the sort of love that one has for one's mother, and there he gardened and wrote and watched his reputation fade. There also he entered county politics, first as a district councillor and for the last two years of his life as a member of the Wiltshire County Council. He wrote a report on wages for the Board of Agriculture, and travelled England to research it; he served on his district housing committee during the difficult post-war years, and wrote angry letters to *The Times* – letters as literary and old-fashioned as Senhouse's letters to Sanchia – about housing policies. He even considered standing for Parliament. 'I write less', he said, 'but do more',[24] and what he did was selflessly in the service of Hodge, and England. His income had shrunk as the novels ceased to sell, and eventually ceased to get written ('I am absolutely dished as a novelist', he wrote to Squire, 'though going strong as man and brother'),[25] and he was never without financial worries; finally he had to let the Old Rectory and move to a cottage nearby. His family had scattered, and he was alone much of the time. Yet he seems to have been more content than at any other period of his life, and the essays that he wrote during these last years are among his most pleasant and unaffected work. They are belles-lettres of the most inoffensive kind – the sort of essays that Chesterton did perfectly, and no one does any more, period pieces even when Hewlett wrote them. In the best of them one gets the open feelings of a very appealing man – his affection for Wiltshire, for his fellow countrymen, and for the natural world, praise for 'the inexhaustible bounty of women', small talk about gardens and wild creatures. Not a brilliant man, and one ill-suited to flourish in the modern world of letters and politics, but a man who praised and loved where he could, was generous and civil, and acted on his own feelings.

Hewlett was a man who came at the end of a tradition in everything he did. At the height of his popularity he was already old-fashioned, and it is perhaps only in the Edwardian era, with its odd mixtures of the old and the new, that he could have enjoyed such status as he did. He was the last Romancer, the last Virgilian, the last poet to have a shot at an Epic (unless we take Pound's word that *The Cantos* is an epic), the last man to write classical tragedies. His ideals – of England, of the English labourer, of Poetic Beauty, of Woman – were all out of the literary past, and sentimentalized in transit into the present. He lived into the modern world as best he could (with Honour, as he no doubt would have put it), but he had no gift for modernity; his Good Society would have been composed of literary gardeners, not of Fabians. He had had hard and lonely times, had come to feel that he has misused his talents, had failed to be recognized as the Poet he wanted to be. Yet he had survived, and at his death his friends remembered him fondly. 'He was an absurd person', Newbolt wrote, 'but an interesting one: very likeable, and very dear to us',[26] and John Freeman judged him 'rather a lonely man, who'd passed the pinnacle of popularity, but hadn't suffered in honesty'.[27]

Perhaps the best epitaph for Hewlett is Pound's reference to him in the Pisan Cantos, for there Pound places him among other writers of his time, in a moving lament for the makers:

> Fordie that wrote of giants
> and William who dreamed of nobility

and Jim the comedian singing:
'Blarney castle me darlin'
you're nothing now but a StOWne'
and Plarr talking of mathematics
or Jepson lover of jade
Maurie who wrote historical novels
and Newbolt who looked twice bathed
are to earth o'ergiven.

Canto LXXIV

In that company there are no discriminations: Hewlett, who wanted an academy of letters to confirm his greatness, but doubted his own talent, stands with his peers in one catalogue of the dead. A man who believed so fervently in the dignity of his calling surely deserves literary companions in death; but the presence in Pound's lament of writers as forgotten as Plarr and Jepson with Ford and Yeats and Joyce is a final ironic comment on the Edwardian man-of-letters dream, and on that moment in 1903 when Hewlett looked round and found himself at the top of Literature.

Notes

1 References to Hewlett's diary are to the typescript of selections from the original manuscript, made by his sister-in-law after his death, and deposited in the British Museum (additional manuscript 41,075). Hewlett's heirs have refused permission to quote from the diary.
2 Yeats wrote to Gosse in 1910 that 'an English Academy would save us, perhaps, from the journalists, who wish to be men of letters, and the men of letters who have become journalists'. *Letters* (London: Hart-Davis, 1954), p. 549. Hardy deplored the decline of pure English, and blamed journalists, and especially woman journalists, in a statement reported in *The Times*, 4 June 1912, p. 7.
3 Laurence Binyon, ed., *The Letters of Maurice Hewlett* (London: Methuen, 1926), pp. 106 and 85.
4 *Letters*, p. 128.
5 *Author*, vol. xxiii (January 1913), 124; the quotation is from Dr Johnson.
6 *Letters*, p. 168.
7 *Letters*, p. 98.
8 *The Forest Lovers* (London: Macmillan, 1898), pp. 1–2.
9 *Open Country* (London: Macmillan, 1909), p. 158.
10 *Letters*, p. 112.
11 *The Times*, 22 December 1910, p. 4.

12 *The Times Literary Supplement*, 22 September 1910, p. 341.

13 *The Times*, 11 October 1911, p. 6.

14 Mrs Belloc Lowndes, *The Merry Wives of Westminster* (London: Macmillan, 1946), p. 109.

15 *Letters*, p. 175.

16 Gertrude Freeman and Sir John Squire, eds, *John Freeman's Letters* (London: Macmillan, 1936), p. 184.

17 *Letters*, p. 173.

18 *Bendish* (London: Macmillan, 1913), pp. 151–2.

19 *Letters*, p. 140.

20 *Letters*, p. 140.

21 *Letters*, p. 165.

22 *Letters*, p. 231.

23 *Song of the Plow* (London: Heinemann, 1916), p. viii.

24 *Letters*, p. 236.

25 *Letters*, p. 207.

26 Margaret Newbolt, ed., *The Later Life and Letters of Sir Henry Newbolt* (London: Faber, 1942), p. 322.

27 *Freeman's Letters*, p. 184.

16

'Mr Pember's Academy'

England has never had an institution comparable in dignity and importance to the Académie Française; no English honour equals election as an Academician, and no English society speaks with equivalent authority on matters of literary usage and literary achievement. For most Englishmen, most of the time, this has not been a worry, but rather a testimony to the sturdy independence of the national character; Frenchmen start academies by instinct, a *Times* leader-writer once remarked, but Englishmen start debating societies. The one occasion when an English academy of letters actually got started proves him right; for though it was conceived as an academy, it lived as a debating society, and died as nothing at all.

The idea of an Academy occurred and reoccurred to English men of letters during the late Victorian and Edwardian years. The issue was raised in (appropriately) the *Academy* in 1897, and a panel of forty academicians was proposed (the Académie Française had forty members, and this number was taken as somehow correct). The list invoked some amusing letters, including one from Shaw nominating Oscar Wilde, and there was comment in the daily press, but nothing further was done. It turned up again in 1901, when the press reported with dismay that there was no English group representing literature at an international conference of scientific and literary societies. It was debated in the pages of the *Author*, the house organ of the Society of Authors, in 1902–3. And it emerged again in 1909, in letters to *The Times*. In all these instances, supporters urged the dignity of letters and the superior arrangements of the French, while opponents noted the difficulties of founding an Academy without a Richelieu, and questioned whether such a body would in fact have anything to do. One does not feel great popular enthusiasm in any of these exchanges; it was not so much that English writers didn't want an academy, as that they could see no strong reason for having one.

But if not many Englishmen wanted an Academy, a few wanted one very much, and at the end of the decade an opportunity arose for these partisans to collaborate, and to bring an English Academy into being. In 1908-9 two events occurred that provided an occasion: 9 December 1908 was the tercentenary of the birth of Milton, and on 18 May 1909 George Meredith died. Both of these occasions seemed to require official attention, of the sort that in France would have been provided by the Académie Française, but in England the best that could be devised was to turn the preparations over to the British Academy for the Promotion of Historical, Philosophical, and Philological Studies. Memorial ceremonies were held, and as reported in the press they seem to have been quite usual and appropriate, but because they were organized by the British Academy, they provided an opportunity for protest; for the British Academy was a society devoted to scholarship, not to creation, and it was constitutionally closed to poets. The protest was slow in coming, but it came. In November an anonymous correspondent to *The Times* used the anomaly of the British Academy celebrating poets as an argument for establishing an academy of letters, and the following week Maurice Hewlett wrote on behalf of his fellow writers to express their 'unanimous and just indignation at the incongruous spectacle of a body which had expressly defended itself from the inclusion of poets in its ranks actively commemorating the centenary of one great poet and superintending the funeral rites of another',[1] and to endorse the idea of a literary academy.

The fact that this expression of indignation came six months after the event suggests that it was not altogether spontaneous, and this indeed seems the case, for at the time that Hewlett wrote he was already engaged in discussions concerning an academy. The discussions were taking place in the councils of a society that, but for its almost total obscurity, might well have been thought the proper one to commemorate poets – the Royal Society of Literature. The RSL had been in existence since 1823, but when it first entered the debate many newspapers professed never to have heard of it. Its membership was largely political and clerical, with a sprinkling of professors and editors; it was presided over by the Earl of Halsbury, former Lord Chancellor and soon, at the age of 88, to lead the 'die hard' Lords against the Parliament Bill. In 1909 its officers and Council included, among 27 members, only two – Hewlett and Gosse – who might reasonably be called literary men.

The Charter of the RSL charged it to maintain the purity of the English language, 'to encourage fellowship and co-operation among those who are disinterestedly striving for the perfection of English literature', to mark the current of literary history by 'Discourses of Reception' and 'Obituary Addresses', and to make Awards of Merit to particular literary works. Of these duties, only the Awards of Merit had been visibly (though irregularly) discharged. For the first seven years of its existence the Society had awarded each year two Gold Medals, and in some cases the choices had been reasonable, and even distinguished: Scott and Southey in 1827, Crabbe in 1828, Washington Irving in 1830. Most of the other recipients are now quite unknown, and many were never men of any literary reputation: Charles Wilkins and James Rennell, for example, and John Schweighauser of Strasburg, Archdeacon William Coxe, and Baron Antoine Isaac Silvestre de Sacy. When George IV died, the funds for the medals died, too, and no more were granted for nearly eighty years. The Society continued to meet, and to distribute money for pensions and prizes – by the end of the century it had disposed of some £85,000 of public money – but it managed in spite of this to remain unnoticed. When an international congress of scientific and literary societies met in 1901, the RSL was not represented because no one remembered that it still existed.

In its late-Edwardian years, however, the Society included three men ambitious for a literary academy: Hewlett, because he disliked being a writer of popular romances, and aspired to the condition of Poet; Edmund Gosse, because he enjoyed literary politics, and saw wider ranges for his talents in an academy; E. H. Pember, because he craved literary immortality, and could only achieve it if he conferred it upon himself. It was Pember who moved, at a Council meeting in December 1909, that a committee be appointed to discuss the creation of an English academy of letters; and when the committee was formed it included Pember, Hewlett, and Gosse. The presence of Gosse and Hewlett seems reasonable enough, but Pember needs some explaining. He was a barrister by profession, who had made a reputation as a parliamentary lawyer, though he was no longer active (he was 76). He was also a poet: 'Widely read in general literature', says the *DNB*, 'and highly critical in taste, he found relaxation and amusement in the making of *vers de société* and of translations and adaptations from the Greek and Latin, especially from Horace and the Greek dramatists'. He wrote in all seven books of verse, which he had privately printed: 'He refrained from publication' is the way the *DNB* puts it, 'and confined the circulation of his plays and poems to a fit and cultured audience.' Since the books bore such titles as *Debita Flacco*, *Echoes of Ode and Epode* and *The Finding of Pheidippides and other Poems*, his decision was probably a wise one. One might say that Pember wrote academician's verse; at least he thought he did, and more than anyone else he wanted an Academy, with a place for himself. He made the first motion, and he put up the money.

It was Hewlett, however, who took the most vigorous action. His letter to *The Times* had claimed for the Society of Authors the right to decide whether an academy was needed, and though the initiative had been taken by the Royal Society of Literature, he insisted that the Society of Authors should be consulted. In the end a joint committee of the two groups was formed, with Hewlett a member twice over (he was the only person on the committee who belonged to both parent organizations).

Hewlett's insistence on the role of the Society of Authors seems at first contrary to the idea of an academy, for the Society was (and is) an organization of professional writers, devoted to professional matters – copyright law, the price of books, royalties; it was, in short, a kind of trade union, and an effective one. In all this, it was the opposite of the gentlemen-scholarly, belletristic RSL, and it is hard to imagine the trade union and the royal society collaborating well together. But if one compares membership lists, one point becomes clear: that it was the Society of Authors that represented the true literary aristocracy of Edwardian England, and it was there that the members of a distinguished literary academy would be found. Hewlett called it a 'real society of men of letters', and so it was. But it was *Edwardian* men of letters, which meant professional writers, living by their pens, and not academicians. Still, for men like Hewlett, commercial writers with artistic pretensions, an academy born of the union of these two societies must have seemed the resolution of a personal problem; for if one were elected to such a body, one would be officially stamped as an Artist without ceasing to be a professional, and art and commerce would be reconciled.

The joint committee met through the winter and spring of 1909–10, and in July announced that a body, to be called the Academic Committee, had been created, 'which shall represent pure literature in the same way that the Royal Academy represents the fine arts, the Royal Society science, and the British Academy learning'.[2] The first twenty-seven members were Alfred Austin, Laurence Binyon, A. C. Bradley, Robert Bridges, S. H. Butcher, Joseph Conrad, W. J. Courthope, Austin Dobson, J. G. Frazer, Edmund Gosse, R. B. Haldane, Thomas Hardy, Henry James, W. P. Ker, Andrew Lang, Sir Alfred Lyall, J. W. Mackail, Viscount Morley, Gilbert Murray, Henry Newbolt, E. H. Pember, Sir Arthur Pinero, G. W. Prothero, Walter Raleigh, G. M. Trevelyan, Arthur Verrall, and W. B. Yeats.

It is, on the whole, a good list, and one might have thought that the Academic Committee was off to a good start. But in fact it was already in trouble. It was in trouble with its own members, and with writers who were not members, it was in trouble with the RSL and with the Society of Authors. Some of these troubles might have been avoided, but others were inherent in the idea itself; founding an academy was like writing in alexandrines – a reasonable idea in seventeenth-century France, but not in Edwardian England.

A sensible analysis of the problems is set down in a private letter from Henry Newbolt to Gosse, dated 9 April 1910. Newbolt wrote:[3]

Hewlett told me yesterday that I have been nominated as an original member of a projected English Academy, and pressed me to 'come in' to it. I was taken by surprise, and carried away by my strong regard for Hewlett, as well as my confidence in his judgment on literary matters. I have since reflected and I am filled with misgivings. I can believe that such an academy, if well founded and once accepted by public opinion, might do good service to the cause of Literature. I also understand the difficulty of devising any method of foundation which shall not be open to criticism. No one is infallible, no one has authority. Yet someone must select. But the penalty of a bad method and a bad selection will inevitably be the destruction of that prestige upon which the possibilities of the new Association depend. I have little to lose myself, but I am afraid for the venture itself. There will be a considerable development of sceptical opinion, and a smaller but more active outbreak of disappointed feeling. The list of members will be scrutinized, and the method of nomination attacked, not only by argument and comparison, but by ridicule – a much more deadly weapon. . . .

I am now reflecting with dismay on the details of the information communicated by Hewlett. It is one thing to join a confraternity of distinguished men of letters, to stand forward,

however audaciously, with people like Hewlett and Robert
Bridges and yourself, for an honest purpose: it is quite another
to be walked out in public as an inmate of Pember's Select
Academy – marching perhaps side by side with a Cabinet
Minister who has drafted an Army Bill and delivered some
popular lectures on philosophy. I am almost tempted to say that
Literature could better bear to be passed over altogether (as by the
Royal British Academy) than to be patronised by a ten and six-
penny Maecenas – a privately printed Sam Rogers – like our
esteemed but eternally obscure friend.

At about the same time Hewlett was writing to Newbolt in distress at
the very thing that had troubled Newbolt, the method of selection
and the role of Pember. 'At a preliminary meeting of the RSL',
Hewlett wrote, '. . . Pember invited Gosse to be a member and Gosse
Pember. Dobson, James, Haldane were "approached" by Gosse on his
own authority: afterwards ('tis true) ratified by the Sub-Committee.
These are the facts.' And in a later letter: 'At present, I take it, it *is*
"Pember's Academy", and none the worse for that – so long as it
doesn't remain so.'[4] It didn't, because Pember died the following year,
but the private intriguing went on, and was evident enough four
years later for Yeats to introduce a resolution forbidding members from
circularizing the committee in favour of private candidates: 'It will
not be passed', he wrote to the Secretary of the Committee, 'but it will
check a form of intrigue that if repeated would break up the committee.'[5] After discussion, the resolution was withdrawn by consent;
whether it stopped such habitual literary politicians as Gosse is uncertain.

Once the Academic Committee had been elected, and the public
announcement made, new problems appeared. *The Times* had suggested, in its report of the original selection of members, that the
Committee might later split off from the Royal Society of Literature,
from which it derived its authority, and become an independent, full-
fledged Academy. This enraged Lord Halsbury, who saw his Society
threatened by its own offspring, and poor Pember wrote anxiously to
the Secretary of the RSL, offering to explain or deprecate; 'I should be
exceedingly sorry', he wrote, 'if Lord Halsbury were to say any thing
that would be likely to set the pre-existing members of the Royal
Society of Literature against the Committee.'[6]

Apparently Lord Halsbury was mollified, but immediately a new problem arose. Mrs Humphry Ward, novelist and anti-suffragette, announced that she would bring before the Council of the Society of Authors a motion expressing her discontent with the fact that no woman writer had yet been elected to the Academic Committee, although the committee included some men whose qualifications for the honour from a purely literary point of view were not at all obvious. And having attacked the composition of the committee, she went on, and in public, to question the methods of selection, and the integrity of Hewlett. In March 1911 Mrs Ward wrote to *The Times* to comment on a report of a Society of Authors meeting at which Hewlett had explained the creation of the Academic Committee.[7]

> When, to the astonishment of many persons connected with the Society of Authors who knew nothing of the matter, the announcement was made last August that an Academic Committee had been selected by a 'joint committee' of that Society and of the Society of Literature, as a member of the Council of the Society of Authors no less surprised than the rest of the world, I took some pains to inquire into what had actually happened. The question was raised by me at a Council meeting of the Society in November last; and from the speeches then made, together with previous correspondence, it appeared – (1) that the Council of the Society of Authors (62 persons) had never been consulted; (2) *a fortiori*, the Society as a whole, numbering some hundreds, had never been consulted. All that had happened had been a communication from Mr. Hewlett as a member of a committee organized by the Royal Society of Literature, through Mr. Hewlett, as Chairman of the Executive Committee of the Society of Authors, to the latter committee suggesting that the Society of Authors should co-operate in what the Society of Literature was doing. Two persons were appointed by the small executive of the Society of Authors – consisting of 12 members – to serve on the joint selecting committee, one of them being Mr. Hewlett, who thus concentrated a truly vast amount of representation, gathered from a very small area, in his sole person. . . . That the selecting committee should afterwards have issued invitations to distinguished men of letters to join the Academic Committee as from 'the two societies sitting in joint session' was surely a little grotesque.

Hewlett replied,[8]

If Mrs. Ward was surprised at learning from your columns that
the Academic Committee had been formed by a joint committee
of two literary societies, it is her own fault. As a member of the
Society of Authors she is put in possession month by month of its
official 'organ,' the *Author*. There, on two separate occasions,
she might read of the action of the Committee of Management.
Again, if she had attended the meeting of council last year, she
would have heard all that I was then at liberty to report. As
to the matter of her present complaint, I will repeat what I
have already told her – (1) that every step taken by me in the
inception of the Academic Committee, so far as it concerned the
part taken in that by the Society of Authors, was taken after
consultation with and under the sanction of the Committee of
Management; (2) that that committee nominated Mr. Freshfield
and myself to represent them upon the joint committee of
nomination; (3) that no invitations to join the new body were sent
out as from the Society of Authors until they had been submitted by
Mr. Freshfield and myself to the Committee of Management and
been approved by them; (4) that two ladies sat, and still sit, upon
that committee.

This is a very disingenuous defence. Clearly what had happened was
that Hewlett, in his dual position as Chairman of the Committee of
Management and a member of the RSL council, was in a position of
unusual power, and that he succumbed to the temptation to use all
of it. He reported to the RSL as representative of the Society of
Authors, and to the Society of Authors as representative of the RSL.
He and Freshfield together made up the list of nominees in the Society's
name, and brought it to the Committee of Management for confirmation (which was given without question). The scheme was never
brought to the Society at large, and no opinions entered into the
selection process except Hewlett's and Freshfield's. Furthermore, the
reports printed in the *Author* omitted the crucial arrangement by
which the entire authority to select academicians in the name of the
Society was delegated to its two representatives, so that Mrs Ward
could not, in fact, have discovered what was going on even if she
had read the house organ carefully.

Mrs Ward fired one parting shot, another letter to *The Times*,
in which, after reviewing the inadequacy of Hewlett's methods, she
concluded:[9]

The management of the whole matter largely accounts for the
tone, half mocking, half hostile, so commonly taken towards
the Academic Committee. It is surely not an easy matter to
establish such a body, with anything like an admitted prestige.
It can be done by an autocrat like Richelieu, or it can be done
with the general consent of the literary class, acting through whatever organization it possesses. The real object of my first letter
was to suggest that it might still be possible to obtain this
consent.

But in fact it was too late, and Mrs Ward, by her protest, had done her
cause no good at all. The Committee by this time existed, and its
members were deep in their own devices for electing their own
candidates. Her objection to the absence of women was treated with
some amusement, coming as it did from a leader of the Women's
Anti-Suffrage League, and the whole things was regarded as one more
example of the troublesomeness of women. 'I think we should leave
her alone for the moment at any rate', Yeats wrote to Gosse; '. . . it is
hard to defend the exclusion of women without saying ungracious
things.'[10]
   The absence of women did nevertheless seem to trouble the Committee, and Mrs Ward was invited to join. When she declined, two
other literary ladies were appointed – Lady Ritchie in 1911, and Mrs
Margaret Woods in 1913 – and for most members that token con-
cession settled the matter. When the name of May Sinclair came up in
1914, Max Beerbohm protested that two women were quite enough;
'I think genius, or at any rate a magnificent distinction, is needed to
enable a woman to add lustre to the Committee and to prevent her
from making it slightly ridiculous', he wrote to Gosse.[11] Both Gosse
and Beerbohm threatened to resign if Miss Sinclair were to be elected.
She wasn't.
   Once established, the Academic Committee spent most of its
meetings electing new members, though not without some difficulties.
The authority of the Committee was not altogether established, either
within or outside its own membership; Trevelyan resigned almost as
soon as he was elected, and it was thought that Bennett, Wells, and
Chesterton were united against joining. The Committee nevertheless
invited Wells, and got this reply: 'I see no useful purpose which your
Committee serves, I am hostile to any attempts to organize art and
literature, which are things necessarily wild and free, and I cannot feel

that I should make a helpful or harmonious member of either your Committee or your Society.'[12] Considering the havoc that Wells had recently created as a member of the Fabian Society, the last clause is undoubtedly true, and the Committee may well have been better off without him; nevertheless, the rejection was distressing, and Henry James set about to persuade Wells to reconsider his decision. James's account of the Committee, and its possible usefulness, is the most generous and intelligent argument that could be made for its existence.[13]

> The thing [he wrote] is a *pleasant* and a plastic, elastic, aspiring thing, greatly appealing to our good-will – by which I especially mean to yours, that of your literary and creative generation; offering us no rigour, offering us opportunities for influence, for pressure in desirable directions and asking no sacrifice worth speaking of or grudging in return. It will be what the best of us shall make it, and it is open to the best of us to make it more interesting and more amusing (if you will – 'in the highest sense of the term') to ourselves, and more suggestive to others. Above all it would be so fortified by your accession that a due consideration for the prestige of current English letters surely ought to move you. You would do something for us that we lack and don't want to lack – and we would do for *you*, I think, that you would find yourself *within* still more moved than without to that critical, that ironic, that even exasperated (if I may call it) play – or reaction! – which is the mark, or one of the marks, of your genius. Don't make too much of rigours and indifferences, of inconsistencies and vows; I have no greater affinity with associations and academies than you – *a priori*; and yet I find myself glad to have done the simple, civil, social *easiest* thing in accepting my election – touched by the amenity and geniality of the thought that we shall probably *make something* collectively – in addition to what we may make individually . . .

But Wells, who had never found the civil, social thing easy to do, and who at this point in his life was most alienated from the literary world, would not be moved; affectionately, but firmly, he declined James's appeal.

Other questions of election were more complicated. James was a member, and therefore the Committee must be open to foreigners, but did that freedom extend to Bengalis? When Yeats proposed Rabin-

dranath Tagore in 1913, Gosse wrote to the Secretary of the Royal
Society of Literature in alarm: 'The Lord Chancellor strongly disapproves of Mr. Tagore as a member of the A.C. I do also. If you
can do anything to prevent this absurd and untoward election, pray
exert your influence'.[14] The Secretary, Percy Ames, was not a member
of the Academic Committee, and had no business influencing its
deliberations; the 'Lord Chancellor' may or may not, depending on
whether Gosse was referring to Lord Haldane, the present Lord
Chancellor, who was a member of the Academic Committee, or to
Lord Halsbury, his predecessor, who was not, but was the President
of the Royal Society of Literature, and a choleric old Tory. In any case,
though Yeats did nominate Tagore on two occasions, he was not
elected.

Though the election of fellow immortals was an engrossing activity
in the early years, the Committee did take, or attempted to take, other
actions, and particularly after the election of its liveliest new member,
Shaw. When his name came up in 1911, Yeats wrote to T. Sturge
Moore in favour of Shaw's candidacy:[15]

A tendency is arising to nominate for an election only safe
men. . . . Are you for the election of Shaw? I think we should
have him, though I think his work arises out of a fundamentally
wrong principle and won't last. Even at that it is better than the
work of some of the people we have and what we want is
vigour. When a man is so outrageously in the wrong as Shaw
he is indispensable . . .

Certainly Shaw did bring vigour to the Committee. He had scarcely
settled into his academic seat when he was up again to propose 'in view
of the received opinion that men of letters are at the climax of their
powers at the age of forty-four, and of the fact that the average age of
the Academic Committee at present exceeds fifty-eight, that the
Committee proceed forthwith to make rules providing for super-
annuation and rejuvenation'.[16] Shaw at the time was fifty-six. The
resolution was judiciously adjourned until the full number of members
were elected, but Shaw returned to the cause in the following year,
when he proposed that only candidates under fifty be considered, and
in 1922, when he urged the introduction of young members, and the
removal of seniors to 'Senatorial inactivity'. The latter motion was
opposed by Gosse, then seventy-three, the former by Yeats, who wrote
from Dublin that if the Committee had existed a bit earlier, and had

elected young men on their promise, they would no doubt have chosen Stephen Phillips and Richard Le Gallienne.

Shaw's activities were not always so light-hearted. It was he, more than anyone else, who spoke to the Committee's charge to concern itself with language. He supported a Commission to consider a common alphabet for the languages of India in 1914, and a Commission to establish a scientific phonetic alphabet in 1915. Perhaps his most serious effort, however, was an attempted action against censorship, and the way it went is significant of what was wrong from the start with the Academic Committee. In January 1912, a group led by St Loe Strachey, editor of the *Spectator* and a fierce foe of indecency in literature, waited upon the Home Secretary to urge passage of a censorship law. Shaw, at the March meeting of the Academic Committee, proposed 'to call attention to the threat of legislation to enlarge the powers of the police to interfere with the freedom of the press on the initiation of common informers and irresponsible private organizations, and to consider how the Committee can most effectively protest against such legislation'. The Minutes of the meeting read:[17]

> There was a full discussion on this subject & it was admitted on all sides that this was a matter peculiarly proper for the consideration of the Academic Committee – but the moment was felt to be inopportune for any action, as the attention of one of the Members, Lord Haldane, had been called to the matter and he had privately expressed the opinion that the time was not ripe for it. It was generally agreed that the Academic Committee will do well to watch any attempt made to interfere with the legitimate freedom of the press.

A group like the Committee, at once professional and honorific, composed of both literary and public men, and with loyalties to the Society of Authors on the one hand, and the RSL (and Lord Halsbury) on the other, was not free to act, and was uncertain as to what direction its action should appropriately take. The time would never be ripe, it is clear, for action of any controversial kind.[18]

If the Committee could not act to preserve its freedom to write, it could fulfil its obligation to make 'Awards of Merit'. Prize-giving, like the election of academicians, is a self-confirming activity, a means of affirming the values of the granting body by adding to it, for to grant a prize is to claim the recipient. The Academic Committee had an opportunity to do so early in its history, when the Princesse Edmond de Polignac (*née* Winnaretta Singer, of New York) offered, through Gosse, to support a prize of £100 each year for an experimental period of five years, for a literary award in memory of her husband. The Committee accepted, and the Polignac Prize immediately became a major issue at Committee meetings: how to choose the winner, how to award the prize, how to assure the continuance of the funds. At the first meeting after the prize was established, Hewlett proposed his candidate, Frederick Manning, for his *Scenes and Portraits*, and at the next meeting was defeated by Newbolt, who reported that the book had been published too early to be eligible, and carried the day with his own candidate, Walter de la Mare. In 1912 Sturge Moore wanted the prize for Forster, but *Howards End* was out of the running, and he had to nominate 'The Road from Colonus', and see the prize go to Masefield's *Everlasting Mercy*. Yeats captured the prize in 1913 for his Irish candidate James Stephens's *Crock of Gold*; in 1914 it went to Ralph Hodgson for *The Bull* and *Song of Honour* (Yeats abstained from voting). The fifth annual prize was postponed because of the war, and though members continued for a year or so to nominate their favourites, in case the prize should some day be given, it was not revived.

Another possible Award of Merit was the Gold Medal, which the Royal Society of Literature had granted only once since 1830. If the Academic Committee assumed responsibility for this award it would enhance its status as an Academy, and Gosse therefore proposed in 1912 that a Gold Medal he presented to Hardy on the occasion of his seventy-second birthday. Hardy accepted the offer, but added that though he did not like to suggest the method of presenting the medal, he would prefer as little ceremony as possible. Yeats and Sir Henry Newbolt were consequently dispatched to Max Gate to make the presentation on Hardy's birthday. They arrived at Dorchester to find, somewhat to their surprise, an empty railway station, without journalists, or curious townspeople, without even a car. Somewhat daunted, they nevertheless made their way to Hardy's home, where they were greeted by Hardy and his wife, and no one else. Luncheon was served to the four of them (plus Mrs Hardy's two cats, who sat on the table throughout the meal), after which Hardy pointedly escorted his wife to the door, closed it behind her, and returned to his seat to await the ceremony. Faced with an audience of two, Newbolt made his way painfully through his presentation speech, followed by an emotional – or perhaps desperate is the better word – peroration from Yeats. Having got through all this, the two were prepared to hand Hardy the medal and escape, but Hardy detained them; he had released his reply to the press, he said, and did not want to make liars out of the journalists who quoted it as delivered. So, while Newbolt and Yeats fidgeted, he drew from his pocket a sheaf of papers and read out his thanks. Then he ushered his guests to the door. The Academic Committee had delivered its first Gold Medal, but in circumstances more suitable to the passing of forged coins.[19]

The problems of this comic incident were products of Hardy's odd character, but other efforts of the Committee to perform its public roles were hampered by obstacles more central to the literary situation. For example, early in the Committee's life, Hewlett had proposed, and the Committee had moved, that the 'Discourses of Reception' and 'Obituary Addresses' by which the Committee was to 'mark the current of literary history in this country' should be published only in the *Transactions* of the RSL. It was an anti-commercial motion, a way of testifying to the high-mindedness of the Committee, and it ran into trouble almost at once; for the members of the Committee were, if not exactly commercial, highly professional, and they resented the loss of their honoraria. The first issue arose over the celebration of the Browning Centenary in 1912. The speakers were to be Pinero, on 'Browning as a Dramatist', and Henry James, on 'The Novel in "The Ring and the Book" '. James set to work, 'tooth and nail', as he put it, on his 'little affair', but was dismayed to learn from the secretary that his essay was to be published in the *Transactions*. Would precedents allow him, he asked, to let his fellow-member, Prothero, also publish it in the *Quarterly Review*? Precedents (if that means Hewlett's resolution) would not, but an arrangement might be made, if copies enough could be provided for the entire Academic Committee and the RSL. Prothero declined, James acquiesced, and the paper was published first as a Transaction, though a revised version appeared shortly after in the *QR*. Here the professionalism, not only of the author-member, but of the interested editor-member, worked against the Committee's intention; how, one wonders, could an Academy hope to operate high-mindedly while its members wrote and edited for their livings?

This point was made again in the following year, when A. C. Benson, who had been appointed by the Committee to a newly-founded Professorship of Fiction, announced that he did not wish to continue in the post. It was, by intention, a considerable honour, but Benson complained that he was wasting his labours. 'If I go to a place like Leeds or Birmingham', he wrote, 'I find that from one thousand to fifteen hundred people will come to hear me, and that being so it seems to me rather a waste of time (if I may use such an expression) to write elaborate lectures for an audience so small and uncritical as that which assembles at Hanover Square; they are kindly and sympathetic enough, but I do not go in for lecturing enough to spend so much time on an audience which does not really take much heed, so far as I can make out, of the quality of what it hears'.[20] He did not mention money in this letter, though it was clearly more profitable to preach to the multitudes in Leeds than to address the few in Hanover Square. In another letter he went directly to the cash question. Like James, he had been offered a fee for publication rights to an address (it was five guineas, from the *Church Times*) and Hewlett's resolution galled him. 'I have a strong inclination', he wrote to Ames, 'to resign my place on the Academic Committee in consequence of this incident, or still more to disobey and let the Committee eject me.'[21] The Secretary granted permission to publish by return post, and the effort to strive disinterestedly for the perfection of English literature by renouncing publication fees was never mentioned again.

In issues like this one, the conflict between two conceptions of the literary life and its rewards – what one might call the honorific vs. the professional – is very clear. In order to exist, the Academic Committee had to pretend that this conflict was not real, and it did so mainly by devoting itself to matters of literary honours, and avoiding the problems of the profession. But its members were nonetheless professional writers, and their sense of their own profession expressed itself in many ways, not only in a vigorous concern for the cash rewards of writing, but also in an independent-mindedness that sometimes clashed with the idea of honours.

There was, for example, the issue of the Laureateship. Alfred Austin died in 1913, and left the post, which he had held with so little distinction, to be filled. Yeats promptly moved that the Academic Committee 'approach the Prime Minister to recommend that the Office of Poet Laureate should be continued, but that the purely honorary character should be emphasized'.[22] By separating the honour from the duties, Yeats was trying to avoid the conflict of literary lives, and to allow the Laureate to go on being an independent professional writer. The Committee amended his motion to read that the Committee expressed its hope that the office would be continued, but that no compulsory duties would be attached to it, and in this form the resolution was circulated to the Academicians. Responses were divided. Supporters of the Laureateship regarded the post as an honour and a subsidy. 'Why should not Southeys and Wordsworths of the future benefit as their predecessors have benefited?' Lady Ritchie asked. 'Poets may not always be rich enough to refuse £100 or £200.' But opponents observed that the Laureate, simply by existing, expressed a relation between public honours and public opinions that was detrimental to the profession of literature. One can see that both sides in the argument were moved by the same impulse that had led to the creation of the Academic Committee – the desire to assert and preserve the dignity of the literary life – but they understood the route to dignity in antithetical ways. On the one hand, traditional, 'Establishment' writers like Lady Ritchie saw dignity as stemming from a common centre in Court and State; on the other, 'liberated' writers like John Galsworthy identified dignity with freedom from commitments.[23] In the end the Committee deferred action on Yeats's resolution; the Laureateship went successively to two Academicians – Bridges and Masefield – but without the Committee's assistance.

I know of no painting or photograph of the Academic Committee in session, but there is one picture – a cartoon by Max Beerbohm – which expresses its existence better than any more literal treatment could. Beerbohm was a member of the Committee when he exhibited his cartoon in 1913, and he clearly drew from experience. The picture shows the Committee members, each with his laurel crown, gathered together in an uncertain group; the caption reads: 'Members of the Academic Committee discussing whether at future meetings an Agenda Paper shall be provided and if so, what on earth to put into it.'[24] It is a shrewd and penetrating statement of the Committee's essential problem. Faced with an irresolvable conflict between its traditional intentions and the actual condition of letters, it could do nothing much except elect new members, and occasionally award prizes. After the first flurry of preparations it attracted little attention, and from the beginning of the First World War until it was dissolved in 1939, it proceeded with ever declining vigour. In its first four years it met twenty-five times, but in the twenty years between the wars only twenty-two times, and only six times after 1930. At one meeting – the only one in 1929 – there were only two members present, Newbolt and Mrs Margaret Woods, and another, in 1931, was sadly adjourned with a note in the minutes, 'no quorum'. It must have been fun, at first to choose one's immortals, and to scheme at getting a friend (or a fellow Irishman) a prize, but these pleasures faded as the importance of the rewards faded. In the minutes of the later years there are lists of possible members, but few members. The last meeting, 4 April 1939, was attended by Henry Nevinson, Ruth Pitter, Edward Marsh, T. Sturge Moore, Binyon, Blunden, and G. Rostrevor Hamilton; it was an unusually large turnout, which voted unanimously to end the Committee.

It is easy to dismiss the Academic Committee as an ill-conceived attempt to control the dignity of literature, which should be, as Wells said, 'necessarily wild and free', but to do so is to miss an interesting historical point. The literary life in the Edwardian period was of uncertain status: was it a noble calling or a business? Did it have a definable national role, or was it of necessity separate and alien to established institutions? Could excellence be agreed upon, and accepted by a large part of the literary profession, and the public at large? The attempt to create an Academy, as I see it, was an Edwardian attempt to assert, and so preserve, a relationship between literature and society in which both were assumed to be stable and homogeneous. The decline of the Committee, then, should take its place in our understanding of modern English history beside the decline of the House of Lords, as one more evidence of the way in which those assumptions of stability failed, and the old life fell apart.

Notes

1 See *The Times*, 2 November 1909, p. 4, and 8 November 1909, p. 8. Hewlett at the time was Chairman of the Committee of Management of the Society of Authors, and thus had some claim to speak for professional English writers.
2 *The Times*, 20 July 1910, p. 10.
3 British Museum, Ashley 5739.
4 In Margaret Newbolt, ed., *Later Life and Letters of Sir Henry Newbolt* (London: Faber, 1942), pp. 161–2.
5 The letter is in the archives of the Royal Society of Literature. It is dated 'Aug. 9'; the year must be 1913.
6 Archives, RSL. dated 11 October 1910.
7 *The Times*, 27 March 1911, p. 11.
8 *The Times*, 28 March 1911, p. 11. Douglas Freshfield, geographer and travel writer, had been Chairman of the Committee of Management of the Society of Authors 1908–9.
9 *The Times*, 31 March 1911, p. 11.

10 Yeats, *Letters* (London: Hart-Davis, 1954), pp. 557–8. The letter is dated 27 March 1911.

11 British Museum, Ashley 5739. Dated 30 June 1914.

12 Archives, RSL. No date.

13 Leon Edel and Gordon N. Ray, eds., *Henry James and H. G. Wells* (London: Hart-Davis, 1953), pp. 157–9.

14 Archives, RSL. Dated 26 June 1913.

15 Ursula Bridges, ed., *W. B. Yeats and T. Sturge Moore* (London: Routledge & Kegan Paul, 1953), pp. 18–19.

16 Minutes of the Academic Committee, 6 December 1911; archives, RSL. At about the same time Shaw withdrew from the executive committee of the Fabian Society, urging that the 'old gang' should give way to younger men. See Kitty Muggeridge and Ruth Adam, *Beatrice Webb: A Life* (London: Secker & Warburg, 1967), p. 197.

17 Minutes, 29 March 1912.

18 For a slightly earlier example of the Committee's incapacity for action, see *W. B. Yeats and T. Sturge Moore*, p. 17, where Yeats regrets that the Committee cannot officially defend Moore, whose story, 'A Platonic Marriage', was under attack from the Vigilance Society for immorality.

19 The story is told, and very well, by Newbolt in his *Later Life and Letters*.

20 Archives, RSL. Dated 1 November 1913.

21 Archives, RSL. Dated 1 December 1913.

22 Minutes, 24 June 1913.

23 The letters from Lady Ritchie and Galsworthy are in the archives of the Society.

24 The drawing is reproduced in *Fifty Caricatures* (London: Heinemann, 1913).